The Criminal Elite

*The Sociology of
White Collar Crime*

The Criminal Elite

*The Sociology of
White Collar Crime*

Second Edition

James William Coleman
California Polytechnic State University—San Luis Obispo

St. Martin's Press

New York

Editor: Don Reisman
Production Supervisor: Publication Services, Inc.
Cover Design: Tom McKeveney
Cover Photo: Ewing Galloway

Library of Congress Catalog Card Number: 88-60531
Copyright ©1989, 1985 by St. Martin's Press, Inc.
Manufactured in the United States of America.
32109
fedcba

For information, write:
St. Martin's Press, Inc.
175 Fifth Avenue
New York, NY 10010

ISBN: 0-312-00976-3

When the courts are decked in splendor
   weeds choke the fields
      and the granaries are bare

When the gentry wears embroidered robes
   hiding sharpened swords
      gorge themselves on fancy foods
         own more than they can ever use
They are the worst of brigands

They have surely lost the way

LAO TZU

Preface

The four years since the publication of the first edition of *The Criminal Elite* have been an exciting time for the study of white collar crime. While there have been no great breakthroughs that have shaken the field to its foundation, there has been a slow, progressive accumulation of knowledge, and with it, I think, a new sense of maturity and direction. I began the introduction to the first edition by rejecting the commonly heard claim that, despite its importance, we really don't know enough about white collar crime yet to understand it and, by implication, to give it the position in criminology it would otherwise deserve. I think it is clear that such claims are even more out of place today than they were then.

In preparing this new edition, my first task was to face the tangled pile of newspaper clippings, notes, and papers I had accumulated since the completion of the original manuscript at the end of 1983. Next, I systematically reviewed the academic journals that I felt were most likely to have published new articles on white collar crime. Not surprisingly, *Criminology*, published by the American Society of Criminology, and *Social Problems*, published by the Society for the Study of Social Problems, proved to be the richest sources of material. Finally, I reviewed all the new books I could locate in this area. Here, I was particularly impressed by John Braithwaite's richly detailed study, *Corporate Crime in the Pharmaceutical Industry*, published in 1984, and Kenneth Mann's insightful analysis of the workings of white collar justice, *Defending White Collar Crime: A Portrait of Attorneys at Work*, published the following year.

Those familiar with the first edition will notice that I have maintained the basic structure of the book unchanged. What I have tried to do was to analyze the large body of new research, reevaluate my earlier conclusions, and integrate the new findings into the book. For the case studies, I weeded out the dated material and brought in as many new cases as space permitted. The heaviest revisions have been made to the chapter on the causes of white collar crime. The section on the structure of opportunity was completely reorganized, both to provide a clearer statement of the factors that most strongly influence the distribution of opportunity and to integrate a great deal of new material, especially on gender and white collar crime. Finally, no matter how many times I go over a manuscript, there always seem to be ways to improve the writing, and I have done my best to make this edition clearer, more concise, and more interesting.

A few words about the structure of the book would, I believe, be helpful to those who intend to use it as a classroom text. The best understanding of white collar crime will naturally come from reading the entire book, but, because of time limitations, some instructors may desire a shorter treatment of the subject to assign to their classes. As with the first edition, I have, therefore, tried to make each chapter as self-contained as possible, so that some parts of the book can be assigned independently of others. The first chapter is a general introduction, which provides enough basic information to enable students to understand any of the subsequent chapters. Rather than giving a summary at the end of each chapter, the concluding chapter contains a restatement of the main points of the entire book, and it should help fill in the gaps for students who have not been assigned the whole book. Thus, an instructor who wishes to give lower division students a good introduction to the subject of white collar crime without dealing with more theoretical issues might assign the introduction, the conclusion, and chapters 2 and 3, which contain many case studies that should maintain students' interest while helping them gain a more realistic understanding of the problem. Students studying criminal justice might be assigned the introduction, conclusion, and chapters 4 and 5, which deal with the origins of the laws against white collar crime and their enforcement. Instructors wishing to familiarize more advanced students with the theoretical issues involved in the study of white collar crime without assigning the entire book might omit chapters 2 and 3 since they contain mostly descriptive material.

My immediate goal in writing this book was to provide a comprehensive summary of this fascinating field and to advance our knowledge wherever I could. But like so many other social scientists, my interest in white collar crime goes beyond academic issues. It seems to me that a calm and unbiased reading of the wealth of material contained in these pages inexorably leads to the conclusion that white collar crime is not only one of the most serious social problems facing us today, but that it is a problem that can be tamed if we have the political will to do so. My hope is, therefore, that the readers of this book will agree with this conclusion and be willing to devote some of their time and effort toward that end.

During the life of the first edition of *The Criminal Elite: The Sociology of White Collar Crime* I received numerous suggestions from readers and users who found ways I could improve the manuscript. More extensive comments for my revision were supplied by the following reviewers: John J. Conrad, Western Illinois University; Robert W. Janes, University of Maryland College Park; Frederick J. Maher, St. Michael's College; Marilynn Cash Mathews, Washington State University; and Alex Taylor, Brenau College. I wish to express my thanks to all the people who contributed to this book.

J.W. Coleman

Contents

1

Introduction

Crime has become one of the greatest public concerns of our time. Television, radio, and the newspapers are filled with shocking accounts of murder and mayhem. Politicians strain to outdo each other with promises to "get tough" on crime and to bring law and order back to the streets. But there is a strange distortion in all this, as though the public has lost sight of the real problem and instead sees only its misshapen reflection. There is no question that common street crime is an important social concern. But our attention has become so fixated upon it that we often ignore white collar crimes that are both more costly and more dangerous to society.

Everyone is familiar with the crimes of the infamous Manson "family," the suicides and murders in Jonestown, and the nicknames the press gives notorious criminals such as "Jack the Ripper" or the "Son of Sam." Yet much bigger and more damaging crimes pass by unnoticed and unpunished. Consider, for example, the havoc wreaked by the asbestos industry. Records of the dangers of asbestos go back as far as the Roman Empire, and modern medical research established its threat to human health decades ago. Yet the major asbestos producers not only fraudulently denied the dangers posed by their product, but launched a concerted campaign to conceal the scientific evidence from their workers. Studies showing the dangers of asbestos were kept secret, many times company physicians failed to tell workers that asbestos might be the cause of their frequent lung problems, and special research was funded to "prove" that asbestos was safe. The ultimate cost of this crime is expected to be staggering. It is estimated that exposure to asbestos in the workplace will cause one hundred thousand deaths from lung cancer, thirty-five thousand deaths from mesothelioma (a cancer of the linings of the lungs and stomach), and thirty-five thousand deaths from asbestosis. In addition, tens of thousands of people who have never worked directly with asbestos will probably die

1

from other sources of exposure. Despite the enormity of these crimes not a single person has faced criminal charges, and the public is largely unaware that they ever occurred.[1]

THE NATURE OF WHITE COLLAR CRIME

Since Edwin H. Sutherland first used the term in his 1939 presidential address to the American Sociological Society, white collar crime has been a focus of controversy. Sutherland, one of the founding fathers of American criminology, widened the scope of his discipline by helping to bring the "upper-world" crimes of business and government into a field that traditionally focused on the crimes of the poor and the underprivileged. Such sweeping changes naturally met resistance, especially since they challenged both traditional political sensibilities and powerful vested interests. Numerous debates broke out over which offenses could legitimately be called white collar crime and whether or not they were "really" crimes.

Part of the problem was of Sutherland's own making. His definition was clear enough: "[A white collar crime is] a crime committed by a person of respectability and high social status in the course of his occupation."[2] Although this definition is a broad one, encompassing everything from embezzlement and industrial espionage to the bribery of government officials, in his work Sutherland focused almost exclusively on the crimes of business, and especially on violations of federal economic regulations. Sutherland's failure to devote more attention to violent white collar crimes probably contributed to the debate that sprang up about whether or not white collar crime was "really" crime. Because such offenses as price fixing and false advertising are usually handled as administrative matters, and violators seldom face criminal charges, Sutherland's critics claimed that white collar crimes weren't crimes at all, or at least that white collar criminals weren't "real" criminals.

By today's standards, it seems rather odd to argue that people who have enough political power to prevent the government from prosecuting them are therefore not criminals, but many people were persuaded by such arguments at the time. Because price fixing was prohibited by relatively new legislation and its victims seldom even knew they were being victimized, it was easy to argue that it wasn't a "true" crime, comparable to theft or assault. Had the argument focused on flammable clothing that burned helpless children, or on industrial poisons that threatened hundreds of people with slow death, that line of argument would hardly have been tenable.

But however Sutherland had conceptualized the problem, he was bound to encounter strong resistance. When he made his famous address, crime was commonly seen as something that happened primarily among immigrants and poor people who had fallen victim to the social pathology of urban society. The idea that many of the fabled "captains of industry" should be considered criminals had a very un-American sound to it, even in the midst of the Great Depression of the 1930s. Perhaps even more threatening was Sutherland's call for tough action to deal with the problem of white collar crime. Proposals to treat powerful corporate executives like "common criminals" were hardly likely to win praise from the upper strata of American society.

Sutherland's use of the concept of white collar crime has also been criticized on more academic grounds. Herbert Edelhertz strongly objected to Sutherland's stipulation that white collar crimes must occur in the course of the offender's occupation.[3] Edelhertz argued that such a definition excludes income tax evasion, receiving illegal social security payments, buying on credit with no intention of paying, and a variety of other offenses that he felt should be considered as white collar crime.

When William Webster was head of the FBI, he defined white collar crime to include virtually any nonviolent crime based on "guile or concealment," no matter what the social status of the offender.[4] While this approach fits far more neatly within the categories of official justice statistics (the social and occupational status of offenders is not included in such figures), it constructs white collar crime so broadly that it destroys the real value of the term. The whole point behind most criminologists' concern with white collar crime is to give the same kind of attention to the crimes of the powerful and the privileged that is given to common offenders. Calling a skid row alcoholic's attempt to trick a friend out of a bottle of wine a white collar crime renders the term virtually meaningless.[5]

Gilbert Geis objected on very different grounds—Sutherland's failure to distinguish between the crimes committed by the corporations as a collective unit and the crimes of their individual members.[6] Following this lead, Clinard and Quinney disposed of the term altogether and replaced it with two others—corporate crime and occupational crime.[7] Although this is a very useful dichotomy, those two kinds of offenses are best seen as varieties of white collar crime, as Clinard himself later recognized.[8] Schrager and Short have proposed the concept of organizational crime as another substitute for white collar crime,[9] but again this term is more useful when seen as one subtype of white collar crime, for it does not include many of the offenses covered in Sutherland's original definition.

In addition to the attempts to replace "white collar crime" with more narrow terms, some criminologists have also proposed broader conceptualizations. Simon and Eitzen[10] use the term "elite deviance," which not only includes most white collar crimes, but also deviant activities of the elite that do not violate the law. It is not entirely clear, however, whether "elite deviance" includes occupationally related behavior alone or encompasses any deviant activity by members of the upper class. Were this ambiguity to be resolved, "elite deviance" and the related concept of "corporate deviance"[11] would certainly be useful; but, once again, these terms cannot replace "white collar crime."

One of the main problems with the deviance approach is the difficulty of determining with any degree of certainty what is and is not deviant. Although criminal law contains ample ambiguities of its own, at least each geographic area is covered by an explicitly stated set of legal norms that can be changed only through certain formalized procedures. There are, on the other hand, a huge number of groups with their own sets of norms defining what is and is not deviant. Not only are many of those definitions contradictory, but the operative norms of such groups are subject to rapid and unpredictable change. The use of so evanescent a concept to define this politically charged field of study is a prescription for endless quarreling. Moreover, the concepts of "elite" and "corporate" deviance are weak in another way. Having dropped any explicit link to the criminal law, the advocates of the deviance approach cannot effectively address the public's deep-seated concern that rich and powerful *criminals* are escaping punishment for their behavior.

But this is not to imply that students of white collar crime must don blinders and ignore all unethical behavior that is not against current law. Indeed, such activities are examined in many places in this book. The point is simply that "white collar crime" is too useful a conceptual tool to be thrown on the intellectual scrap heap. Because it clearly identifies a specific problem of great concern to people around the world, "white collar crime" has become one of the most popular phrases ever to come out of sociological research. Not only is Sutherland's term widely used in criminology, but it has become part of everyday English and has been adopted in several other languages as well. It would be a serious mistake to try to replace it with other, less powerful concepts.

Some of the critics of Sutherland's definition do, however, have valid objections, and a revision is necessary to clarify the ambiguities in the original and stake out the broadest reasonable parameters for our study. First, the fact that responsibility for some white collar offenses can be attributed only to a group, and not its individual members, must be explicitly recognized. Second, financial crimes that are not directly part of the offender's occupation must be included. Third, we must broaden Sutherland's stipulation that white collar crime is by persons of "high social status and respectability," for many of the white collar offenses examined in these pages were committed by persons from the middle levels of the status hierarchy. Thus, we arrive at the following definition: *white collar crime is a violation of the law committed by a person or group of persons in the course of an otherwise respected and legitimate occupation or financial activity.*

This new definition is broader than Sutherland's in two important respects. First, white collar crime is no longer restricted to persons of high social status. This definition still requires, however, that the criminal hold a respectable job, and as we shall see, crimes by those in positions of high status and power still comprise the core of the problem of white collar crime. Second, financial crimes such as income tax evasion are now included. Organized crime, on the other hand, is beyond the scope of this definition. Although there are many similarities in the operation of a group of organized criminals such as the Cosa Nostra and the criminal activities of a corporation such as General Motors or Exxon, respectability is the key difference. Whereas the Cosa Nostra is considered a deviant organization explicitly organized to carry on criminal activities, Exxon and General Motors are accepted as legitimate businesses seeking legitimate ends despite any illegal activities in which they may have engaged. So-called career criminals, such as con-men or burglars, whose principal occupation is some kind of criminal activity, are likewise excluded by this test of respectability.

Academic criminologists seem to relish debates about what should and should not be counted as a white collar crime. A great deal of time and energy has been devoted to such arguments that could have been far better spent investigating the problem itself. But at the risk of adding more fuel to this fire, one more point about our definition still needs clarification: Exactly what qualifies as a violation of the law? One of the central issues of the early debates about the definition of white collar crime was whether it included violations of civil as well as criminal law. As the study of white collar crime has matured, more and more criminologists have accepted Sutherland's contention that it should include both. [12] As Blum-West and Carter pointed out, the distinction between torts (civil offenses) and criminal offenses is not in the acts themselves but in the administrative response to them. Most white collar offenders violate both types of laws, and the decision to pursue a case in civil or criminal court is made largely on extralegal grounds. [13]

The latest definitional problem has its roots in the increasingly international character of the modern economy. Deviant actions by individuals or organizations may be subject to several different sets of national laws or may manage to stay in the cracks between different jurisdictions. How then do we classify such actions? Any behavior that violates the law of the country in which it occurs is obviously illegal, even if it is carried out by foreigners or foreign multinationals. In some cases, the actions of multinationals in foreign countries may also be subject to the "extraterritorial" jurisdiction of their country of origin. Although this standard is a good starting point, it is inadequate to deal with the activities of foreign multinationals in poor Third World countries. As Michalowski and Kramer have pointed out, the multinationals are often far wealthier and more powerful than the Third World countries in which they do business and can exercise great influence over the laws those countries do or do not enact.[14]   It is therefore necessary to include internationally agreed upon principles of human rights and national sovereignty in deciding what is and is not criminal behavior. Although these international laws are not as clearly defined or as widely accepted as the statutes in most individual nations, the basic principles governing the conduct of nations and multinational corporations are well established. They have been codified in such United Nations documents as the Universal Declaration of Human Rights, the Guidelines for Consumer Protection, and the Draft Codes of Conduct for Transnational Corporations; violations of the standards in these documents will therefore be included in our definition of criminal behavior.

COUNTING THE COSTS

The lawlessness of the privileged and the powerful causes subtle damage to the social fabric that is impossible to measure in precise, quantitative terms. Even the economic damage of white collar crime is extremely difficult to gauge, and most of the few numerical estimates we have date back to the 1970s. The Senate Judiciary Subcommittee on Antitrust and Monopoly, one of the only bodies with the temerity to attempt such an estimate, concluded that corporate crime cost the public between $174 billion and $231 billion a year in the early 1970s.[15] As staggering as those figures are, they represent only part of the problem of white collar crime. A 1974 estimate put the cost of another type of white collar crime—employee theft and embezzlement—at $7 billion a year.[16] According to another widely quoted estimate, "inventory shrinkage" (retailers' loss of merchandise from employee theft and shoplifting) adds about 2 percent to the cost of an average product, while a different expert held that employee theft and the cost of insurance to protect against it add a full 15 percent to consumer costs. [17] The Internal Revenue Service has estimated that U.S. corporations fail to report over $1 billion a year in income, and another estimate from the early 1970s put the annual loss from all forms of tax evasion at $30 billion. [18] Although such figures have a reassuring ring of authenticity, they represent little more than educated guesses and may be far off the mark. Social scientists have a difficult enough time measuring such public events as births, deaths, and migrations; the measurement of criminal behavior obviously poses much more difficult problems.

Whatever the exact total, economic losses from white collar crime dwarf the losses from street crimes such as larceny, robbery, and burglary. The Equity Funding swindle alone is believed to have cost the public as much as all the street crime in the United States for an entire year, [19] and other white collar crimes have cost many times more. In comparison to these billion-dollar crimes, the biggest robbery in U.S. history, the 1978 robbery of the Lufthansa warehouse at New York City's Kennedy Airport, netted only $4 million, and the average take for a robbery that year was a paltry $434. [20] The Joint Economic Committee of the U.S. Congress put the yearly losses from street crimes at about $4 billion—less than 5 percent of the estimated losses from corporate crime. [21]

Yet despite such facts, most people are still more concerned about street crime than about white collar crime. Much of this attitude can be attributed to simple ignorance. The media focus so much attention on street crime that most people don't realize how much more costly white collar crime actually is. But even those who are aware of the enormous financial burden of white collar crime often do not understand the true scope of the problem. The cost of white collar crimes may be high, the argument often goes, but at least they are nonviolent crimes that pose no direct threat to the public. Even though this argument has been voiced by some reputable criminologists, it too is based on ignorance, for white collar crime can produce as much violence as any street crime.

The National Safety Council has estimated that fourteen thousand people a year are killed in industrial accidents, and another government estimate puts the yearly toll of deaths from occupationally caused diseases at one hundred thousand. [22] It is difficult to determine how many of those deaths result from violations of the law and how many are caused by hazardous conditions the law does not prohibit, but data from Wisconsin indicate that 45 percent of the industrial accidents in that state result from violations of state safety codes. [23] And since inspectors from the Occupational Safety and Health Administration have found violations of health and safety codes in 75 percent of the firms investigated, it seems likely that illegal activities of some kind are involved in many of these deaths. [24]

Nor are workers the only ones killed by white collar criminals. The National Product Safety Commission has estimated that twenty million serious injuries and thirty thousand deaths a year are caused by unsafe consumer products. Again, it is unclear how many of the products involved violate safety laws or are fraudulently represented by manufacturers or merchants, but it seems likely that illegalities are involved in the majority of those cases. Most difficult of all to estimate are the human costs of illegal environmental pollution. Not only is it hard to find the exact cause of environmentally related health problems, but the ultimate source of the pollutants can be just as difficult to track down. Since the government still permits many dangerous substances to be released into the environment, most environmental problems probably arise through a combination of legal and illegal contaminants. But whatever the sources, environmental pollution has deadly consequences. The National Cancer Institute estimates that as much as 90 percent of all cancer may be environmentally induced, and cancer is now second only to heart disease as the leading cause of death in North America. [25]

By virtually any criterion, then, white collar crime is our most serious crime problem. The economic cost of white collar crime is vastly greater than the economic cost of street crime. And although it may be impossible to determine exactly how many people are killed and injured each year as a result of white collar crimes, the claim that such crimes are harmless, nonviolent offenses can hardly be taken seriously. Since only about twenty thousand murders are reported to the police in an average year, "nonviolent" white collar criminals probably kill considerably more people than all the violent street criminals put together.

VARIETIES OF WHITE COLLAR CRIME

There are so many kinds of white collar crime that a book of this length could be devoted merely to describing them. It is all too easy to be overwhelmed by an avalanche of facts, stories, and anecdotal reports and to lose sight of the fundamental issues. Moreover, there are political and ideological reasons to focus on some types of white collar crime and to ignore others. When business or civic leaders talk about white collar crime, they usually discuss crimes against business, such as embezzlement or computer crime. But sociologists, criminologists, and other observers of a more critical persuasion often focus their concern on the crimes committed by business—price fixing, false advertising, and environmental pollution, for example.

A typology is obviously needed that encompasses all important white collar crimes. But what sort of typology? From a humanistic perspective, our paramount concern must be the effects white collar crimes have on the victims. Using such a standard, we can divide white collar crimes into two large groups: property crimes, which cause only economic damage; and violent crimes, which cause injury, sickness, or death. This distinction is obviously of great importance in the formulation of social policy, but it has serious deficiencies as a device to help us understand the crimes themselves. Even though these two types of white collar crime have different consequences, their etiologies and internal dynamics often are virtually identical. For example, an executive who claims that a deadly product is "as safe as milk" usually has the same motivation and works under the same organizational pressures as an executive who lies about the durability or effectiveness of a product.

A sociology of white collar crime can be more effectively organized around the differences between the offenders rather than around the differences between the victims, and the next two chapters use such an offender-oriented classification. Chapter 2 deals with *organizational crime*—white collar crimes committed with the support and encouragement of a formal organization and intended at least in part to advance the goals of that organization. *Occupational crime*—white collar crime committed by an individual or a group of individuals exclusively for personal gain—is examined in chapter 3.

Because occupational crimes are similar to many familiar street crimes, the concept can be easily understood. An occupational crime is an illegal act committed in the course of an otherwise legitimate occupation without the encouragement or support of the offender's employer. Although employers may tolerate some occupational offenses, illegal acts intended to benefit the employer are classified as organizational crimes. Thus, the unique feature of organizational crime is that it is supported, encouraged, and oftentimes even required by the operational norms of the organization in which it occurs. Like occupational crimes, the individuals involved in organizational crime are usually seeking some personal benefit—an increase in pay, a promotion, or perhaps only continued employment. But unlike occupational criminals, they are also seeking to benefit a larger organization.

The fact that many organizations publicly proclaim a different set of goals from those they actually pursue, or even have official policies forbidding illegal activities, is of little importance here. What counts are the *operational* norms that define the organization's real goals and guide its employees' behavior. For example, the fact that the General Electric Corporation had a rule prohibited price fixing did not deter the directors of the company's heavy electrical equipment division from participating in just such a conspiracy. When the guilty executives testified in court, they said that, despite the written policy, it was clear that the company expected them either to fix prices or to find some other way to equal the big profits that price fixing provided. [26]

In General Electric's case, there was ample evidence that the top managers knew or should have known about the illegal activities of their subordinates. However, that is not always so. In many corporations, subsidiaries and divisions operate with great independence from the central hierarchy, and executives may make an intentional effort to avoid knowledge of the illegal activities of their subordinates in order to shield themselves from criminal liability. But whether or not a particular offense can be traced back to top management, it still represents an organizational crime if it is supported by the operational norms of a significant segment of the organization and is intended to advance the organization's goals. By the same token, illegal activities carried out solely for the benefit of the offenders are not organizational crimes even if they have wide support among other employees or are committed by top corporate leaders. For example, after financier Robert Vesco took over control of a Swiss mutual fund known as IOS, he allegedly siphoned off over $200 million in cash and securities for his personal use. [27] If the charges are correct, Vesco's activities must be labeled occupational crime, despite the fact that he ran the company.

PREVIEW

The next two chapters present a typology of white collar crime and illustrate it with numerous case studies and examples. From the huge number of examples that might have been included, I have selected what I believe to be the most important or best-documented cases that fit the various categories. A few cases of unethical behavior in which the participants managed to stay just within the boundaries of the law are also included, both to point out inadequacies in the current legal codes and to clarify the parameters of criminal behavior. The remainder of the book uses this foundation to build a sociology of white collar crime. Chapter 4 examines the laws that define white collar crimes and the social forces that led to their enactment. The legislative struggle, however, represents only half the battle. The way the laws are enforced is equally important, and chapter 5 describes the enforcement effort and appraises its effectiveness. Chapter 6 tackles the most difficult subject of all—the causes of this diverse set of phenomena known as white collar crime. Finally, chapter 7 presents a summary of the main themes of the book and allows the author to indulge in the arrogance of telling the world how it ought to change.

NOTES

1. Joseph A. Page and Mary Win-O'Brien, *Bitter Wages: Ralph Nader's Study Group Report on Disease and Injury on the Job* (New York: Grossman, 1973), 22; Richard T. Cooper and Paul E. Steiger, "Occupational Health Hazards: A National Crisis," *Los Angeles Times,* 27 June 1976, I: 1 *passim;* Daniel M. Berman, *Death on the Job: Occupational Health and Safety in the United States* (New York: Monthly Review Press, 1978), 85.

2. Edwin H. Sutherland, *White Collar Crime* (New York: Dryden Press, 1949), 2.

3. Herbert Edelhertz, *The Nature, Impact, and Prosecution of White Collar Crime* (Washington, D.C.: U.S. Government Printing Office, 1970).

4. William H. Webster, "An Examination of FBI Theory and Methodology Regarding White-Collar Crime Investigation and Prevention," *American Criminal Law Review* 17 (Winter 1980): 275–286.

5. It should be pointed out that the Bureau of Justice Statistics did not adopt this kind of definition in its *Dictionary of Criminal Justice Data Terminology* (2nd ed., Washington, D.C.: U.S. Department of Justice, 1981) and continues to include the characteristics of the offender. According to the dictionary, a white collar crime is a "nonviolent crime for financial gain committed by means of deception by persons whose occupational status is entrepreneurial, professional or semi-professional and utilizing their special occupational skills and opportunities; also nonviolent crime for financial gain utilizing deception and committed by anyone having special technical and professional knowledge of business and government, irrespective of the person's occupation" (p. 81).

6. Gilbert Geis, "Toward a Delineation of White Collar Offenses," *Sociological Inquiry* 32 (Spring 1962): 162.

7. Marshall B. Clinard and Richard Quinney, *Criminal Behavior Systems,* 2nd ed. (New York: Holt, Rinehart and Winston, 1973).

8. Marshall B. Clinard and Peter C. Yeager, *Corporate Crime* (New York: The Free Press, 1980), 17–19.

9. Laura Shill Schrager and James F. Short, Jr., "Toward a Sociology of Organizational Crime," *Social Problems* 25 (April 1978): 407–419.

10. David R. Simon and D. Stanley Eitzen, *Elite Deviance* (Boston: Allyn and Bacon, 1982). See especially pp. 5–6.

11. See M. David Erdmann and Richard J. Lundman, *Corporate Deviance* (New York: Holt, Rinehart and Winston, 1982).

12. Gilbert Geis, "Upperworld Crime," pp. 114–135 in Abraham Blumberg, ed., *Current Perspectives on Criminal Behavior* (New York: Alfred Knopf); Stanton Wheeler, "Trends and Problems in the Sociological Study of Crime," *Social Problems* 23 (1976): 523–534; Schrager and Short, "Sociology of Organizational Crime"; John Braithwaite, *Inequality, Crime and Public Policy* (London: Routledge and Kegan Paul, 1979); Clinard and Yeager, *Corporate Crime;* John Hagan and Patricia Parker, "White Collar Crime and Punishment," *American Sociological Review* 50 (June 1985): 302–316.

13. Steve Blum-West and Timothy J. Carter, "Bringing White-Collar Crimes Back In: An Examination of Crimes and Torts," *Social Problems* 30 (June 1983): 545–554.

14. Raymond J. Michalowski and Ronald Kramer, "The Space Between the Laws: The Problem of Corporate Crime in a Transnational Context," *Social Problems* 34 (February 1987): 34–53.

15. Cooper and Steiger, "Occupational Health Hazards."

16. Clinard and Yeager, *Corporate Crime*, 8.

17. Chamber of Commerce of the United States, *A Handbook on White Collar Crime* (Washington, D.C.: Chamber of Commerce of the United States, 1974), 6.

18. Norman Jaspan, *Mind Your Own Business* (Englewood Cliffs, N.J.: Prentice-Hall, 1974), 201.

19. Arthur B. Shostak, *Modern Social Reforms* (New York: Macmillan, 1974), 246; Public Citizen Staff Report, *White Collar Crime* (Washington, D.C.: Congress Watch, 1974), 17–18.

20. John M. Johnson and Jack Douglas, eds., *Crime at the Top* (Philadelphia: Lippincott, 1978), 151.

21. Clinard and Yeager, *Corporate Crime*, 8–9.

22. Nicholas A. Ashford, *Crisis in the Work Place: Occupational Disease and Injury* (Cambridge, Mass.: M.I.T. Press, 1976), 114.

23. U.S. Congress Joint Economic Committee, *The Cost of Crime in 1976* (Washington, D.C.: U.S. Government Printing Office, 1976), 8.

24. U.S. Department of Labor, *The President's Report on Occupational Safety and Health* (Washington, D.C.: U.S. Government Printing Office, 1973).

25. This figure is based on data from 1972. See Paul Brodeur, *Expendable Americans* (New York: Viking Press, 1974), 75.

26. Gilbert Geis, "The Heavy Electrical Equipment Antitrust Cases of 1961," in Gilbert Geis and Robert F. Meier, eds., *White Collar Crime: Offenses in Business, Politics and the Professions*, rev. ed. (New York: The Free Press, 1977), 123.

27. Lester A. Sobel, ed., *Corruption in Business* (New York: Facts on File, 1977), 51, 163–167.

2

Organizational Crime

Few events have had a more profound effect upon the pattern of modern life than the growth of bureaucracy. Huge organizations dominate today's social landscape in a way that could hardly have been imagined a few centuries ago. The unprecedented size and complexity of the modern state and the enormous number of tasks it has assumed have wrought profound changes in our social structure. But the most revolutionary transformation has come in economic organization.

The capitalist world's most fundamental economic unit—the private corporation—did not even exist four hundred years ago. The Dutch East India Company, usually cited as the earliest ancestor of the modern corporation, was not formed until 1602, and many more decades passed before the corporation began to take on its present form. But by the middle of the nineteenth century, almost all major businesses were operating as corporations.[1] And since that time, major corporations have undergone phenomenal increases in size. In 1986 the annual sales of the firms in *Fortune* magazine's list of America's five hundred largest industrial corporations totaled more than $1.7 trillion ($1,723,419,611). The revenues of the General Motors Corporation alone exceeded $100 billion—greater than the income of any government in the world except those of the United States and the Soviet Union.[2]

But the power of the corporations does not come from sheer size alone. The corporate giants have also won control of the key markets through which the lifeblood of the U.S. economy flows. In the early part of the nineteenth century, no single enterprise in the United States produced as much as 10 percent of the total output of a particular manufacturing industry. By the early twentieth century, seventy-eight companies supplied over half of the production in their respective industries, and twenty-eight of those companies supplied over 80 percent.[3] The antitrust crusaders of the late nineteenth and early twentieth centuries succeeded in dismembering a few of the most blatant monopolies and prevented a few other firms from achieving monopolistic domination of their markets. But the monopolies of the nineteenth century were replaced by oligopolies (a few giant firms working together to control a market) in the twentieth century, and the growth of economic concentration continued unabated. Today the one hundred largest U.S. corporations control a larger percentage of all manufacturing assets than was controlled by the two hundred largest firms in 1950 or the one thousand largest in 1940.[4] Less than 1 percent of U.S. manufacturers now hold 88 percent of all industrial assets and earn about 90 percent of all profits, and the one hundred largest manufacturing firms receive a significantly greater share of all profits than all 370,000 other manufacturing firms put together.

The story is much the same for the major financial institutions that wield so much power over the activities of other business firms. A fraction of 1 percent of all banks holds 70 percent of all deposits, and a mere nineteen banks control the majority of the bank trust business, which comprises the single largest pool of financial resources in the world today.[5] Moreover, government reports have shown that the major shareholders in the nation's largest banks are other banks, thus weaving America's financial institutions together in a tightly meshed fabric of interlocking ownership and control.[6]

As the corporate sector has grown, so have the size and scope of the government. In 1900 the federal government employed only about 1 million people; today, its employees number well over 12 million. And as in the case of the corporations, the government's influence in our social and economic life has grown along with its size. In addition to such traditional duties as national defense and law enforcement, the government has taken on many other heavy responsibilities including environmental protection, social welfare, public health, and regulation of the economy. Today, the life-styles and well-being of millions of people, along with billions of dollars in profits, often hang in the balance of a single government decision.

The importance of these changes can hardly be overestimated. Although American culture continues to give the highest esteem to the values of individualism and self-determination, the organizational revolution has transformed the social geography of American life, opening up a yawning chasm between America's myths and aspirations and its realities. Our dreams continue to be those of the yeoman farmers and independent merchants and businesspeople who settled a vast continent. But we are increasingly a nation of employees, working in one or another of the vast bureaucracies and fearfully dependent upon the boss or the boss's boss. The "invisible hand" of the open marketplace is now often attached to an awesome amalgamation of corporate and governmental power. Even democracy itself has a different meaning in a society in which public opinion is shaped by the bureaucracies of mass communication and the growth of economic concentration has placed so much power in the hands of the few.

The legal response to this organizational revolution has been slow and ineffectual. Traditionally the law has been based upon the principle that criminal responsibility rests with autonomous individual actors. But in many ways, the organizations themselves, and not individual employees, are the real perpetrators of organizational crimes. In many cases, criminal activities are rooted in an organizational subculture and a set of attitudes that have developed over many years, and they cannot be traced to any single individual or group of individuals. Of course, individual actors must still carry out the criminal deeds, but there is ample evidence to show that the attitudes and characteristics of those individuals are often of little importance. Those who refuse to carry out the illegal activities demanded by their organization are simply replaced by others who will.

The organizational crimes examined in this chapter fall under five general headings: fraud and deception, attempts to control the marketplace, violent white collar crimes, bribery and corruption, and violations of civil liberties. This clarification is used purely for heuristic purposes and is not intended to represent an exhaustive typology of organizational crime. The perceptive reader will notice that many of the case studies presented in these pages are drawn from the same industries. This stems in large measure from the distribution of the crimes themselves. The industries with highest crime rates—petroleum, automobile manufacturing, and pharmaceuticals—naturally provide us with more examples of corporate crime.

FRAUD AND DECEPTION

False Advertising

False advertising is one of the best known forms of fraud and deception. Who hasn't seen an advertisement that seems patently false or bought a product whose performance fell far short of the claims of it promoters? But the legal definition of false advertising is much more generous to the advertisers than most people assume. Although common sense would tell us that false advertising consists of the use of untrue statements in advertising, the law uses a different standard. It is not *falsity* but *deception* in advertising that is illegal. According to Section

15 of the Federal Trade Commission Act, deceptive advertisements are those that are "misleading in material respect," and this has been interpreted by the courts to mean that the deceptive advertisement must somehow affect the purchasing decisions of the customer. Although there is usually little doubt about what makes a statement true or false, determining whether or not a statement is deceptive is a much more complex business, because one must not only examine the nature of the statement but also judge its potential effect upon the listener.

This "deception" standard certainly has a logical rationale. For example, when Esso claimed that its gasoline put a "tiger in your tank," it was making a statement that was literally false yet not deceptive, since no reasonable person would believe that a tiger could actually materialize in a gas tank. The flaw in this approach is that complex legal standards that are difficult to apply tend to be interpreted in favor of those with the money to build the best legal case. And, of course, it is the advertisers, not the consumers, who command such resources. As a result, a body of case precedent has built up which allows salespeople and advertisers to lie to potential customers, as long as they use only broad, general lies (e.g., "This is the finest soap in the world."), on the grounds that such claims have no effect upon purchasing decisions. If this were actually true, and such exaggerated claims ("puffery," as they are called) did not sell products, they would hardly have remained a mainstay of advertising for so many years.

But even with the wide latitude given advertisers to "puff" their products, violations of the law are still common. In one Rise shaving cream commercial, for example, a man was shown shaving first with an "ordinary" lather that dried out quickly after application, and then with Rise which fulfilled its advertising slogan by staying "moist and creamy." What the television audience was not told was that the "ordinary lather" was not shaving cream at all, but an aerosol especially concocted to come out in a big attractive puff and then quickly disappear.[7] A similar case involved Campbell's "chunky style" soups. The bottom of the soup bowl used in a television commercial was filled with marbles, which pushed the pieces of meat to the top, thus making the soup look a lot chunkier than it really was. Many other cases of false advertising involve claims manufacturers made about the specific characteristics of their products. The manufacturer of Anacin ran into trouble with the Federal Trade Commission for claiming that its product relieved nervous tension, stress, and depression, was stronger than aspirin, brought relief within twenty-two seconds, and was more effective than other non-prescription analgesics.[8] The makers of Listerine mouthwash ran into similar problems with claims about their product's ability to prevent colds.

Such deceptive advertising can be devastating to small competitors who cannot afford major campaigns of their own, but most victims are consumers deceived into thinking that an expensive brand name product is better than less expensive substitutes. False advertising can also have far more serious consequences. In July 1974, under pressure from the Federal Trade Commission, twenty-five companies and the trade association of the plastics industry agreed to stop claiming that cellular plastics were nonflammable or self-extinguishing. In fact, these products produce denser smoke, faster spreading flames, and more extreme heat than do alternative products. To make matters worse, cellular plastics also give off toxic gases as they burn, and such gases are believed to have caused numerous deaths in aircraft accidents in which cellular plastic seats were set afire. Despite the fact that the industry had known of the dangers of the products for years, no criminal complaints were brought against the companies or any of their employees.[9]

The response to the cellular plastics case was typical of most false advertising. Even in particularly blatant cases, the toughest sanction commonly imposed is to require "corrective" advertising. More often, however, offenders merely sign a consent decree in which they agree to stop their illegal activities. Thus, even if detected, corporate false advertising almost always goes unpunished, for these measures aim to stop further criminal actions or reduce the damage already done, not punish the offenders.

A common form of false advertising used by retail stores is known as "bait and switch." The idea is to "bait" the customers into the store with advertising that offers merchandise at an extremely low price and then to switch their attention to a more expensive product. When customers ask about the sale merchandise, retailers either claim that "the last one was just sold" or point out some obvious flaw that the advertising failed to mention. Sometimes the customer is not informed of the switch until it is too late to do anything about it. For example, one firm advertised an offer to repair automobile transmissions for only $69.50. But once the mechanics actually dismantled a transmission, they claimed to find new "problems" that would substantially raise the price.[10]

Fraud

In contrast to false advertising, more blatant business frauds are usually handled as criminal offenses, but the severity of the punishment varies greatly with the type of offense and the size and influence of the company involved. Take the case of the Holland Furnace Company. With sales of about $30 million a year, Holland was certainly not one of America's corporate giants, but neither was it a "mom and pop" operation with only a couple of employees. As Christopher Stone put it, Holland "seems almost to have been born crooked."[11] Holland's standard sales technique was to send a representative to a private home who would claim to be an inspector from the gas company. Once inside, he would dismantle the heater as part of his "inspection," then flatly refuse to put it back together, claiming there was grave danger of explosion. In the middle of the family crisis that inevitably ensued, a solution would present itself magically at the door—in the form of a Holland furnace salesman, who would make a quick sale. Twenty-two years of legal problems and consumer complaints passed before the company president and two vice-presidents were found guilty of criminal contempt, and the president was sentenced to six months in jail.[12]

The Holland Furnace Company and other shady home-improvement businesses are part of what Philip Schrag called the "commercial underworld"—small and medium-sized firms that operate on the fringes of the law.[13] Such businesses typically prey on the poor and on minorities through door-to-door sales schemes, high-pressure credit sales, and other marginal ventures. One typical approach involves the sale of cheap merchandise or promised home repairs on "easy credit" terms to low-income buyers. The loans then are quickly sold at a discount to finance companies, and by the time the customers realize that they have not gotten their money's worth, it is too late. According to the law, a "holder in due course" of a note is entitled to collect on it, even if the original holder did not keep up his agreement with the borrower.

But those with low incomes and little education are not the only victims of the commercial underworld. Land fraud schemes, for example, prey on more affluent victims. These schemes typically involve high-pressure sales of retirement or vacation lots that are described in lavish brochures as having all utilities and being set in beautiful locations. Unsuspecting customers are often persuaded to buy the property sight unseen, and when they finally visit their property, they find barren desert or swampy marshland. One such racket advertised Lake Mead "rancheros" for which electricity, water, and phone service were available. In reality, the power and phone lines were six miles away, and to reach the nearest water, a homeowner had to make a twelve-mile trip to a coin-operated pump.[14]

Although such schemes are usually quite profitable, they pale in comparison to the major frauds worked in the corporate world. Certainly the most famous example was the Equity Funding case. Estimates of the total losses vary, but they run as high as $3 billion—

one hundred times the Holland Furnace Company's total yearly sales. Unlike the small and medium-sized firms in the commercial underworld, the Equity Funding Corporation moved in the glittering world of high finance. The take from its fraudulent operations was much larger, but retribution was also more severe when the day of reckoning finally came. After Equity Funding finally went bankrupt, there was too much publicity and too many influential victims demanding justice for Equity's top management to escape the full measure of the law.

The Equity Funding Corporation was founded in 1960 and flourished in the heady economy of what are sometimes known as the "go-go" years. From the beginning, Equity was based on a "funding concept" that was designed to appeal to customers' greed. In most cases, customers bought mutual fund shares and an insurance policy from Equity. They were then given a loan with their shares as collateral, that in turn was used to pay the insurance premiums. After ten years the program was to end with the customers making a large cash payment to clear up the loan—presumably from the money they had made from the increasing value of their mutual fund shares. Of course, the whole scheme would work only as long as the stock market never went down, but an economic decline seemed very unlikely amid the buoyant optimism of the times.

The Equity Funding Corporation itself lost money practically from the beginning. Its directors soon resorted to one of the most common techniques of business fraud to keep the company afloat: they juggled to books to give the company a false veneer of success, thus increasing the value of its stock and the willingness of bankers to provide loans. Five years after Equity Funding went public, the value of a share of their stock had risen from $6 to an astronomical $80. Equity stock was, however, virtually worthless in another five years.

Whether motivated by company loyalty, greed, or fear, over 130 Equity executives knew of the fraud and said nothing to the authorities. The scandal finally broke when an employee, disgruntled by his layoff, leaked damning information to a securities analyst. The subsequent investigation showed that Equity had written fifty-six thousand bogus insurance policies, created $120 million in phony assets, and even "killed" some of its phony insurees in order to collect on their policies. The entire corporation collapsed soon after the facts came to public light. A federal judge later gave Equity's president, Stanley Goldblum, an eight-year sentence for his role in the case, and numerous other conspirators received shorter terms. [15]

Such clean solutions to corporate crimes are, unfortunately, a rare occurrence. Fraud and deception have become accepted business practices throughout many "legitimate" industries, and that makes them extremely difficult to root out. One well-known example of this phenomenon can be found among American automobile dealers. A public opinion survey found that, while 74 percent of the public believed that bankers were honest, only 3 percent felt the same way about new-car dealers.[16] Common complaints against car dealers include false claims made in the sale of new automobiles, the forcing of unordered accessories on customers, the selling of used cars as new cars, and excessive finance charges.

Most people are quick to attribute these problems to the personal character of the dealers, who are depicted as shady, dishonest characters—the type you wouldn't want living next door. But the real cause of the problem lies in the economic structure of the automobile business. In 1921 there were eighty-eight automobile manufacturers in the United States; now there are only a handful. The small number of potential suppliers makes the loss of a franchise a serious threat and keeps the new-car dealer heavily dependent on the manufacturers. And these manufacturers place intense pressures on dealers to sell as many cars as possible, while caring little about dealers who excel in the performance of their service and warranty obligations. The system of sales bonuses for the dealers who sell the most cars puts a heavy burden on small dealers, who are forced to cut their profit margins to the bone in order to compete with the large dealers who receive those lucrative cash rewards. Since most dealers make so little profit from the sale of new cars, many of them feel compelled to make up the difference from their service departments. The manufacturers thus inadvertently promote such illegal practices as charging for more hours of labor than were actually needed for a job, installing new parts when the old ones needed only minor repairs, and charging for work that was never done. Part of the widespread failure among dealers to live up to their warranty obligations can also be attributed to the manufacturers. The factory pays only about two-thirds the amount that dealers charge private customers for the same repairs, on top of which dealers are often required to fill out lengthy paperwork and to tag and return parts replaced under warranty.[17] Manufacturers are sometimes directly involved in such fraudulent schemes as well. In 1987 the Chrysler Corporation admitted that it had allowed executives to drive its cars and had later reset the odometers and sold the cars to the public as new.[18]

Nor are automobile dealers and manufacturers the only source of difficulty for motorists. A 1979 study by a federal agency found that the average motorist was overcharged $150 a year for car repairs. The investigators concluded that fifty-three cents of every car repair dollar were wasted because of faulty repairs, overcharging, and other problems.[19] A study by the National Highway Traffic Safety Administration concluded that consumers waste almost $20 billion a year on automobile repairs. [20]

Tax Evasion

Business organizations have the same motivation to avoid paying their taxes as individual citizens (see chapter 3). But there is one essential difference between individual and corporate taxpayers: because the latter have vastly more political influence, they are able to obtain specific, industry-by-industry tax breaks and loopholes that make most corporate tax avoidance completely legal. According to the 1976 Corporate Tax Study conducted by the U.S. House of Representatives, the top 148 U.S. corporations paid less than half of the official tax rate on their profits. Ten percent of those corporations paid virtually no income tax at all, including Ford Motor Company, Western Electric, and Bethlehem Steel. [21] As a result of the proliferation of loopholes and special tax breaks, the proportion of the tax revenue derived from corporate taxes dropped from 33.6 percent in the mid-1940s to 10.4 percent in the early 1980s. [22] A comprehensive tax reform program designed, among other things, to increase the corporations' share of the tax bill was phased in beginning in the 1987 tax year, but at the time of this writing, it is still too early to gauge its impact.

One thing that is clear is that the bewildering complexity of the tax laws is a major ally of corporate tax dodgers. It often takes years of litigation to determine if a new corporate tax strategy is legal or not. As a result, most corporations are shielded from criminal prosecution even when their actions are apparently intended to defraud the government. For example, one important tax dodge available only to multinationals involves foreign tax shelters. Under the law, money made by U.S. companies abroad is not taxed until it is brought back to the United States; if it is not returned, it is not subject to U.S. taxes. Taking advantage of this loophole, big corporations often set up subsidiaries in countries with low corporate tax rates and manipulate their books to make it appear that most of their U.S. profits were actually earned in the "tax haven" country. For example, a product produced in the United States may be sold to a foreign subsidiary at virtually no profit, then resold for a much higher price. The profit on the resale is therefore recorded on the books of the foreign subsidiary based in a country such as Switzerland, which has only a 7 percent corporate income tax. As long as the money is not "repatriated" to the United States, the higher U.S. tax rate is avoided. [28] Such manipulations clearly violate Internal Revenue Service guidelines requiring that transfer prices between the different branches of a multinational be set at the same level as they would if independent companies were dealing at "arm's length." However, it is extremely difficult if not impossible for the IRS to determine what the "arm's length" transfer price would have been, and as a result, great latitude is created for corporate abuse and manipulation without fear of criminal penalties. [24]

The Internal Revenue Service does not even seem very concerned about many of the most blatant and unquestionably illegal claims of powerful corporate taxpayers. The General Accounting Office recently estimated that 42.4 percent of American corporations fail to report all their interest earnings, and that the total amounts to about $7 billion a year in untaxed income. Yet 1987 testimony before the House Sub-committee on Commerce, Consumer and Monetary Affairs revealed that the IRS has no interest in applying the sophisticated computer system it uses to track the interest income of private citizens to the major corporations. [25]   Indeed, the IRS's enforcement efforts are so weak that many of the criminal cases brought against corporations stem from the investigations of entirely different activities. For instance, the 1977 indictment of Phillips Petroleum company for tax fraud came about only because of the company's failure to pay taxes on the $3 million it kept in a Swiss bank for the purpose of making illegal political contributions. The indictment charged that Phillips used "international couriers, code names, misleading (bookkeeping) entries, and false invoices and billing" to conceal the company's true expenses from the IRS. [26]   Had Phillips not been under investigation for illegal payments, its tax evasion never would have come to light. Moreover, Phillips was not alone in such illegal activities. Almost half of the ninety-five companies that admitted making various kinds of illegal payments during the bribery scandals of the mid-1970s said that they would have to make adjustments in their federal income tax. [27]   Certainly, most of those "adjustments" involved the cover-up of overseas bribery and fraudulent tax deductions claiming bribe money as a legitimate business expense.

CONTROLLING THE MARKETPLACE

The insecurity of competition is an inherent part of a capitalist economy, but so are the efforts of business to escape competition through monopolistic control. The corporation that can take over an important market not only can reduce its risks but also can virtually guarantee itself a high level of profitability. Although the public is often unaware of the intricate webs of interlocking control corporations weave to restrain competition, the benefits reaped from monopoly are clearly made at its expense. When competition disappears, so does the motivation for innovation and improvement. Research and development dims in importance, production stagnates, and complacency replaces the competitive spirit. Worst of all, the public suffers because the monopolists can charge whatever price they choose for their products.

In response to these problems, the United States and most other Western nations have enacted "antitrust" legislation that aims to protect competition in the marketplace through the use of civil and criminal sanctions (see chapter 4). But as the statistics cited at the beginning of this chapter show, antitrust enforcement has by and large failed to deter economic concentration. Year after year, corporate concentration has increased and competition has declined.

Today's corporations use many of the same techniques to win market control that were employed by their predecessors of a century ago, despite that fact that new laws have made most of those techniques illegal. These business crimes fall into three categories. First of all, a corporation seeking to control its market can employ such unfair competitive practices as exclusive dealing (an agreement by two or more firms to exclude others from their business dealings), price discrimination, and bribery. Or, instead of trying to destroy competitors, it can buy them out; an approach that has gained increasing popularity despite the provisions of the Clayton and the Celler-Kefauver Acts outlawing mergers that might tend to restrain competition. Finally, once a few giant firms come to dominate a market, they can enter into illegal conspiracies to restrict competition and fix prices. Private businesses are not, however, the only ones that enter into such conspiracies. Powerful professional organizations, such as the American Medical Association and the American Bar Association, have also been involved in price fixing and other violations of the antitrust laws.

Unfair Competition

The line between "good" and "dirty" business is a fine one. The competitive spirit that antitrust legislation was intended to protect indirectly promotes many kinds of criminal activities including antitrust violations themselves. Critics of antitrust legislation have often held it to be unfair, because a competent, well-run firm can accidentally create an illegal monopoly simply by doing a better job than its competitors. However, this argument ignores the basic facts of monopolies and antitrust enforcement. The historical record shows that the great monopolies of the late nineteenth and early twentieth centuries were all established through the use of ruthless business tactics that would be illegal today. It is highly doubtful that any of the great monopolies could have been created if their founders had lived up to the spirit of modern legal standards. Furthermore, the courts require proof of "intent to monopolize" before handing down an antitrust conviction—that is, evidence showing either that a company has exploited its monopolistic advantage or that it has used illegal means to establish it. A company that establishes a monopoly through fair competition and does not use its monopolistic position to exploit the public or other firms has not violated the antitrust laws.

One of the earliest and most effective techniques used to build monopolies was price discrimination—the sale of the same goods or services at different prices to different customers. Although this sounds like an innocent enough practice, it has led to the demise of many small firms. John D. Rockefeller's huge Standard Oil monopoly was built upon a foundation of price discrimination. When Rockefeller was laying the first stones of his empire, he concluded that the way to dominate the oil industry was not by producing oil but by refining and distributing it. By winning secret rebates from the railroads, he gained a decided price advantage over competing distributors, who had to pay much higher transportation costs. [28] As the Standard Oil Empire grew, Rockefeller used other price manipulations to subdue his competitors. Whenever a small local competitor sprang up, Standard would slash its price below its own cost. The small firm would soon be facing bankruptcy, while Standard could simply make up its losses with its profits in other markets.

Because these abuses occurred decades ago and have long since been outlawed, they may seem to be only of historical interest. But the laws have not been effectively enforced, and the techniques pioneered by Rockefeller and his contemporaries are still in common use, even among the same multinational corporations that were spawned in the breakup of Rockefeller's Standard Oil empire. A typical example comes from the major petroleum corporations' attack on the so-called private branders in the 1960s.

In contrast to the oligopolistic giants of the oil industry, the private branders, who buy gasoline from any available sources, are small, fragile, and fiercely competitive. Quicker to recognize the changes suburbanization brought to the oil market after World War II, they revolutionized gasoline retailing by erecting large, multipump stations along main suburban highways, doing away with much of the service given in "service stations," and creating the first self-serve pumps. As a result of these innovations, they were able to undersell the majors by as much as five to six cents a gallon. The public responded, and by the early

1960s, the private branders had captured about 20 percent of the retail gasoline market.

The giants of the oil industry were slow to react to the challenge of these small firms. But in the mid-1960s, the domestic earnings of the majors began to decline, and it became clear that something had to be done. Once again the majors resorted to the time-tested techniques that Rockefeller pioneered. The majors' first response was to give special discounts to their dealers in areas of high competition, while continuing to sell gasoline at the regular price in other areas. When the private branders responded with price cuts of their own, the conflict often escalated into a "price war" in which each station tried to match the price cuts of its competitors. One price war studied by the Federal Trade Commission lasted almost four years, during which time gasoline sold below cost for 572 days. Because small, independent companies obviously lack the financial resources of the integrated multinationals, many were driven into bankruptcy. A substantial number survived, however, and the private branders continued to win an increasing share of the retail market.

In the middle of 1972, the tactics of the majors abruptly changed. They discontinued giving price allowances to their stations, and the independents watched in amazement as their giant competitors stopped responding to their price cuts. The reason for this unexpected action soon became clear, as the independents found it harder and harder to buy gasoline in the following months. Starting in early 1972, the majors made significant reductions in their refinery operations and slashed the sales they had traditionally made to the "lesser majors," who, in turn, cut their sales to independents. Excluded from many of their sources of supply, the independents were forced to cut back on their operations, and their share of the retail market has declined ever since.[29]

Both phases of the majors' attack on the private branders appear to contain obvious illegalities. Price discrimination seems to have been used in the first phase, while the second phase involved an illegal conspiracy to restrain trade. However, the government took no action to enforce the antitrust laws in either case.[30]

The majors used these techniques again in 1979 to justify a precipitous jump in the price of gasoline. Following the Iranian revolution, which disrupted the production of Iranian crude oil, U.S. refinery output dropped, and a serious gasoline shortage developed. Long lines formed around open stations, and frustrated motorists frequently had to wait hours to fill up. Most important for the oil companies, the shortages could be invoked to justify large increases in the retail price of gasoline. The majors blamed the shortages on the cutbacks in Iranian production and panic buying by consumers—an explanation that seemed logical enough at the time. It was not until many months later, when the gasoline lines had been nearly forgotten, that reports suppressed by the Carter administration showing that there had been no gasoline shortage at all began to surface. According to the evidence, other sources had made up for the reductions in Iranian production, and crude oil imports to the United States had not dropped at all. But if the oil shortage was pure deception, the enormous increases in profits reported by the oil companies for 1979 were undeniably real. Some petroleum companies reported increases of over 200 percent in their already substantial profits. [31]

Ironically, some of the major corporations' most important allies in their battle against small competitors can be found in the same government bureaucracy that is responsible for antitrust legislation and its enforcement. American tax laws, for example, strongly favor big business. In the early 1970s, U.S. Representative Charles Vanik estimated that the actual tax rate on the one hundred largest U.S. corporations was only half as high as it is for smaller firms. [32]   A more recent study by Lester Salamon and John Siegfried also concluded that larger firms pay lower taxes than small firms and that the reason for the differential was the political power of the large corporations. [33]

Mergers and Acquisitions

Despite the unequal battles they must wage against the major corporations, many smaller firms manage to survive and prosper. Along with all the advantages—resources, power, influence—that go with the great size of the major corporations, there are also some inherent disadvantages. A large, diversified concern is seldom able to respond to changing economic conditions as quickly as a small company concentrated in a single market. Large, successful bureaucracies tend to follow conservative policies, assigning the highest priority to protecting the status quo and casting a dubious eye toward proposals for sweeping change. The most vigorous of the small to medium-sized firms are, in a word, "hungrier" than their larger competitors. The managers of the smaller firms are more willing to try out radically new ideas, for they know that to survive, they must take risks.

As a result, big corporations have often found it easier and more effective to buy out smaller competitors than to drive them under. Most of the increase in the concentration of assets in the hands of the largest corporations has resulted from mergers and take-overs, not from the competitive advantages enjoyed by the big firms. In the two decades following the end of World War II, for example, the two hundred largest U.S. corporations increased their share of all manufacturing assets from 42.3 percent to 60.9 percent. Yet, without the acquisition of smaller companies, their share of total manufacturing assets would have increased to only 43.2 percent—less than a 1 percent gain.[34] Moreover, there is little doubt that many, if not most, of those mergers could have been held to be illegal, for the Celler-Kefauver Act of 1950 expressly forbids mergers that "may lessen competition or tend to create a monopoly."

Illegal mergers are given different legal treatment from that accorded most of the other white collar offenses examined up until now. Whereas such activities as price fixing and bribery are criminal offenses, monopolistic mergers are handled entirely as administrative matters. This approach makes sense, because many mergers among smaller firms are harmless or even beneficial to the economy, and business executives who fail to judge the monopolistic impact of their merger plans correctly can hardly be held to be criminals. Moreover, criminal sanctions are not needed to stop monopolistic mergers. Because mergers are highly visible public events, it should be sufficient for enforcement agencies to examine each proposed merger and take civil or administrative action against those that may have significant, anticompetitive effects.

Federal enforcement agencies have failed to do much to enforce the restrictions on corporate mergers, however. From 1914 to 1969 there were over thirty thousand mergers in the United States, yet the Justice Department and the Federal Trade Commission together brought only about three hundred antimerger cases to trial.[35] Part of the failure to block anticompetitive mergers can be attributed to flaws in Section 7 of the original Clayton Act (see chapter 4). But even after those flaws were corrected by the Celler-Kefauver Act, mergers continued unabated. Ironically, three of the biggest waves of mergers in U.S. history came immediately after the passage of legislation designed to prevent such monopolistic combinations (the Sherman Act of 1890, the Clayton Act of 1914, and the Celler-Kefauver Act of 1950).[36] This fact alone says a great deal about the failure of the enforcement effort. Certainly the wave of mergers and acquisitions in the 1980s has been virtually ignored by those in charge of antitrust enforcement. Yet it has included some of the biggest mergers ever proposed—for example, the $14 billion merger of Standard of California and Gulf Petroleum and the $10 billion merger of Texaco and Getty Oil—and numerous cases in which corporate giants have bought out major rivals, such as Texas Air's purchase of Eastern Airlines and General Electric's acquisition of RCA.

Conspiracies

The success of the giant corporations in buying up or squeezing out their smaller competitors has left many of the largest markets in the United states in the control of oligopolies, usually made up of three to five firms. Because antitrust laws specifically forbid the monopolization of an entire industry by a single firm, and because the prospects of attacking a large and firmly entrenched competitor are generally unattractive, most oligopolists are content to achieve market control through cooperation with their supposed competitors.

One essential task for any oligopoly is to erect the strongest possible barriers to prevent new competition from entering the market. The huge outlays of capital usually necessary to begin production of a new product, along with the intimidating political and economic power of the established firms, normally suffice to ward off new challengers. But most oligopolies also use other techniques to strengthen entry barriers—control of the supplies of essential raw materials, costly advertising campaigns to establish name-brand recognition, and governmental protection in the form of tariffs, import quotas, and favoritism by federal regulatory agencies.

Once their market has been secured, the oligopolistic firms can turn their attention to the creation of a system of mutual cooperation that will keep profits up and competition down. All of the different devices used to achieve this goal are, strictly speaking, illegal, because the Sherman Act forbids "every contract, combination. . .or conspiracy in restraint of trade." Enforcement agencies, however, have tended to focus upon only a few of the most obvious types of offenses—especially conspiracies to divide up markets or fix prices. And there is strong evidence that such illegal conspiracies are common in many different industries. In a survey conducted by the Ralph Nader organization, 58 percent of the presidents of the one thousand largest U.S. industrial firms felt that such conspiracies were a "way of life" in U.S. industry. [37] Although only a few criminal antitrust cases are prosecuted each year, they have involved all types of enterprise, from the milk, bread, shrimp, and cranberry industries to those that produce sheet steel, plumbing fixtures, and uranium. One early attempt to estimate the extent of price fixing concluded that it was "quite prevalent" in U.S. industry, [38] and another more recent study of corporate crime reached a virtually identical conclusion. [39]

The petroleum industry once again provides many excellent examples. Although most people think of the international oil cartel as a child of the OPEC sheiks, the international oil companies began conspiring to fix prices at least as far back as 1928, decades before many of the Middle Eastern oil fields were even discovered. The problem that originally led to the creation of an international oil cartel was a worldwide surplus of oil, which was accompanied by one of the rare outbreaks of vigorous competition between the major oil companies. Alarmed by the rapid decline in prices, the heads of the world's three largest oil-companies—now known as Exxon, Shell, and British Petroleum—met at Achnacarry castle in the Scottish Highlands, for what they claimed was some "grouse shooting." The real business at hand, however, was the negotiations that laid the foundation for the international oil cartel that helped shape the economic destiny of the modern world. The goal of the "Achnacarry Agreement" was to establish a framework for international cooperation among the major oil companies, based upon the principle that each company accept and strive to maintain its existing share of the market "as is." But because a cartel that included only the three biggest companies was obviously inadequate, all the important participants in the international oil trade were soon brought into the deal.

One of the most striking things about these secret cartel agreements was the great sophistication and specificity with which the participants set down the operating procedures for their criminal conspiracy.[40]   Three successive agreements laid out both the functions of each of the local cartels that were to be established in consuming countries and the ways in which the "as is" principle was to be maintained. The preferred method of correcting changes in market shares was by transferring customers from the overtrader to the undertrader. If such an adjustment were impossible, the undertrader was to receive the net profits the overtrader realized from selling more than its allotted share. So sophisticated were these agreements that even the possible increase in profit margin resulting from the overtraders' greater total volume was recognized and ordered transferred to the other members of the cartel. There was also a formula designed to punish habitual undertraders through a slow reduction in their allotted shares.

Aside from dividing up the petroleum market, the conspirators also agreed upon a price-fixing arrangement forbidden by U.S. law. Oil prices were set at the price of American oil—at that time the most expensive in the world—plus the cost of shipment from the Gulf of Mexico to the point of sale. Thus, even oil purchased in the Middle East at half the U.S. price and shipped only a short distance was to be sold at the full American price plus the "phantom freight" charge from the Gulf of Mexico. Expensive American petroleum was thus protected from foreign competition at the expense of consumers in the United

States and around the world. Moreover, by artificially encouraging the production of U.S. oil, these agreements accelerated the depletion of U.S. reserves, just as import quotas were to do in later decades. [41]

The "Draft Memorandum of Principles" of January 1, 1934, was the last of the three supplementary agreements that oil companies signed after the Achnacarry meetings. It was clearly part of an exclusive trading agreement—another violation of American law. In the words of this document, "No participant shall be free to sell to outsiders either crude oil or finished products." [42] The document goes on to recommend that the majors buy out their competition in order to maintain their market control:

> *Purchase of Outsiders.* It is recognized that it is desirable to convert uncontrolled outlets into controlled class; in view of this the purchase by the "as is" members of going distributing concerns outside the "as is" is to be recommended as tending to improve the stability of the markets. [43]

There is some dispute about how long this carefully constructed cartel actually lasted. The oil companies claimed it came to an end in September 1939, with the outbreak of World War II. But a special investigative committee reporting to the Swedish parliament found evidence of "continued cooperation among the three major companies" after the war. [44] And there is other evidence that difficult issues were brought before a high-level, intercorporate committee of oil executives as late as 1971. George Henry Schuler, a representative of a minor oil company with concessions in Libya, reported that when his proposal for dealing with problems in that country proved too big for the "London Policy Group" to handle, he presented his arguments to a "meeting of the chiefs" held in Mobil's New York headquarters and presided over by the president of Exxon. [45] Such damning testimony, combined with clear evidence showing a continued pattern of parallel actions among the major oil companies, indicates that they are still working together to control the world market for oil. This does not necessarily mean, however, that the oil companies still hold regular high-level meetings to fix prices and conduct other illegal activities. As Ralph Nader put it when surveying the general problem of price fixing, "What begins as conspiracy frequently develops into conditioned response, with only occasional explicit coordination required." [46]

Collusion in the Professions

Large corporations are not the only organizations that violate the antitrust laws. Many medical and bar associations encourage the same monopolistic behavior. Until recently, it was common practice for local bar associations to publish schedules of minimum fees and to punish attorneys who charged less. And because they hold the power to control licensure, such associations actually have a much greater ability to enforce their price schedules than do business associations. The American Bar Association used to hold that: "The habitual charging of fees less than those established in suggested or recommended minimum fee schedules, or the charging of such a fee without proper justification, may be evidence of unethical conduct."[47] Accordingly, a lawyer could be disciplined or even disbarred for failing to charge customers a high enough price. In defense of this practice, the American Bar Association claimed that its members were not covered by antitrust law, even though the courts had repeatedly held that fee schedules set by business associations were illegal and the Sherman Act contained no exemption for professional associations.

The case that finally forced the application of the antitrust laws to the legal profession was brought by Lewis and Ruth Goldfarb. When the Goldfarbs purchased a home in Fairfax County, Va., they began to shop around for title insurance. The first lawyer they approached told them he charged 1 percent of the total selling price of the house. Thinking that too high a price, the Goldfarbs sent letters to thirty-six other lawyers. All nineteen of the replies they received quoted the identical price of 1 percent of the selling value, which the Goldfarbs later discovered to be the minimum price listed in the local bar association's fee schedule. Lewis Goldfarb was himself an attorney, and he brought suit to stop Fairfax County lawyers from fixing their prices. The case ultimately wound up before the Supreme Court, which unanimously held the mandatory fee schedules to be illegal, noting that they represented "a classical illustration of price fixing."[48]

In addition to such fee schedules, both the legal and medical associations have employed numerous other techniques to exploit their professional monopolies. One good example was the American Medical Association's effort to restrict the number of medical school graduates and keep the demand for medical services higher than the supply of physicians.[49] Another was the legal profession's prohibition on advertising. Although advertising and the increased competition it brings might be expected to produce substantial benefits for those in need of legal services, lawyers saw it as a threat to their standard of living. Recognizing the obvious monopolistic intent behind such restrictions, the Supreme Court struck down the prohibition on advertising in 1977.

Legal and medical associations have also fought against the advent of group practices that handle large volumes of clients at lower cost. For example, the first comprehensive group medical practice in the United States, organized by Dr. Michael Shadid in Elk City, Okla. in 1929, ran into fierce opposition from the local medical association. After an unsuccessful attempt to expel Shadid on charges of unethical practice in 1931, the Beckham County Medical Association disbanded itself, waited six months, and then re-formed without Shadid. Futile efforts also were made to get the state legislature to revoke the licenses of the physicians working at Shadid's clinic, and the AMA refused to admit them to the organization. Twenty years of conflict finally reached a climax in 1950, when the clinic filed suit against the medical society, charging it with conspiracy to restrain trade. Eventually the society settled out of court and admitted the clinic's doctors to membership. There was, moreover, nothing unique in this case. The other early group practices, such as Ross-Loos and Kaiser-Permanente, also faced similar problems.[50]

The same determined opposition was also encountered by the original group legal practices. One of the first such low-cost practices was the Legal Clinic of Jacoby & Meyers. The two lawyers opened up their "clinic" in an inexpensively furnished storefront office in a suburban shopping center, offered unusually long hours of service, and made extensive use of paralegal assistants to cut costs. Within six months of its September 1972 opening, the clinic was handling 1 percent of all the divorce work in Los Angeles, and the more traditional, higher-priced lawyers were getting worried. Their response was to charge Jacoby and Meyers with violating the state bar's code of ethics. After several years of maneuvering, their license was suspended for forty-five days, and they were ordered to change the name of their clinic. However, in May 1977, more than four years after the charges had first been filed, the California Supreme Court exonerated Jacoby and Meyers of all charges.[51]

In their defense, professional societies have advanced elaborate explanations purporting to show how such innovations are actually harmful to the profession and its clients. They also strenuously object to the notion that they are simply trade associations out to advance the financial interests of their members (and thus subject to antitrust laws), claiming instead that their only goal is to improve the quality of the professional services they control. But the historical record, from the AMA's bitter opposition to government-financed medical care for the aged to the bar's battle against no-fault insurance, shows that the pecuniary interests of their members has usually taken precedence over the welfare of the public in their deliberations.

VIOLENT WHITE COLLAR CRIMES

No matter how skeptical they may be about the motives of big business, few Americans see corporate executives and managers as violent criminals. It is easy to believe that a vast reservoir of violence lies behind the defiant visages of the young blacks trapped in the ghettos or the haggard features of heroin addicts, but corporate executives would seem to be another story entirely. Hardworking, competitive, and successful, these men and women typify the aspirations and ideals of the middle class and seem worlds apart from the violence and disorder found in big-city streets.

But the differences between the criminals of the upper world and those of the underworld are as much matters of form as of substance. Although the techniques may be different, the results are often the same. The young robber who accidentally kills a store clerk displays the same disregard for human life as shown by engineers who falsify test results to conceal a deadly flaw in an automobile or airplane manufactured by their employer. The engineers' distance from their victims allows them the luxury of preserving their self-respect by pretending that no one will really be hurt by their crimes, but the damage is just as real.

As we have already seen, white collar offenders kill and injure many more people than do street criminals. Industrial corporations, for example, have displayed a consistent pattern of irresponsibility in dealing with dangerous substances such as PCBs, beryllium, cotton dust, coal dust, dioxin, Kepone, mercury, asbestos, cadmium, lead, chlorine, and arsenic. This pattern of irresponsibility goes far beyond merely ignoring safety warnings. Corporations have attempted to suppress evidence that these substances were dangerous, funded biased research to "prove" false conclusions, lied to their workers and to the public, battled against adequate safety standards, and obstructed enforcement efforts. The record of corporate irresponsibility in matters of product safety is much the same. Time and again, corporations fail to adequately test the safety of their products, and when the dangers finally come to light, they stonewall their critics and deny that any problems exist.

Unsafe Production

One well-known example of corporate irresponsibility with toxic chemical occurred in Hopewell, Va., where the Life Sciences Products company set up a chemical manufacturing plant in a converted garage. After only a few weeks in the plant, many workers began to suffer dizzy spells, blurred vision, and tremors. One worker reported that his hands were shaking so badly that he had to have a friend hold his glass when he stopped off for a beer after work. Most of the local physicians blamed these problems on nerves and overwork. But one young cardiologist, Yi-Nan Chou, decided to send specimens of one patient's blood and urine to the Center for Disease Control in Atlanta. Researchers there found the specimens to have a high concentration of Kepone, the toxic

insecticide manufactured in the converted garage.[52] Subsequent investigations disclosed that Life Science Products was set up by two former
employees of the Allied Chemical Corporation to supply it with the
dangerous chemical it used to manufacture under its own auspices. Yet
neither the workers nor the community were told anything about the
dangers of Kepone. Although Allied denied responsibility for the damages, Life Science Products was shut down, a federal court fined Allied
$5 million, and Allied agreed to donate $8 million to a Virginia environmental fund after Kepone all but destroyed the fishing industry on
the St. James River. In addition, Allied paid approximately $15 million
more as a result of civil actions involving the Kepone case.[53] Many of
the chemical workers employed at the plant suffered far greater losses,
including sterility and other serious disabilities, and because Kepone
builds up in human and animal tissues, there is considerable concern
that what one conservationist has called a "chemical time bomb" may
have been released among those living near the plant.[54] Ten years
after Life Sciences Products was shut down, the St. James River was
still closed to most commercial fishing.[55]

The story of vinyl chloride, the foundation of a multibillion dollar
plastics industry, is much the same. Evidence of the dangers of vinyl
chloride began accumulating soon after the end of World War II, when
studies from the Soviet Union, Romania, France, and the United States
linked vinyl chloride to liver damage. Although employees exposed to
the chemical frequently complained of sore and weak fingers, company
physicians in the United States repeatedly denied that the problem had
anything to do with their work. As the number of workers subject to
long-term exposure increased, evidence of a serious new problem began
to emerge. An extremely rare form of cancer, angiosarcoma of the liver, began to show up in an alarming number of vinyl chloride workers.
Although angiosarcoma is so rare that, according to one report, not
a single case was found in over two hundred thousand liver specimens examined at the Bronx Veterans Administration Hospital, four
cases were found in a single American plant employing only 250 people in vinyl chloride and PVC (polyvinyl chloride) work.[56] In 1971,
Cesare Maltoni, a researcher working for the Italian chemical industry, found that vinyl chloride produced angiosarcoma in laboratory animals at levels of exposure far lower than those to which American workers were being exposed. The Manufacturing Chemists Association (the
trade association of the American chemical industry) quickly joined with
the European firm that had done the research in an attempt to keep
these findings secret. But the growing incidence of this otherwise rare
cancer could not be hidden from public attention.[57]

As is so often the case with industrial hazards, the damage done by
vinyl chloride extends far beyond the work force directly involved in its

production. A study by researchers from Bonn University found serious liver disease in workers who turned PVC plastics into floor tile, thus indicating that some of the roughly seven hundred thousand workers who handle some form of PVC may be at risk. Moreover, a study by the Environmental Protection Agency concluded that more than 300 million pounds of vinyl chloride escape into the environment each year. Although the long-range effects of this pollution are difficult to gauge, a study of three Ohio towns in which vinyl chloride was manufactured disclosed an abnormally high incidence of birth defects in infants and tumors of the central nervous system among adult men.

The corporate response to the asbestos problem followed much the same pattern. Asbestos is unique only in that its dangers were recognized much earlier than were those of most other industrial hazards. The Roman naturalist Pliny the Elder mentioned a lung disease suffered by slaves who mined asbestos and described the makeshift respirators they used to protect themselves from injury. The first modern report of a worker's death from exposure to asbestos was made by a British physician in 1906, and in 1918, U.S. and Canadian insurance companies stopped selling individual life insurance policies to asbestos workers. By 1935, asbestos had been linked to lung cancer and to asbestosis, another crippling lung disease,[58] and by 1955 the causal link between asbestos and lung cancer was conclusively established.[59]

Yet all this scientific evidence seemed to have little impact on the asbestos industry, whose members repeatedly denied that any problem existed. Although company physicians at the nation's leading asbestos producer regularly diagnosed lung problems among asbestos workers, company policy prevented doctors from informing their patients about abnormal chest x-rays or recommending outside treatment. After the publication of the 1955 study establishing a link between asbestos and lung cancer, the industry took the offensive, hiring numerous researchers to "prove" that asbestos was harmless. By 1960, sixty-three scientific papers had been published on the problems of asbestos exposure. The eleven studies funded by the asbestos industry all rejected the connection between asbestos and lung cancer and minimized the dangers of asbestosis. All fifty-two independent studies, on the other hand, found asbestos to pose a major threat to human health.[60] Such evidence suggests that the asbestos industry knowingly perpetrated a massive fraud on its workers and on the public.

Apologists for such corporate crimes argue that "everything causes cancer" and that the risks of getting the disease from exposure to most carcinogens is really very slight. But that line of reasoning will not work on the problems of asbestos. According to estimates from Mount Sinai Hospital's Environmental Sciences Laboratory, nearly *one-half* of all deaths among asbestos insulation workers are directly caused by exposure to that substance.[61] Of the half-million living workers who have been exposed to significant doses of asbestos, it is estimated that one hundred thousand will die from lung cancer, thirty-five thousand from mesothelioma (a rare cancer of the lining of the lungs and stomach), and thirty-five thousand from asbestosis.[62] There is growing evidence, moreover, that those living near asbestos factories are also at risk. A study conducted by physicians from the Department of Occupational Health of the London School of Hygiene and Tropical Medicine found that, of the seventy-six confirmed deaths from mesothelioma studied, thirty-one of the victims had worked with asbestos, eleven had lived within half a mile of an asbestos factory, and nine others were relatives of asbestos workers (including seven wives of asbestos workers, one of whom regularly brushed her husband off when he came home from work covered with asbestos powder).[63]

As the case of asbestos demonstrates, the release of dangerous industrial pollutants into the environment can transform a problem of industrial safety into a problem of public health. The dangerous, often deadly consequences of environmental pollution have become an everyday fact of life for citizens of the industrialized nations. There are far too many examples to permit us to do more than present some general statistics and a few cases of especially well-documented crimes.

Toxic wastes pose one of the industrialized world's most serious environmental problems. American industry alone produces eighty-eight billion pounds of toxic wastes a year, and the EPA estimates that 90 percent of it is disposed of improperly. Huge quantities of deadly substances have already built up in 50,000 dumps and 180,000 open pits, ponds, and lagoons around the country.[64] Oftentimes the operators of these sites have already gone out of business by the time the public becomes aware of the problem, and even when this is not the case, the records of which chemicals the sites contain are often completely inadequate. Many of these sites hold a veritable witch's brew of toxic chemicals mixed together in unknown combinations. Although obviously irresponsible, many of the dumpers' actions were legal at the time they were taken. But as the laws have grown more restrictive, corporations have become increasingly involved in criminal misbehavior.

According to an article in the *Los Angeles Times*, for example, officials of the Occidental Chemical Corporation, a subsidiary of Occidental Petroleum, permitted the illegal dumping of dangerous pesticides from their Lathrop, Cal., plant to go on for years with the full knowledge that they were poisoning local drinking water. In addition, the *Times* charged that Occidental Chemical intentionally withheld this information from California officials, repeatedly filed misleading reports on their waste dumping activities, and made false statements to the press to cover up their crimes. Intercompany memos written by Occidental's engineering and technical services manager provide damning evidence of corporate irresponsibility. According to one memo,

> California state water quality control laws clearly state that we cannot per-
> colate chemical to ground water. . . .We percolate all of our gypsum water,
> our pesticide wastes, and 1% to 3% of our product to the ground. To date
> the water quality control people do not know about our pesticide waste
> percolation. Our neighbors are concerned about the quality of the water
> in their wells. Recently water from our waste pond percolated into our
> neighbor's field. His dog got in it, licked himself, and died. Our laboratory
> records indicated that we are slowly contaminating wells in our area, and
> two of our own wells are contaminated to the point of being toxic to animals
> or humans.[65]

Yet Occidental took no corrective action even after this clear-cut warn-ing, and continued to dump pesticides from the Lathrop plant for at least two more years.

Another subsidiary of the Occidental Petroleum Corporation, Hooker Chemical, was involved in a similar scandal on the other side of the country on the Love Canal in New York State, an old dump-ing ground that Hooker gave to the Niagara Falls School Board in the early 1950s. In June 1958, three schoolchildren were burned near the dumping site, and internal memos indicated that Hooker officials attributed the problem to the toxic chemicals left there. But this informa-tion remained secret for twenty years, until massive leaks from the site contaminated a group of nearby homes with a potent mixture of toxic chemicals. By the end of 1980, the state had been forced to evacuate 239 families and demolish their homes, and law suits worth $15 billion were making their way through the courts. Another 311 homes were eventually condemned, and the Love Canal disaster cost the Ameri-can taxpayer about $200 million. Yet, six years after those initial evacu-ations, the government had still not issued an official ruling on whether Love Canal was habitable, apparently because it feared setting a prece-dent that would require evacuations around the hundreds of other toxic dumps in the United States.[66]

Another notorious case of industrial contamination was the Chisso Corporation's poisoning of Minimata, Japan with the mercury emissions from its local plant. The first symptoms of mercury contamination at Minimata surfaced in the early 1950s. Local birds began to lose their sense of balance and fly into buildings or simply fall out of the trees, while some cats began walking with a strange, stumbling gait and then suddenly went mad, running in circles and foaming at the mouth until they collapsed. Local fishermen and their families were the next to fall victim to this plague. Unusual tenderness in the gums and mouth would be followed by trembling that grew progressively worse, until the victim began violently thrashing about and eventually lapsed into unconsciousness. But, most frightening of all were the mental effects of "Minimata disease"—confusion, hallucinations, and mania. By 1975, health surveys had uncovered thirty-five hundred victims and more than 120 deaths.[67]

When faced with the violence it had done to the people of Minimata, the Chisso Corporation responded in the same way its American counterparts did in similar situations: it denied responsibility, and when that position became untenable, it fought bitter court battles to avoid paying compensation to the victims and their families. Not until 1973 was Chisso finally forced to admit its guilt and pay reasonable compensation.[68]

It seems that the widely publicized tragedy in Minimata would discourage other corporations from being so negligent with their mercury discharges, if for no other reason than to avoid the near-bankruptcy that faced Chisso. Unfortunately, this was not the case with American mercury producers. Mercury pollution in the Hackensack Meadowlands in New Jersey is so bad that one environmental expert has described the region as "more severely contaminated with mercury than any other area known in the world."[69] Nevertheless, the companies that had owned the nearby mercury processing plant during its operating years (1937 to 1973) followed the familiar pattern and denied all responsibility.[70]

Charges of even more blatant misconduct in the handling of mercury emissions have been lodged against the Olin Corporation, whose continuous dumping of mercury into the Niagara River was severe enough to attract the attention of the federal government's understaffed investigative agencies. After a federal suit, Olin agreed to limit its emissions of mercury into the Niagara River to 0.5 lb. a day, and several years later the allowable level of emissions was further reduced to 0.2 lb. per day. But the U.S. Justice Department subsequently filed another lawsuit, in which it charged that Olin had vastly exceeded the mercury emission limits to which it had agreed and then falsified its report to the government in order to cover up its crimes. In one report filed with the EPA, for example, Olin stated it had discharged 0.11 lb. of mercury on one day in July 1972, but other evidence showed that the company's mercury emissions actually amounted to 330 lb. Olin was ultimately fined $70,000 for its offenses, and two of its employees were each given fines and three years probation.[71]

Since the passage of federal legislation regulating the disposal of hazardous wastes in 1976, manufacturers have turned increasingly to private contractors to get rid of the dangerous substances they produce. Although the law requires the licensing of firms that dispose of hazardous wastes, there has been so little supervision or control that blatantly illegal techniques are commonly used to get rid of the unwanted chemicals. Indeed, many of the firms that rushed into the hazardous wastes control business were actually run by organized crime.[72] And no matter who controls those companies, this is a profitable venture for both parties: disposal firms make fat profits by illegally (and inexpensively) dumping the wastes, and the large corporations get rid of their pollutants cheaply and easily, while avoiding any financial responsibility for them. The public is, once again, the principal loser.

New Jersey, with America's largest chemical industry (and, not coincidentally, its highest rate of cancer mortality), is experiencing especially severe problems with such illegal dumping. Legal testimony indicates that some waste disposal companies send out tanker trucks in the dead of the night to find empty streets, vacant lots, or quiet streams, and simply open the valves and let their dangerous cargo pour out. Not only do such crimes contribute to New Jersey's alarming incidence of cancer, but many of the chemicals are flammable and thus pose the additional threat of fire and explosion.[73] One illegal dumping site was discovered when an empty lot suddenly burst into flames. Another was discovered by a fire inspector who found that his shoes were being eaten away by the chemicals dumped in a lot he happened to walk across.

In one of the worst cases to date, the small town of Times Beach, Mo., was virtually destroyed by pirate dumping. The problem arose from a hexachlorophene plant's efforts to dispose of wastes contaminated with dioxin, one of the most toxic substances known to science. The plant hired a local waste hauler to do the job, and he sprayed the waste-oil mixture on horse arenas, streets, parking lots, and farms throughout the state. The problem was so bad in Times Beach that the EPA found dioxin levels one hundred times those considered safe for long-term contact. Intense national publicity eventually forced the federal government to buy up the entire town and move the people out.[74]

Unsafe Products

Consumers undoubtedly were complaining about shoddy merchandise thousands of years before the creation of the first modern corporation. Traditionally, the law has merely warned the buyer to be careful, and little was done to redress consumer grievances. Even today, there is nothing illegal about selling cheap merchandise at exorbitant prices, provided that no fraudulent claims are made. The same is true of the sale of most unsafe products, although the manufacturer of such products may still face substantial civil liability. Most of the cases we are about to examine involve not only the manufacture of dangerous products but also fraudulent or deceptive statements made by corporate officials to avoid a sales disaster or costly civil suits. These fraudulent statements turn corporate irresponsibility into corporate crime.

The potential for harm varies greatly from one type of product to another. The hazards of an improperly made hat and an improperly made airplane are obviously quite different. But of all consumer products, automobiles and other motor vehicles have proven to be the most dangerous. There have been well over 2 million traffic deaths since the first recorded U.S. automobile fatality in 1899 and perhaps ten times that many injuries. However many of those casualties can be attributed to defects in the vehicles, the fact remains that automobiles are extremely dangerous machines, and one would expect that responsible manufacturers do everything possible to make them safer. Unfortunately, the conventional wisdom in the automobile industry has been that "safety doesn't sell." Alfred P. Sloan, the former president of General Motors, expressed the position of his industry in replying to the urgings of the DuPont Corporation to use its safety glass in the Chevrolet:

> I am trying to protect the interest of the stockholders of General Motors and the corporation's operating position—it is not my responsibility to sell safety glass. . . .You can say perhaps that I am selfish, but business is selfish. We are not a charitable institution—we are trying to make a profit for our stockholders.[75]

It would be interesting to know how many of Mr. Sloan's stockholders died because GM cars did not have safety glass. But whatever the number, it is clear that the automobile industry has not merely been indifferent to proposals to improve vehicle safety but in many cases has actively opposed them.

This attitude was clearly reflected in the industry's response to the National Traffic and Motor Vehicle Safety Act of 1966, which required automobile makers to notify their customers about safety-related defects in their products. Time after time, the manufacturers have put up vehement opposition to the recalls until forced to make them by the regulatory agencies or the courts. One typical case involved GM's line of "X-cars" (Chevrolet Citation, Buick Skylark, Pontiac Phoenix, and Oldsmobile Omega). The X-cars, GM's first small front-wheel-drive cars, were plagued with mechanical problems from their introduction in 1980. They were subject to numerous recalls, the most serious of which involved a brake defect that was alleged to have caused the deaths of thirteen persons. Documents obtained by the House Commerce Committee show that tests by the National Highway Traffic Safety Commission identified the problem long before it gained media attention. The results of those tests were never made public, however, presumably because of pressure from GM—the nation's largest private employer. A recall of 240,000 cars was finally made on March 30, 1983, but only after numerous press reports about the problem and strong congressional pressure.[76]

The most highly publicized automotive safety defect of recent times was the unsafe gas tank in the 1971 through 1976 model Ford Pintos and Bobcats. According to the National Highway Traffic Safety Administration, "Low to moderate speed rear-end collisions of Pintos produce massive full tank leaks due to puncture or tearing of the fuel tank and separation of the filler pipe from the tank."[77]   There is evidence that Ford knew about these safety defects before the Pinto was ever put on the market but declined to make the necessary changes for economic reasons.[78]   For example, internal company documents uncovered by investigative reporters showed that in secret crash tests of the Pinto, Ford found the gas tank ruptured in every crash that occurred at over twenty-five miles per hour. Nevertheless, Ford later denied that the tests had ever been made,[79] and it repeatedly claimed that the charges against the Pinto were unwarranted.

The original charges against the Pinto came from Ralph Nader's Center for Automotive Safety. A subsequent article in the muckraking magazine *Mother Jones* presented substantial new evidence against the Pinto. As the publicity increased, the National Highway Traffic Safety Administration finally issued an "initial determination" that the Pinto's gas tank was unsafe. Ford continued to vehemently deny the charges against the Pinto until a week before the public hearings were scheduled to begin and then suddenly agreed to recall the Pintos and Bobcats.[80] Although the entire cost has never been totaled, Ford's decision to cut corners on the gas tank safety of the Pinto-Bobcat and to continue to deny the dangers of the vehicle for years after they became apparent probably cost the company well over $100 million. In addition to the cost of the recall, Ford was subject to dozens of civil suits, some of which brought multimillion dollar judgments. But, of course, Ford's losses were slight compared to the more than fifty people who are believed to have died as a direct result of automobile accidents involving gas tank ruptures.[81]

The case of the Firestone 500 steel-belted radial tire bears substantial similarities to the Pinto case. Firestone began production of the tire in 1972, and the first signs of trouble appeared before that year was over. An intracompany memo to a Firestone vice-president warned that "we are in danger of being cut off by Chevrolet [which was using the tire] because of separation failures."[82] This problem of sudden blowouts or loss of pressure caused by separation of the tread from the steel-belted inner layer was to plague the tire throughout its five years of production. The Atlas Tire Company, which sold the Firestone 500 under its own name, wrote to Firestone in 1973 complaining about the tire's high rate of failure: "In the eyes of Atlas, it appears Firestone is coming apart at the seams, and drastic action is required."[83] Complaints poured in from numerous other firms that sold or used the 500, including the Ford Motor Company. In 1976, Montgomery Ward, which had been selling the 500 under the name Grappler 8000, told Firestone that customer returns had reached "epidemic proportions" that "amplified the fact we were given a bad product." Firestone also had ample evidence of the 500's defects from its own staff. A Firestone engineer who set out to investigate complaints about the tire in 1973 found that 32 percent of the new tires he examined at one location showed separation of the steel belting.[84] Whereas a return rate of much over 5 percent is considered a sign for serious concern in the tire industry, the 500 had an average return rate of 17.5 percent, and the return rate in one year reached 27 percent.[85]

Firestone's top management responded to the overwhelming evidence against the 500 with a concerted campaign to keep the truth from the public. When a government survey of tire safety produced damning evidence against Firestone's tire, the company filed a suit to block the survey's release, claiming it was inaccurate and would create the impression that there were widespread defects in radial tires.[86] In July 1978, a Firestone representative had the temerity to claim that "the 500 is providing reliable service to millions of motorists today as it has for many years. There is no safety-related reason for the public to be concerned about continuing to use Firestone steel-belted radial 500s or any other properly maintained Firestone-made tire."[87] In light of the evidence in Firestone's possession at the time, this statement and the numerous others like it can only be considered acts of blatant fraud.

By the time Firestone stopped production of the 500 at the end of 1977, over 23 million of them had been produced. The whole fiasco was a devastating blow to the Firestone Corporation. Its president resigned for "personal reasons," and the company was hit with hundreds of damage suits, a $234 million bill for the recall the government forced upon it, and a huge loss of public confidence. But once again, the public was the real loser. Tens of thousands of 500s failed on the road, contributing to numerous accidents and at least forty-one deaths.[88]

As bad as the safety record of the automobile industry has been, that of the pharmaceutical industry has been even worse. Time after time, respected pharmaceutical firms have shown a cavalier disregard for the lives and safety of the people who use their products. Industry salespeople are trained to routinely downplay the dangerous and some- times even fatal side effects of their products, and many pharmaceutical manufacturers apparently see nothing wrong with encouraging their representatives to make deceptive statements that stop just short of fraud. The former medical director of E. R. Squibb and Sons described his reasons for resigning as follows: "I reached a point where I could no longer live with myself. I had compromised myself to the point where my back was to the wall, and I had to choose between resigning myself to total capitulation or resigning as medical director." He went on to say that a drug company doctor "must learn to word a warning statement so it will appear to be an inducement to use the drug rather than a warn- ing of the dangers inherent in its use."[89] Of course, such behavior is not illegal, and as defenders of the industry point out, the same kind of sales approach is used for countless other products. But a company manufacturing products upon which many lives depend must assume a greater burden of responsibility than other firms, and the pharmaceu- tical industry has largely ignored this obligation, choosing instead to pursue the maximum possible profit.

Although the major pharmaceutical firms certainly attempt to stay within the law, this exploitive philosophy has inevitably lead to numer- ous criminal activities—particularly in the falsification of the tests the Food and Drug Administration requires before certifying a new drug and the use of fraudulent and deceptive advertising. One of the best- documented of these frauds involved a new drug from the Richardson- Merrell Company, MER/29—a cholesterol inhibitor intended for use by heart patients. When the drug was first developed, Richardson-Merrell foresaw a multimillion dollar sales potential, and the company was anx- ious to win FDA approval as quickly as possible. Richardson-Merrell's economic calculations were certainly accurate, for MER/29 was used by about one hundred thousand people in the first seven months after its introduction, but the company's rush to exploit that lucrative mar- ket proved its undoing. While top management was preparing a major marketing campaign, bad news began to come in from the research department. In one laboratory test, all the female rats given a high dose of MER/29 died, and all the rats in a later test involving a lower dosage of the drug had to be destroyed before the experiment was completed. Autopsies revealed abnormal blood changes in the rats, and these dis- turbing results were confirmed from tests with other animals. Monkeys, for instance, suffered blood changes, loss of weight, and serious visual problems.

Richardson-Merrell's response to this clear evidence of problems with MER/29 was not to withhold the potentially dangerous drug from the market but to falsify the data. One laboratory technician testified that she was ordered by a Richardson-Merrell executive to change the reports on the health problems experienced by test animals and to make up data for nonexistent animals showing no harmful effects from the use of MER/29. When the technician complained to her supervisor, she was told, "He [the executive] is higher up. You do as he tells you, and be quiet."[90] Richardson-Merrell's application to the FDA was thus full of fraudulent statements. The report on one study claimed that only four of eight experimental rats had died, when in fact they all did. Completely fictitious body weights and blood tests were made up for dead rats, as though they were still alive and taking MER/29. Shortly before the license to sell MER/29 was granted, Richardson-Merrell completed another study in which nine of ten experimental animals developed eye opacities (cataracts) and then told the FDA that eight of twenty rats had developed a mild inflammation of the eye.

Clinical data about the dangers of MER/29 began building up as soon as the drug hit the market. But the discovery of Richardson-Merrell's fraud came about quite by accident, when an investigator for the FDA happened to share a ride with the husband of one of the laboratory technicians who was asked to falsify data. Had the husband not felt talkative that day, Richardson-Merrell might never have been caught—indeed, it seems quite likely that most cases of the falsification of data by pharmaceutical manufacturers never come to light. As the FDA inspector who first uncovered the MER/29 fraud put it, "I didn't think the [MER/29 case] was typical, but I was wrong. . . .They were totally geared to the dollar sign. I am sure there are many other firms similar to them—even today. I suspect [Richardson-Merrell] got away with the same thing many times before."[91]

By the time MER/29 was finally taken off the market, over four hundred thousand people had used the drug, and at least five thousand users had suffered serious side effects—usually the "classic triad" of hair loss, severe skin problems, and cataracts.[92] Criminal charges were brought against a Richardson-Merrell vice-president and two laboratory supervisors. Each could have received five years in prison and a $10,000 fine, but instead the judge gave them only six months' probation. After pleading no-contest to eight of twelve counts against it, the Richardson-Merrell company was given the maximum fine of $80,000—hardly a severe punishment for a company that made a profit of $17,790,000 that year.[93] Indeed, the $80,000 represented only a small fraction of the money Richardson-Merrell made from its crime: in its first year of production MER/29 brought in over $7 million in gross revenues.

The MER/29 case is exceptional only because Richardson-Merrell was caught red-handed falsifying data. A more common ploy by pharmaceutical companies is to conceal the data they have about the hazards of their products. This was the case, for example, with Oraflex, a painkiller marketed to arthritis patients by Eli Lilly and Company. The use of Oraflex has been linked to the deaths of at least sixty-two patients, and the evidence shows that the company knew about twenty-six of these deaths in foreign countries before it applied to the FDA for permission to sell the drug in the United States. Lilly did not reveal any of this information to the FDA, however, and Oraflex was approved for sale in April 1982. By August, the drug had to be withdrawn from the market when reports of these deaths and of a growing number of new ones began circulating in the media.[94] Three years later, in August 1985, Lilly pleaded guilty to misdemeanor charges arising from its attempts to conceal the hazards of Oraflex. The total punishment handed out for a crime that is believed to have killed 49 people and injured 916 more was a $25,000 fine for Lilly and a $15,000 fine for one executive.[95]

The case of the Dalkon Shield was far more devastating to its perpetrator, the A. H. Robbins Company. The Dalkon Shield was an extremely popular intrauterine birth control device in the late 1960s and early 1970s. But as it turned out, every woman who used it was risking serious complications. The most dangerous of several problems was that the wick used to insert and remove the device also served as a pathway for bacteria-laden fluids to travel up into the uterus. It is estimated that at least 17 women were killed and as many as 200,000 more injured by complications involving the Dalkon Shield.[96]

A. H. Robbins was involved in a web of unethical dealings right from the beginning, when it relied on safety tests conducted by a physician who had a substantial financial interest in the Shield. As evidence of the dangers of the Shield mounted, the company, in the words of two court-appointed "special masters": "engaged in an ongoing fraud by knowingly misrepresenting the nature, quality, safety, and efficacy of the Dalkon Shield."[97] A quality control supervisor for Robbins reported that when he told his boss that he must speak up about his concerns with the safety of the Shield, he was accused of "insubordination" and was warned that if he valued his job he had better do as he was told.[98] A former Robbins attorney, Roger L. Tuttle, later stunned the lawyers at a routine pretrial deposition in 1984 when he admitted that boxes of memos relating to the Sheild case had been burned in order to keep them out of the hands of the victims' attorneys. [94] By 1985 Robbins had paid out more than $378 million dollars to settle 9,200 suits from the victims, but those cases were only the tip of the iceberg. In August of that year, Robbins declared bankruptcy, indefinitely postponing compensation to the 40,000 to 50,000 more women who legally deserve it. In July 1987, Robbins proposed to merge with the Rorer Group of pharmaceutical companies, and they offered to create a $1.7 billion fund for the victims. However, critics estimate that the total cost of the claims may actually be closer to $5 billion, and they charge that if this deal is approved, many of the later claimants may get nothing. [100]

Another unethical practice in the pharmaceutical industry is the "dumping" of unsafe products in poor nations with lax drug-safety regulations. Although U.S. law forbids the export of any drug that has not been approved by the FDA, manufacturers have often found ways to skirt the law. A. H. Robbins, for instance, continued to market the Dalkon Shield overseas long after the publicity about its side effects had made it virtually impossible to sell in the United States, and those sales continued until the Shield was officially ruled unsafe by the FDA. [101] The same tactic was used by the manufacturers of birth control pills containing high dosages of estrogens. After the publicity about the dangers of these contraceptives made them unsalable in the United States, at least two manufacturers sold off their stocks of pills at cutrate prices for distribution to women in Third World countries. Some pharmaceutical companies have also taken advantage of a loophole in U.S. law that allows antibiotics to be exported without FDA approval. For example, the Upjohn Company continued to export the antibiotic Panalba, even though it was taken off the American market in 1970. The case against Panalba is a convincing one: not only do 20 percent of the people who use novobiocin, one of Panalba's two ingredients, suffer allergic reactions, but in addition, Upjohn's own tests showed that Panalba's safer ingredient, tetracycline, was more effective than Panalba when used alone. Although Panalba is believed to have been related to the deaths of at least twelve patients in the United States, it was still exported to thirty-three other countries. Upjohn, however, did take the precaution of changing Panalba's trade name to Albamycin-T. [102] Another common form of dumping practiced by the multinationals is to ship old drugs whose shelf life has expired to unsuspecting Third World countries. [103]

Another reflection of the pharmaceutical companies' priorities can be seen in the fact that they tend to admit the harmful side effects of their drugs only when forced to do so by the countries in which the drugs are sold. From the information supplied by pharmaceutical companies, it would appear that some drugs are safer when they are sold in poor countries with weak controls on the operations of pharmaceutical manufacturers. Consider the adverse reactions listed by the Searle Company for their oral contraceptive, Ovulen. In the United States, Searle lists "nausea, loss of hair, nervousness, jaundice, high blood pressure, weight change, and headaches" as side effects. The farther south the product is sold, however, the safer it seems to become. In Mexico, only two side effects, nausea and weight change, are named, and in Brazil and Argentina, Searle would have physicians believe that Ovulen has no harmful side effects at all. [104] Such deception is, moreover, a much more serious matter in Third World countries. Since Third World physicians often do not have access to current journals or the latest medical information, they must rely more heavily on the information supplied by drug companies and their salespeople. [105]

BRIBERY AND CORRUPTION

In West Africa it is known as *dash*; in Latin America, *la mordida* ("the bite"); in Italy, *la bustarella* ("the little envelope"); in France, *pot de vin*; in the United States, "grease." Under whatever name, bribery is a universal phenomenon with roots that stretch far back into human history. The Code of Hammurabi, created by the king who founded the first Babylonian empire almost four thousand years ago, held that if a man was bribed to give false witness against another, he must bear the penalty imposed in the case. An edict by one Egyptian pharaoh proclaimed the death penalty for any official or priest who accepted a bribe for the performance of his judicial duties. References in Greek and Roman laws, as well as in the Bible, show that bribery was condemned with harsh penalties in other ancient societies as well. [106]

Although the record of American history cannot match those others in terms of antiquity, it, too, is replete with references to the problem of corruption. In 1918, for example, an investigation by the Federal Trade Commission found widespread bribery in American business. The FTC reported to Congress that "the commission has found that commercial bribery of employees is a prevalent and common practice in many industries. These bribes take the form of commissions for alleged services, of money and gratuities and entertainments of various sorts, and loans—all intended to influence such employees in the choice of materials." [107] These practices had become so accepted among some workers that one corrupt employee even approached a representative of the commission to ask for his assistance in collection of a "commission" that he said was due him.

Many students of bribery in the present day United States have concluded that it is not only widespread but also is accepted as a normal business practice in many segments of the economy. [108] There is, however, no reliable way to gauge the true extent of the problem, and estimates of the total amount of money involved differ widely. In 1974 the Chamber of Commerce of the United States put the cost of bribery at about $3 billion a year, [109] but another estimate put the cost of bribery in just three industries—food, retail, and building—at $5 billion to $8 billion a year. [110] A 1976 estimate published in *The New York Times* put the yearly figure at $15 billion. [111] Whatever the exact number, there is no question that bribery involves large amounts of money and has a major impact upon the economy.

Many criminologists categorize bribery on the basis of its intended target. Thus, they distinguish bribery directed at private firms and individuals from bribery directed at government employees. From a sociological standpoint, however, it makes more sense to include the payoffs made to win government contracts in the same category as the payoffs made to win private business, for the motivations and *modus operandi* of the offenders are often identical. Accordingly, we will distinguish between *commercial bribery* intended to promote sales or obtain confidential business information and *political bribery* intended to influence government policy.

Commercial Bribery

The bribery of judges and other government officials is an ancient crime, but the concept of commercial bribery is a much more recent development (see chapter 4). And although it is illegal, many people are willing to brush commercial bribery off as a normal business practice that causes little real harm. Supporters of this position argue that the total amount of money paid out in bribes is relatively small and has little effect on the average consumer. One analysis of thirty-four U.S. corporations that admitted paying overseas bribery concluded that, whereas the bribes involved totaled $93.7 million, the total sales revenues of the companies amounted to $679 billion. Thus, the bribe money composed only 0.014 percent of the sales of those companies. [112] The question of how much more bribery went undetected, however, remains unanswered. And even if the total amount of money involved in commercial bribery is small, the practice creates a climate of corruption and disrespect for the law and gives major corporations with vast financial resources an unfair advantage over their smaller competitors.

When firms attempt to buy sales for their products, their first targets are often the purchasing agents who are paid to make those decisions. But such corrupt employees are clearly occupational criminals, and this problem will be examined from their perspective in the next chapter. Our attention here will be focused on the organizations that offer corrupt payments and the techniques they employ.

Corporate payoffs are often made through dummy firms set up to act as conduits for illegal transactions. Under this arrangement, the parent corporation can write off bribe money as a legitimate business expense and can claim it knew nothing about the payoffs. One such dummy firm was the Economic and Development Corporation, which the Northrop Corporation established in Switzerland, ostensibly as a sales corporation. In reality, the EDC was a conduit for funds kept in Swiss bank accounts that were used to make various sorts of bribes and "questionable payments." The recipients included numerous political and governmental agents in the Netherlands, Iran, France, the Federal Republic of Germany, Saudi Arabia, Brazil, Malaysia, and Taiwan. [113]

More often, however, businesses distribute payoff money through sales agents. Because many multinational corporations find it difficult and expensive to set up an office in every country in which they do business, they often employ local sales agents who know the people involved in making major purchases. Such agents also provide an excellent conduit for the distribution of bribe money, for they know who is likely to accept bribes and what kind of inducements they prefer. In addition, the use of local sales agents allows foreign multinationals to avoid direct involvement in the illicit payments. The sales agents do not volunteer information about the recipients of their largess, and the multinationals don't ask.

The case that touched off the most notorious international bribery scandal of recent times involved the Lockheed Aircraft Corporation. Although the $25 million that Lockheed admitted giving out in "questionable payments" certainly represented a substantial amount of money, other corporations later admitted even larger payments. (Exxon's total, for instance, was well over $46 million.) [114] But no other firm seems to have fostered corruption in such high circles as did Lockheed. Among those named in bribery charges were the former prime minister of Japan, Kakuei Tanaka, and Prince Bernhard of the Netherlands.

Although Lockheed apparently made a number of direct bribery payments, it too preferred to work through sales agents. Lockheed's corrupt activities in Indonesia not only illustrate this technique but also seem to show tacit support for Lockheed's sales tactics from the U.S. government. When Indonesian President Sukarno was deposed in a coup, Lockheed officials became concerned about the status of their sales agent with the new government. Lockheed documents show that they consulted the U.S. embassy for help and that "embassy CIA personnel" checked out the matter and found the agent to be "well connected" with the new regime. Other documents show that Lockheed bribes may have reached all the way to Sukarno himself and later to his successor, President Suharto. The evidence also indicates that Lockheed officials were worried about the demands that the bribes be paid directly to high Indonesian military officers, both because the bribes might be discovered and "could be damaging to Lockheed's name and reputation" and because sales commissions are tax-deductible but bribery is not. Lockheed memos show that the company tried to convince the officers of the need to take bribes through agents because of the "significant protection provided for them as well as for us."[115]

Officials in Iran, the Philippines, Italy, West Germany, Turkey, Mexico, Colombia, and Venezuela all received Lockheed bribe money, but the biggest scandals involved the Netherlands and Japan. Lockheed's "questionable payments" in the Netherlands won worldwide attention because Prince Bernhard, the husband of the Dutch queen, was implicated. Although an investigative committee appointed by the Dutch government did not find sufficient grounds for a criminal indictment, numerous serious charges were made against the prince. A former Lockheed sales agent charged that Prince Bernhard had received regular secret payments to promote the sales of the Lockheed F-104 fighter, and other sources indicated that the total may have reached $1.1 million. Other charges centered around the sale of Lockheed's P-3C patrol plane. According to some evidence, Bernhard was offered a $1 million bribe by Lockheed, but the deal fell through when he demanded a commission of from $4 to $6 million. None of these charges resulted in civil or criminal action against the prince, although he was forced to resign from a number of official positions, including his job as the Inspector General of the Dutch armed forces.[116]

Lockheed's criminal activities in Japan also reached to the highest levels, and they involved much larger sums of money and a wider network of corruption. Most of the charges centered around the $7.1 million paid to Yoshio Kodama to act as a Lockheed sales agent. Described by Senator Frank Church as the leader of the "ultra right-wing militarist faction" in Japan, Kodama was a war criminal who had served three years in prison after World War II. In addition to Kodama, other Lockheed agents are believed to have given out $12.6 million more in payoffs. These bribes spanned many years and involved numerous different aircraft, but the biggest scandal erupted over the sale of twenty-one Lockheed L-1011 TriStar passenger planes to All-Nippon Airways. When Lockheed's successful bribery attempt came to public light, three executives of All-Nippon were arrested on various perjury and foreign-exchange law violations, and there were charges that Prime Minister Tanaka had accepted $1.6 million to facilitate the sale. An extensive investigation led to the arrest of Tanaka, his secretary, Toshio Enomoto, and two top executives of the Marubeni Trading Corporation (Lockheed's national trading agent) for accepting bribes. [117]

Some of the most persistent questions about corruption in the American government surround the Department of Defense's huge yearly purchases of equipment and supplies for the U.S. military. Although the Department of Defense has long been notorious for its waste and inefficiency, it has become increasingly clear that much of the problem can be traced to bribery and corruption. In 1986 the U.S. attorney for a region in Southern California with a heavy concentration of defense contractors testified that: "Kickbacks on defense subcontracts are a pervasive, longstanding practice which has corrupted the subcontracting process at most, if not all, defense contractors and. . .defense procurement programs." [118]   A coordinated attack on corruption in defense procurement involving the Department of Defense, the FBI, and the Internal Revenue Service lead to legal action against dozens of individuals and corporations in 1987. Most of the corporate defendants were small to medium-sized subcontractors, but employees of such corporate giants as Martin Marietta and General Dynamics were also involved. In addition to bribes and kickbacks, other charges concerned the submission of false claims for payment and the sale of substandard merchandise that often had false quality certifications. The list of such merchandise contains everything from aircraft ejection seats to clothing and tools. Several price-fixing conspiracies were also uncovered, involving such widely diverse areas as steel springs and pipeline dredging contracts. [119]

Political Bribery and Corruption

Special-interest groups use a host of different techniques to bend government policy to their ends. And despite their corrosive effects upon the democratic process, many of those techniques are completely legal. For example, one of the most persuasive rewards private industry has to exchange for political favors is the lure of a high-paying job when a cooperative official or politician leaves government service. Although some restrictions have now been placed on this practice, there is little doubt that it is still a highly effective tool used to influence government officials without breaking the law (see chapters 4 and 5).

Lavish parties and free entertainment are other common devices used to curry favor among elected officials. Although the lobbyists' big entertainment budgets raise few eyebrows in Washington, the process of corruption becomes more apparent when their largess involves free trips and all-expense-paid vacations. The Northrop Corporation's attempts to win favor with legislators and high-ranking military personnel provide a typical example. The Senate Watergate committee's investigation of an illegal $150,000 contribution Northrop made to President Richard Nixon's campaign touched off a stockholder suit and a special audit by the corporation's accounting firm, Ernst and Ernst. Among other things, the audit revealed that between 1971 and 1973 the corporation rented a posh goose-hunting lodge on Maryland's eastern shore that had been visited only 120 times by Northrop officials but 123 times by military personnel, 21 times by civilian Pentagon officials, 11 times by members of Congress, and 85 times by congressional staffers. A subsequent congressional investigation disclosed that hunting lodges were used for similar purposes by other defense contractors, including Rockwell International and the Remington Arms Company. [120]

But the most popular legal method of purchasing political influence is still through campaign contributions (see chapter 3). Restrictions on direct corporate contributions to political candidates, however, have created some problems for organizational influence seekers and led to many illegal attempts to skirt the law. Corporations sometimes provide free services directly to sympathetic candidates, in the hope that such assistance will be less obvious than illegal monetary contributions. For instance, a corporation may provide a candidate with free stamps or mailing services, free use of company facilities such as duplicating machines, telephones, and computers, or the assistance of employees on company time. Some corporations make large loans to candidates that may or may not be paid back. Others secretly pay campaign expenses by shifting part of a candidate's advertising bills to their own accounts. [121] Republican President Dwight Eisenhower observed that corporations "lend office equipment and the services of their public relations experts and lawyers; they make it easy, through bonuses and expense accounts, for executives to contribute substantial sums; and they buy advertising space at ridiculously high rates in political pamphlets and brochures." [122]

Corporations have not always been content to operate through such indirect methods, and there have been numerous revelations of direct corporate payments to finance election campaigns. Among the many illegal campaign contributions that came to light during the Watergate investigations, the dairy cases not only involved the largest amounts of money, but several of those contributions were apparently linked to specific administrative actions, thus violating bribery statutes as well. Associated Milk Producers, Inc. (AMPI), the nation's largest dairy co-op, made numerous illegal payments to support such major political figures as President Lyndon Johnson and Democratic Presidential candidate Hubert Humphrey. But the dairy industry's biggest payoffs were given to Richard Nixon, the man who defeated Humphrey in 1968. And while the other contributions were, as far as is known, intended to purchase general goodwill and political influence, some of the contributions to the Nixon campaign were apparently tied directly to an increase in the price support of dairy products. According to court documents, AMPI lobbyist Robert Lilly admitted making a commitment of campaign funds to President Nixon's reelection campaign "in conjunction with" the 1971 price support increase authorized by Nixon. [123] The executive director of another major dairy co-op, Dairymen, Inc., reported a secret meeting with two other co-ops called to raise $300,000 that had been requested for immediate use in Nixon's reelection campaign. They were able to come up with only $25,000 in cash, which they turned over with a renewal of their pledge to contribute a total of $2 million to the campaign. The following day the Nixon administration announced a substantial increase in dairy price supports. [124]

A similar case came to light in March 1975, when the Securities and Exchange Commission accused the Gulf Oil Corporation of funneling more than $10 million into a Bahamian subsidiary for use as illegal political contributions. According to subsequent Senate testimony, the head of Gulf's Washington lobbying effort decided who was to receive the funds and then ordered the controller of the Bahamian firm to send up the cash for disbursement as campaign contributions. [125] Most prominent among those alleged to have received illegal contributions from Gulf was the minority leader of the Senate, Hugh Scott. According to the charges, Scott received up to $100,000 in illegal contributions, much of which he handed out to other candidates he supported. Although the Senate spent months trying to figure out what to do about the charges against Scott, it finally decided not to investigate the matter, and he retired from the Senate a few months later. [126] Only one, much less powerful congressman, James R. Jones, was indicted; and after pleading guilty, he was fined a mere $200. Ironically, Gulf's Washington lobbyist escaped all charges because Congress, frightened by the Watergate investigations, had reduced the statute of limitations on illegal campaign contributions from five to three years, and the special prosecutor was unable to act quickly enough to meet the deadline. [127]

Gulf also made political contributions in numerous other countries. In some cases, such as those involving Sweden and Canada, the contributions were not in violation of national laws. But in other instances, they violated U.S. tax and financial reporting laws as well as the laws of the host country. Gulf's largest contributions were made in South Korea, where the company had invested over $200 million in an oil refinery, a fertilizer plant, and other projects. In Senate testimony, Gulf's chairman admitted making over $4 million in political contributions to the ruling party of South Korean President Park Chung Hee—a clear violation of Korean law. In defense of their activities, Gulf officials claimed that they had been threatened with serious reprisals if they did not make the payoffs. Unfortunately, the Korean government used its censorship power to prevent its press from reporting the bribery incidents and never responded to Gulf's charges. Gulf's chairman also admitted buying a helicopter worth over $100,000 for former Bolivian President René Barrientos and donating another $360,000 to his political party. Other evidence indicates that Gulf also made payments to lower-level officials in South Korea, Bolivia, Italy, Turkey, Switzerland, Kuwait, Venezuela, Nigeria, Gabon, Angola, Ecuador, and the Netherlands. [128]

There was nothing particularly unique in Gulf's activities; dozens of other major corporations have admitted to similar involvement in international bribery and corruption. In Italy, Gulf actually entered into cooperative agreements with other multinational petroleum corporations to coordinate their efforts at political corruption. The Exxon Corporation admitted that it made almost $50 million in political payments over a ten-year period, and that its subsidiary, Esso Italiana, had acted as a collection agent for payments made by other companies. Each multinational was expected to contribute a *pro rata* share of the payoff money based upon its sales volume, and each firm was allowed to specify who was to receive the funds. Virtually no Italian political parties were neglected—Exxon even gave $86,000 to the Communists. Although no Italian laws clearly prohibited such payments, most of the multinationals did violate U.S. law by falsifying their books to make the bribes appear to be legitimate business expenses eligible for tax deductions. [129]

Perhaps the most damaging form of international bribery is that aimed at the leaders of Third World countries. The bribes and financial incentives the major multinationals offer are enormously attractive to those living in such poor nations, and many local leaders have been only too happy to sell out the interests of their country for a share of the booty. Typical were the activities of the United Brands Company in Honduras. In 1974, that small, poverty-stricken nation attempted to recoup some of the losses it had suffered from increases in the price of imported oil by placing a tax on its banana exports. United Brands saw this tax, which amounted to about one cent a pound, as a serious threat because many of its competitors were based in countries that did not impose such a tax. So the company turned to bribery to protect its profits, paying out $1.25 million to highly placed Honduran officials. In return, United Brands won a reduction in the tax that cost that impoverished nation $7.5 million in the first year alone. [130]

VIOLATIONS OF CIVIL LIBERTIES

Assaults on individual liberty take many forms. In authoritarian regimes, they involve direct and often violent repression of dissenting views. In the liberal democracies, political repression assumes more subtle guises. Corporations commonly hire investigators and informants to spy on their political opponents. Government agents work behind the scenes and out of public view, oftentimes violating the laws they claim to be protecting. This seeming paradox is a reflection of the fact that while the ruling elites in contemporary industrial societies have enormous power, it is not unlimited power. The strength of tradition, public opinion, and opposing political groups has been sufficient to create legal limits on the abuses of the elite, even if those forces have been unable to win effective enforcement action against such influential criminals (see chapters 4 and 5).

Corporate Violations

Violations of civil liberties are usually associated with governments, not private businesses. But the growing size and influence of today's corporations have led them to take on many quasi-governmental roles and become more and more deeply involved in the political process. The mere concentration of economic control has transformed some long-standing business practices into new threats to civil liberties. For example, many nineteenth-century businesses refused to hire particular individuals because of their political beliefs. But in that era of independent farmers and small businesses, there were usually other employers to be found. The present-day centralization of economic control has made the risks of offending one of the major corporations greater by the year—and perhaps more significantly, it has made the demand for conformity so often associated with life in the corporate world that much more powerful. The Senate Subcommittee on Constitutional Rights recently heard estimates that up to one-fourth of the major U.S. corporations require polygraph tests as a condition of employment. The questions were reported to involve the job-seeker's sex life, political preferences, and family relations—questions even the FBI is prohibited from asking its applicants. [131] Detectives are also employed to carry out background checks on prospective employees or on those up for important promotions.

The latest trend in employee surveillance is the use of urine analysis to detect illegal drug usage. According to a survey by the American Management Association, half of America's largest corporations now test every job applicant, and other surveys indicate that about one-fifth of all businesses have some kind of drug-testing program. [132] Moreover, drug testing is not limited to job applicants. Many current employees are being subjected to random drug tests, even if they have had no problem at work. There is an obvious threat to personal freedom when workers are hired and fired on the basis of their private lives and not their performance on the job. And to make matters worse, the results of both the polygraph and urine analysis tests are unreliable and have blackened the reputation of many innocent persons.

The corporations have not, however, limited the targets of their surveillance to their own employees. Private firms also use hired agents to investigate outsiders who for one reason or another appear to threaten their interests. The most famous of these cases was certainly General Motors' attempt to smear Ralph Nader. This episode began in November 1965, with the publication of Nader's book attacking the safety of GM's Corvair. In January of the following year, Nader noticed he was being followed. He also began receiving anonymous phone calls, even though his number was unlisted. The night before Nader was scheduled to testify before Senator Abraham Ribicoff's subcommittee on auto safety, he received harassing phone calls until 4:00 A.M. warning him to "cut it out, now!" [133] Nader's landlady was questioned about how promptly he paid his bills, and other friends and associates were asked about Nader's sex life, his political affiliations, and whether he was anti-Semitic.

By this time Nader was convinced that someone was trying to dig up or even create information that could be used to discredit him. With the help of some reporters from the *New Republic*, he discovered that he was the subject of an investigation by Vincent Gillen, the head of a successful detective agency. After being apprised of this information, Senator Ribicoff and Senator Gaylord Nelson asked the Justice Department to look into the possible harassment of a witness before a congressional committee—a felony punishable by a $5,000 fine and up to five years in prison. Ford, Chrysler, and American Motors issued quick denials that they had been involved, but GM made no public comment. Put on the spot by reporters, GM was eventually forced to admit that it had ordered the investigation. In later testimony before the Senate, GM president James Roche claimed that the investigation was intended to find out if Nader had ties with the other attorneys who were suing

GM for damages caused by Corvair accidents and was thus making improper public statements about a case in litigation. Roche stated, "The investigation was limited only to Mr. Nader's qualifications, background, expertise, and association with such attorneys [those working in the suit against GM]. It did not include any of the harassment or intimidation recently reported in the press."[134]

But this portrayal of GM's actions as simply a casual, if rather unwise, investigation of an attorney who might be participating in a suit against them did not hold up long. In court papers relating to a suit Nader brought against GM, Gillen finally admitted that the actual purpose of the investigation was to discredit Nader and to "shut hum up." It turned out that Gillen had secretly recorded the instructions he received from Richard Danner, the lawyer acting as liaison between GM and the Gillen Agency. Among other things, GM's lawyer was reported to have said that

> they [GM] wanted to get something somewhere on this guy to get him out of their hair and to shut him up. He's Syrian or something, and maybe you will find an anti-Semitic angle. . . .That will be interesting to Ribicoff. There's something somewhere; find it so they can shut him up. His stuff is pretty damaging to the auto industry. [135]

No criminal charges were brought against Roche, Gillen, or anyone else in the case. But GM did not emerge entirely unscathed. For one thing, the congressional reaction to GM's behavior in the Nader affair was one of the primary reasons the auto safety laws GM was fighting were finally passed. Also, GM eventually had to make substantial payments to the numerous victims of Corvair crashes. And perhaps most bitter of all for the company, Nader won a $425,000 court settlement that he used to establish a "continuous legal monitoring of General Motors' activities in the safety, pollution and consumer relations area."[136]

The question of how common such direct personal assaults on corporate "enemies" actually are is difficult to answer. The Nader case was certainly not an isolated incident, but neither is there enough evidence to say that such behavior is common practice among American corporations. In his court statement, Vincent Gillen said he had been conducting investigations for GM since 1959. His cases included an examination of the "morals, character and political beliefs" of actor Danny Kaye to see if they were suitable "for identification with General Motors" in a proposed advertising campaign, a two-year surveillance of a women who said she had had an affair with a GM executive, an investigation of a United Auto Workers official, and an investigation of a Harlem antipoverty worker who charged GM with discrimination. Of course, not all these cases necessarily represent violations of individual civil liberties. It seems that GM was within its rights to investigate an entertainer who was to be used in a national advertising campaign—provided, of course, that he was informed about the investigation. It is much harder to imagine a legitimate justification for the investigations of union officials or minority activists, and it appears the goal of such inquiries was pure harassment.

Numerous similar incidents involving other corporations have also come to light. The International Telephone and Telegraph Company has an especially bad reputation in this regard. For instance, ITT was found to have conducted an organized campaign to repress news stories the company considered unfavorable to its efforts to acquire the American Broadcasting Company. The campaign even included investigations of the personal lives of reporters who were writing articles ITT disliked.[137] The popular opposition to the use of nuclear power has led many utility companies either to create their own network of spies and informers or to hire private detective agencies to do it for them. Securities and Exchange Commission records showed that the nuclear utilities are paying several million dollars a year for such intelligence efforts. The list of the firms that have admitted carrying on surveillance programs against their political opponents at their rate-payers expense include such household names as Pacific Gas and Electric, Boston Edison, and the Philadelphia Electric Company. Other utilities have continued to deny their involvement in such activities despite testimony from disgruntled employees to the contrary. A former employee of Georgia Power charged that the firm spent at least $700,000 a year to maintain a surveillance program on "subversives," who were defined as anyone "who for any reason would be against the rate increases or would have some type of critical opposition to the operation of the power company."[138] Some utility companies also provided dossiers on their political opponents to trade associations, which in turn distributed them to other companies, thus expanding the network of private spies.[139]

Governmental Violations

While uncovering information about corporate violations of civil liberties is no easy matter, the problem is vastly more difficult where the government is concerned. The government agencies involved in domestic spying wrap themselves in a cloak of secrecy and often claim that "national security" is being threatened whenever attempts are made to strip away their cover. Until the Watergate investigations of the 1970s, the officially sanctioned system of illegal wiretaps, surveillance, dirty tricks, character assassination, political harassment, and violence directed against the government's political opponents was almost entirely hidden from public view. And although those investigations revealed many abuses of official power, there is still no guarantee that government agents were not successful in covering up other illegal activities. Moreover, now that the Watergate era has passed, there are many indications that police and intelligence agencies have returned to "business as usual."

The available data indicate that the institutionalized system of political surveillance and harassment brought to public light in the 1970s is a relatively new phenomenon. Until the 1930s, domestic intelligence operations were put together on an ad hoc basis in response to specific problems.[140] The political developments that culminated in the inferno of World War II also spurred an unprecedented expansion in the effort to gather domestic and international intelligence. But unlike past conflicts, the intelligence apparatus was not dismantled after the war but redirected against citizens who for one reason or another were deemed subversives. The Cold War, the "Red Scare" so skillfully manipulated by Senator Joseph McCarthy, the civil rights movement, and the war in Vietnam provided ample justification to maintain and expand wartime surveillance and political intervention, even though this involved many activities that were clearly illegal in peacetime. Reports from the FBI, CIA, IRS, Army Intelligence, and other agencies involved in domestic "operations" show a surprising indifference to their duty to obey the law. Illegal activities were considered a problem only if there was a danger they might be detected and produce political problems for the malefactors or their bosses.[141]

The objects of illegal government surveillance and harassment have included the Ku Klux Klan and the American Nazi Party on the right, Democratic and Republic opponents of presidential incumbents in the center, and various communist and socialist groups on the left. But if individuals of all political persuasions have been victimized at one time or another, most of the government's efforts have been directed against the left. The evidence shows that leftist groups have been riddled with government informers and agents provocateurs, while right-wing extremists have usually been ignored and in some cases even used as tools against the left. In examining thirty-four cases of such infiltration, Gary T. Marx found that eleven involved white campus groups, eleven involved white peace and/or economic groups, ten were directed against black and Chicano groups, and only two involved right-wing groups.[142]

ILLEGAL SURVEILLANCE.   It is clearly illegal for the government to engage in any sort of political harassment or "dirty tricks" against its citizens, but the legality of domestic surveillance is a matter of debate.

Some experts argue that the government has no constitutional right to do any sort of spying on its own citizens, while others disagree. But the Bill of Rights is only one of the legal restraints on government surveillance. Several statutory restrictions have been placed on specific techniques of information gathering, and the government is, of course, bound by the criminal statutes covering such offenses as burglary and breaking and entering.

Wiretapping, one of the most common techniques used to gather information on U.S. citizens, was first declared illegal in 1934. However, the FBI simply ignored the law and continued listening in on private phone conversations on the flimsy theory that the prohibition on "any person" wiretapping was somehow not meant to apply to FBI agents. In 1937 the Supreme Court rejected this argument and held the law to be applicable to federal agents. In response to this decision and another one in 1939, Attorney General Robert Jackson issued an order prohibiting all FBI wiretaps, but it stood in force for only two months, until President Franklin Roosevelt unilaterally decided the FBI still had the power to wiretap in "national security" cases. Illegal wiretapping remained a common practice until the law was changed in 1968 to allow wiretapping during criminal investigations if a prior court order were obtained. A second law, passed in 1978, allows court-ordered domestic wiretaps to gather foreign intelligence information. Although these laws opened the door for some legal wiretaps, the use of this technique for general surveillance and information gathering was still prohibited. Other techniques of electronic surveillance, such as those involving hidden microphones, are not specifically mentioned in statutory law, but an illegal entry is usually necessary to plant such devices. [143]

Although former FBI director J. Edgar Hoover expressed some concern about the negative publicity that would occur if an FBI agent was caught illegally planting a "bug," Hoover's FBI showed little concern for its obligation to obey the laws it was supposed to be enforcing. The frequency of burglaries and break-ins to plant listening devices fluctuated with the political climate of the times, but such activities have been part of FBI operations for more than three decades. In 1953 the FBI allegedly planted fifty-two microphones; the number increased to 99 in 1954 and 105 in 1955, before leveling off at about seventy-three a year for the rest of the Eisenhower administration. During Robert Kennedy's years as attorney general, the number of new bugs installed jumped to an average of more than ninety-two per year. The use of bugs declined significantly during Ramsey Clark's tenure as attorney general, then increased sharply in the Mitchell-Nixon era, and once again under the Reagan administration. [144]

The use of legal wiretaps also reached an all-time high during the Reagan presidency. In the first three years of his term, President Reagan approved more than double the number of wiretaps authorized by his predecessor, Jimmy Carter. In the last year of the Carter administration the Justice Department obtained authority to use 118 wiretaps and listening devices, but by 1983 the number of such devices in place had risen to 359. Moreover, those figures do not include wiretaps authorized to gather foreign intelligence information, which increased from 319 in 1980 to 473 in 1982. [145]

In addition to planting bugs, government agencies also use burglaries to gather physical evidence and information. In 1948, FBI agents broke into the offices of Thomas Emerson, Yale University professor and the president of the leftist National Lawyers Guild, and photographed an article he was writing for the *Yale Law Journal*. There is evidence that the FBI broke into the National Lawyers Guild offices three other times in order to microfilm its membership lists along with another article exposing FBI wiretapping. [146] Along with the wiretaps, such burglaries apparently grew increasingly common in the 1960s and early 1970s. A freedom-of-information suit filed by the Socialist Workers Party uncovered documents showing that the FBI regularly burglarized the SWP's national offices as part of the notorious COINTELPRO program. According to those documents, the FBI burglarized the Socialist Workers' offices at least ninety-four times between 1960 and 1966 in order to photograph, and in some cases steal, documents outlining the organization's membership, contributions, and political strategy. These break-ins occurred on an average of once every three weeks for six and one-half years. [147] The documents also revealed that the FBI paid 316 different informers over $1.5 million to spy on the SWP's youth affiliate, the Young Socialist Alliance. At least forty-two of the informers held office in one of the two organizations, and two informers ran for public office as members of the Young Socialist Alliance. [148]

Many people see such activities as an aberration brought on by the social upheavals surrounding the civil rights movement and the war in Vietnam. However, there is strong evidence that such activities are still going on today, in an era more noted for self-centered apathy than revolutionary fervor. In 1987 a former FBI informant named Frank Varelli testified before the House Judiciary Subcommittee on Civil and Constitutional Rights that he was paid by the FBI to infiltrate the Committee in Solidarity with the People of El Salvador (CISPES). He said that his FBI handler had told him they had broken into the Dallas offices of CISPES. The subcommittee also heard evidence that fifty-eight unexplained burglaries had occurred since 1981 in the offices of groups opposed to the Reagan administration's Central American policy, and that in most cases nothing more than membership lists was taken. [149]

The FBI also has illegally tampered with the U.S. mails. According to federal law, mail can be opened by law enforcement agencies only after a federal court has issued a warrant authorizing such activities. But in 1975 it was revealed that the FBI had been illegally opening private mail for over twenty years in at least eight major cities. In New York City alone, FBI agents examined 42 million pieces of mail from 1959 to 1966. [150]

One of the most disturbing uses the FBI made of its intelligence data was to compile lists of "dangerous" or "potentially dangerous" subversives who were to be rounded up and imprisoned in the event of a national emergency. Originally begun by the FBI in the late 1930s, the list was maintained until the 1970s, when the heat from the Watergate scandals caused officials to fear its exposure. During some periods, Director Hoover maintained the list against the wishes of his superiors, but most of the time the various attorneys general that Hoover worked for gave their enthusiastic support to the program—even though there was no legal authorization for such a program for over a decade after its inception, when the Internal Security Act of 1950 was ratified. This act also set much stricter legal limits on who could be included in the lists of potential political prisoners and gave the "subversives" more procedural protections than the FBI program allowed. Hoover simply ignored the law. Moreover, when Title II of the act was repealed in September 1970, the FBI once again violated the specific mandate of Congress and continued to maintain its lists of candidates for concentration camp. [151]

The FBI was more heavily involved in domestic surveillance than were other government agencies, but it was by no means alone. Numerous local police departments engaged in surveillance operations of their own. The Madison, Wis., police force, for instance, infiltrated agents into the Black Panthers, a welfare mothers organization, and other leftist groups at the University of Wisconsin. Perhaps the most notorious local intelligence operations of the 1960s and early 1970s were conducted by the so-called Red Squad of the Chicago Police Department, which carried on a literal shooting war with black militants. More recently, the Los Angeles Police Department was found to be compiling lists of leftists, antinuclear activists, and critics of police activities. In one case, the Los Angeles City Council was shocked to discover that the LAPD had sent a photographic team into the press gallery to take pictures of those who testified against nuclear power at a 1978 council meeting. As a result of such revelations, together with civil actions taken by the victims of the investigations, the LAPD agreed to destroy the "subversives" files its Public Order Intelligence Division had accumulated. However, the files apparently were not destroyed but were taken to the home of a police sergeant who leaked their contents to a right-wing political organization known as the Western Goals Foundation, which is alleged to have distributed the files through its computer network.[152]

Other federal agencies have also engaged in domestic intelligence activities. The Internal Revenue Service compiled political files on eight thousand individuals and three hundred groups during the 1960s and 1970s. The National Security Agency scanned millions of private telegrams sent to foreign countries by U.S. citizens. In the late 1960s, U.S. Army Intelligence launched a campaign to collect information on "predisturbance activities"; by 1970, it had compiled files on one hundred thousand civilians. Even the CIA got involved in domestic intelligence in the 1960s and 1970s. The CIA illegally opened and photographed the contents of 216,000 letters sent to and from the Soviet Union and created a computerized index of 1.5 million names derived from those mail openings. In addition, the agency prepared dossiers on the political activities of seventy-two hundred individuals and one hundred groups and had data on three thousand more people stored in computers. And all this activity was carried on despite specific legislation forbidding the CIA to engage in domestic political surveillance.[153]

The White House occasionally has bypassed existing agencies and become directly involved in illegal surveillance. President Nixon organized the "Plumbers" to act as his own secret intelligence agency. Nixon operatives engaged in a variety of illegal activities, including the break-in at the office of Daniel Ellsberg's psychiatrist and, of course, the famous Watergate burglaries.

HARASSMENT AND POLITICAL REPRESSION.   The American government's campaign against the left, however, went far beyond mere surveillance to encompass a program of direct political harassment and intimidation. The roots of the most recent government attacks on the left go back to the early 1940s, when the FBI began systematically leaking defamatory reports about various leftist leaders and their organizations and preparing anti-leftist speeches, articles, and books at government expense. In 1956 FBI Director Hoover began COINTELPRO (shorthand for "counter-intelligence program"), which was to be involved in a host of criminal activities over the next two decades. The original target was the U.S. Communist Party, but the program was soon expanded to include virtually all political groups on the left and even a few groups on the extreme right.

One prominent FBI target was Dr. Martin Luther King, the civil rights leader who not only championed nonviolence but also won the

Nobel Peace Prize. Once King rose to prominence in the civil rights movement, he was kept under constant surveillance, and his phone was illegally tapped by FBI agents with the explicit approval of Attorney General Robert Kennedy. The FBI attempted to stop Marquette University from awarding King an honorary degree and tried to prevent Cardinal Spellman, the archbishop of Boston, from appearing at a joint speaking engagement with him. When the FBI uncovered evidence about an alleged extramarital affair, it attempted to plant incriminating stories with two journalists. When that ploy failed, the Bureau sent a tape recording, presumably containing incriminating evidence, and the following anonymous letter to King and his wife, Coretta, in an apparent attempt to drive him to suicide:

> King, there is only one thing left for you to do. You know what it is. You have just 34 days in which to do it. (This exact number has been selected for a specific reason.) It has definite practical significance. You are done. There is but one way out for you.

The "34 days" in the message referred to the fact that King was to receive the Nobel Peace Prize the following month.[154]

The FBI apparently sent hundreds of letters containing similar personal attacks on other political activists. The Bureau sent a letter to the wife of Elijah Muhammad, the leader of the Black Muslims, in which it accused Muhammad of having an affair with his secretary. It sent a letter to a Black Panther party youth group leader accusing Fred Hampton and another top Panther leader of having "sex orgies" in party headquarters. In St. Louis the FBI tried to distract a civil rights worker from her political activities by sending her husband a vicious letter accusing her of carrying on affairs with the men in the civil rights organization for which she worked. A subsequent FBI report claimed credit for the breakup of their marriage a few months later.[155]

Another goal of these anonymous letters was to foment discord and division in leftist movements. In the late 1960s, when the Black Panther party was attempting to develop closer ties with a Chicago street gang known as the Blackstone Rangers, the FBI sent a letter to the head of the Rangers warning him of a fictitious Panther plot against his life, signing it, "A black brother you don't know." In a similar attempt to break up the alliance between the Black Panthers and the white radicals of the Students for a Democratic Society, the FBI sent poison-pen letters to Panther headquarters alleging that the "lily-white" SDS was out to control the Panthers. In San Diego the FBI created a series of political cartoons in an attempt to spark trouble between the Black Panthers and US, another prominent black organization. A subsequent FBI memo, written under the heading "Tangible Results," noted that "shootings, beatings, and a high degree of unrest continues to prevail in the ghetto area" and that "it is felt that a substantial amount of unrest is directly attributable to this program."[156] The FBI also used cartoons to encourage a split between the New Mobe (a large antiwar group) and the Socialist Workers Party, to brand activist Tom Hayden as a CIA plant, and to accuse Oakland Black Panther leader Bobby Rush of skimming off the profits from the sale of party newspapers.[157] In a variation of this technique, the FBI sent the National Mobilization Committee 217 fake forms offering housing for visiting demonstrators during the 1968 Democratic Convention. The FBI later boasted that this trick produced "chaos" in the demonstrator housing program, and the same technique was used again during the Washington peace march of 1969.[158]

The FBI often enlisted other organizations and agencies in its campaigns against the left. For example, the Bureau persuaded the phone company to cut off the long-distance phone service of the New Mobe before the Democratic Convention in 1968 and urged other peace groups' creditors to press for delinquent payments. On several occasions the FBI attempted to get the military to draft political activists on the left, and it even passed word to the Mafia about activist-comedian Dick Gregory's public attacks on their criminal activities, apparently in hopes of inciting a violent reprisal. Not surprisingly, local police departments were a favorite FBI tool. The Bureau attempted to have several SDS activists picked up on minor charges before their 1969 convention and had the work release of two jailed SDS members canceled after a surveillance team spotted them stopping for a swim on their way back to prison.[159]

One of the most shocking incidents to come to light was the FBI's cooperation with the Chicago police and state's attorney in what, to all appearances, was the political assassination of two Black Panther leaders, Fred Hampton and Mark Clark. William O'Neal, Hampton's personal bodyguard and an FBI infiltrator, gave the agency a detailed floorplan of the Chicago apartment in which the Panther leaders were staying and the information that it contained two illegal shotguns. In response to this unsubstantiated report of illegal firearms, Chicago police conducted a predawn raid on December 4, 1969 and shot Hampton and Clark to death while they were still in their beds.[160] Nor did the FBI limit its activities to inciting violence by other agencies. Between 1971 and 1976, according to a report in *The New York Times*, FBI agents engaged in direct physical assaults on radicals and burned or disabled their cars. The burnings were done with Molotov cocktails so that they would appear to be the work of other leftists.[161]

On several occasions, FBI agents incited right-wing groups to attack leftists working for various political causes the Bureau opposed. One of the best-documented cases of this kind occurred in San Diego in the late 1960s and early 1970s. According to evidence submitted to the Senate Select Committee on Intelligence, the FBI succeeded in resurrecting a previously disbanded right-wing paramilitary organization known as the Minutemen and placing an FBI informant, Howard Godfrey, in a leadership position. Not only did the FBI pay Godfrey a regular salary, but it also provided the Secret Army Organization (the group's new name) with firearms, explosives, and other equipment, and supplied at least 75 percent of the SAO's operating expenses. An SAO cell directed by Godfrey engaged in repeated acts of violence and terrorism against the left, including the destruction of newspaper offices and bookstores, the firebombing of cars, and assaults on political activists. In one incident, Godfrey and another SAO member fired two shots into the house of a well-known leftist, seriously wounding a young woman. The following day, Godfrey turned over the gun and the jacket he wore during the assault to his FBI supervisor, who helped conceal the evidence from San Diego police. Even after this information came to light, the FBI succeeded in protecting its operatives from prosecution. [162]

The FBI also used provocateurs to encourage violence by leftist groups; here, however, the goal was to incite the members of the group to commit a crime, so they could be arrested. In Seattle, for instance, FBI infiltrators participated in a campaign of arson and bombings of university and civic buildings. And in 1970, the FBI hired Charles Grimm to serve as an undercover agent at the University of Alabama. Grimm openly urged student radicals to commit acts of violence, encouraged the setting of fires on campus, solicited dynamite from other students, and made Molotov cocktails. Local police agencies have also engaged in similar activities. For example, William Frappoly, an agent for the Chicago police intelligence division, infiltrated the Students for a Democratic Society at a local university and later worked in the protests at the 1968 Democratic Convention in Chicago. When Frappoly was a witness at the Chicago Eight conspiracy trial, he publicly admitted that he attempted to persuade radicals to sabotage public facilities during the convention. [163]

In his study of agents provocateurs in the American left, Andrew Karmen found a recurring pattern in the actions of these police agents. [164] First, the FBI or local police agency selects a group, territory, or situation for infiltration. Next, the agency finds an agent whose background is compatible with that of the intended victims. He or she is then sent in to join the appropriate group and begins doing minor jobs to help win acceptance. After this goal is achieved, the agent seeks out militant individuals and begins urging them to commit their violence. Oftentimes the agents provide guns, bombs, and other materials and even personally participate in the crimes themselves. Finally, the police close in at the most compromising moment. The agent then withdraws, only to return for the trial with a carefully conceived story admitting complicity with the criminal events but denying entrapment. After examining over four thousand reports obtained from a freedom-of-information suit, a *Chicago Sun-Times* reporter summarized the FBI's goals in the 1960s and early 1970s as follows: "The Bureau set out to exterminate the so-called New Left and militant or high-profile black civil rights groups, and even sought to provoke injury or death among their leaders."[165]

The reports that surfaced after the death of J. Edgar Hoover frequently described him as a kind of megalomaniac obsessed with animosity toward left-wing activists. As a result, some have blamed the FBI's illegal activities solely on Hoover's personal hatred of the left. But an examination of Hoover's relationship with his superiors in the federal bureaucracy shows otherwise. Although Hoover often concealed, or at least downplayed, the full scope of the FBI's illegal activities, the various attorneys general and presidents he worked for knew and approved of the general principles behind the programs of illegal surveillance and political harassment he carried out. Often, Hoover's superiors issued direct orders specifically requesting the FBI to carry out some sort of criminal activity.[166] Moreover, the FBI was not the only agency engaged in the campaign against the American left. We have already mentioned the illegal activities carried out by local police departments and by the CIA. In addition, the Internal Revenue Service not only illegally supplied the FBI with tax returns of political dissidents but also undertook punitive tax audits against leftists from as far back as the 1950s up to the time of the Watergate investigations.[167] The Nixon administration's "Plumbers" organization engaged in illegal surveillance activities directed against radicals and liberals, and its "Incumbency Responsiveness Program" explicitly sought to use the power of the presidency to reward Nixon's political allies and punish his opponents. Thus, there is little doubt that Hoover's actions were part of a systematic pattern of political repression aimed at the American left.

International Violations

Before examining the crimes committed by American agents in other nations, we must take another look at our definition of criminal behavior. Because these activities occur outside the United States, they do not always violate U.S. law. However, U.S. agents have often violated the canons of international law mentioned in the first chapter, as well as the laws of the countries in which they carry on their activities.

When examining domestic violations of civil liberties, there are clear heuristic advantages to distinguishing between corporate and governmental crimes. However, this distinction breaks down when applied to international offenses because the international objectives of the U.S. government and those of the major corporations are often so tightly interwoven as to be almost identical. [168]   U.S. multinationals commonly support illegal government activities by providing cover for CIA agents, as well as other services in such areas as international finance and transportation. There is also convincing evidence that the goals of U.S. foreign policy often are determined by the needs of the multinationals. Numerous CIA operations, for example, have been launched in response to corporate concerns about the safety of their overseas investments. [169]

Although the U.S. government has the legal right to pursue any foreign policy it chooses, many of the techniques that have been used to achieve those objectives are clearly illegal. In fact, there is a real question as to whether or not the CIA actually has the legal authorization to conduct the "covert operations" for which it has gained worldwide notoriety. The original intent of Congress was clearly that the CIA was to be an intelligence agency, not an international secret police. The Senate Select Committee on Intelligence has noted that "authority for covert action cannot be found in the National Security Act" (the act that created the CIA). [170] The CIA, on the other hand, has claimed that its covert actions are authorized in Section 102 of that act, which directs the agency "to perform such other functions and duties related to intelligence affecting internal security as the National Security Council might from time to time direct." Despite the flimsy nature of its legal authority, the CIA still spends more than two-thirds of its budget on covert actions. [171]

The CIA has shown a similar disregard for the explicit constitutional provisions granting exclusive power to declare war to Congress. Acting entirely on presidential directives and without congressional authorization, the CIA has waged a number of secret wars around the globe. In the early 1950s, for example, CIA-sponsored guerillas led raids against China and launched an invasion of Guatemala. The Eisenhower administration ordered the Guatemala invasion when a leftist government took power there, demanded higher wages for the workers in U.S.-owned banana plantations, and expropriated land owned by the powerful United Fruit Company. In response, the agency organized a secret army in neighboring Honduras and backed its successful invasion with its own fleet of bombers. [172] In the late 1950s, CIA aircraft carried out similar bombing missions in support of a revolt against President Sukarno of Indonesia, and the agency was also involved in the coup that finally succeeded in ousting Sukarno in 1965. [173] The 1960s also saw the ill-fated attempt by a group of CIA-backed guerillas to invade Cuba at the Bay of Pigs. But by far the largest of the CIA's secret wars was carried on in Southeast Asia, where its involvement started as far back as 1954 and reached its peak in the late 1960s and early 1970s. Among other activities in the region, the CIA recruited at least two separate armies—one that fought along the South Vietnamese borders with Cambodia, Laos, and North Vietnam, and a second, larger one that operated inside Laos. When casualties and desertions crippled the original force of Laotian tribesmen, the CIA hired seventeen thousand Thai mercenaries, despite an act of Congress specifically forbidding the use of mercenary troops. By 1971 almost fifty thousand Americans were involved in the secret war, yet this huge operation was successfully hidden from the public and even from most members of Congress. [174] The agency has had much less success, however, in concealing its latest military adventure in Nicaragua. The fact that the CIA organized, funded, and directed, the antigoverment rebels in that country has become public knowledge in the 1980s.

The CIA was involved in plots to murder many leftist politicians. Direct assassination attempts were launched by the agency against Patrice Lumumba, the leftist leader of the Congo, and against Washington's perennial Cuban antagonist, Fidel Castro. The CIA also encouraged plots that resulted in the deaths of Rafael Trujillo in the Dominican Republic, Ngo Dinh Diem and his brother, Nhu, in South Vietnam, and General Rene Schneider of Chile. The most bizarre of these schemes was surely the campaign against Castro. Aside from the eight different assassination attempts uncovered by the Senate Select Committee on Intelligence, the CIA concocted numerous other schemes to discredit Castro, including a plan to dose him with a strong psychedelic drug before a major speech and a ludicrous scheme to dust his shoes with tallium salts—a strong depilatory the CIA hoped would make his beard fall out and thus ruin his revolutionary image. The assassination plots involved equally bizarre techniques, including poisoned cigars, an exploding seashell, and a wetsuit dusted with a deadly bacteria. The agency even turned to the underworld, persuading important syndicate figures to organize an assassination attempt. [175]

The bloody popular revolution that ousted the Shah of Iran and brought the Ayatollah Khomeini to power has focused new attention on the CIA-backed coup that helped launch the Shah's reign in 1953. The trouble originally began when the Shah, who had assumed the throne after World War II, was forced to name Mohammed Mossadegh as premier in 1951. Mossadegh quickly pushed the youthful king into the background and began steering his country on a leftward course. He nationalized the Anglo-Iranian Oil Company and took over the huge

Abadam refinery on the Persian Gulf. This move was a blow not just to British Petroleum (as Anglo-Iranian was later to be called), but to all the immensely powerful petroleum multinationals. Their response was to organize a boycott of Iranian oil—an effort that won strong support from the U.S. State Department and its help pressuring independent oil companies to go along. The value of Iranian oil exports dropped from over $400 million in 1950 to less than $2 million for the two-year period following the boycott. [176]

The disastrous economic effects of the boycott inevitably pushed Mossadegh closer to the Soviet Union. In May 1953, he warned the United States that, unless Iran got more financial aid, he would go elsewhere for assistance. President Eisenhower refused the request and ordered preparations made for clandestine intervention in Iran. The CIA then persuaded the Shah to issue an order removing Mossadegh from office. But the officer who served the notice was jailed, and the Shah fled the country. The CIA's project director, Kermit Roosevelt, responded by hiring a group of agitators to organize anti-Mossadegh demonstrations. The mobs, together with pro-Shah factions in the armed forces, succeeded in overthrowing Mossadegh and returning the Shah to power. After the coup, a new agreement was struck with the oil companies, and British Petroleum was returned to the Iranian market. However, its monopoly was ended, and an equal share of the concession was given to an American consortium and a smaller share to Dutch and French interests. Interestingly enough, all the major figures in the American government's plot had financial ties with the multinational petroleum corporations. Eisenhower's close relations with the oil companies are discussed in chapter 3. Allen Dulles, the director of the CIA at the time, was a former attorney for the Anglo-American Oil Company, and Kermit Roosevelt, who directed the clandestine operations in Iran, quit the CIA in 1958 to become a vice-president of Gulf Oil in charge of "government relations." [177]

Of all the CIA attempts at covert intervention in the affairs of other nations, the campaign against the Chilean leftist Salvador Allende is certainly the best-documented. Although Chile had a long democratic tradition, dating back to its independence in 1818, the U.S. government repeatedly felt it necessary to intervene in domestic Chilean affairs. When Allende ran for president in 1958 and again in 1964, the CIA launched secret campaigns to insure his defeat. But the real trouble began in the late 1960s, when it began to look as if Allende might actually win the next election. As the political winds began shifting in Allende's direction, "leaders of American multinational corporations with substantial interests in Chile. . .contacted U.S. government officials in order to make their views known." [178]   Foremost among these firms was the International Telephone and Telegraph Company, a major American multinational with heavy investments in Chile. One of ITT's directors, John McCone, was a former head of the CIA, and he returned to his old employers to offer a million dollar ITT slush fund to be used against Allende. Although it refused to directly accept the money, the agency told ITT how to funnel the funds into the hands of Allende's opponents. ITT repeatedly urged the CIA to take tough action against Allende, traded information with the agency, and tried to persuade other U.S. corporations to bring economic pressure to bear against Chile.

The U.S. government employed what was termed a "two-track" effort to prevent Allende's election and later to force him from office. Track one involved a wide variety of covert techniques aimed at manipulating the Chilean political system. To this end, the CIA paid out millions of dollars to the Chilean media to spread anti-Allende propaganda and encourage civil disorder. At one point, $25,000 in bribe money was authorized to pay Chilean legislators to vote against Allende's confirmation as president, but the money was apparently never spent. Once Allende became president, the U.S. government tried to, in the words of President Nixon, "make the economy scream." [179] This governmental-corporate assault on the Chilean economy included (1) a sharp reduction in American economic aid (however, military aid was continued at its previous level); (2) the virtual termination of short-term credits to Chile from U.S. banks; (3) reductions in funds from the World Bank and other international development agencies; (4) the withholding of supplies necessary for Chile's industry, such as parts for Chile's many American-built industrial machines; and (5) pressure on other Western countries and corporations not to trade with Chile.

Track two employed a more direct approach, for its aim was to foment a military coup and end Chilean democracy. Some evidence indicates that the CIA was working to "politicize" the Chilean Army as early as 1969, but it was certainly deeply involved by 1970. According to the Senate Select Committee on Intelligence, the CIA made twenty-one contacts with key Chilean military and police officials in October 1970, and "those Chileans who were inclined to stage a coup were given assurance of strong support at the highest levels of the U.S. government, both before and after a coup." [180] The CIA also encouraged several Chilean plots to assassinate General Rene Schneider, who was strongly committed to the Chilean constitution and refused to be involved in subversive activity. After three unsuccessful attempts, General Schneider was finally killed in October 1970. The coup that killed Allende and ended Chilean democracy did not come until three years later, when the Chilean economy was reeling from American economic pressure and from strikes and paramilitary terror supported by CIA money. [181]

The actions the U.S. took against the Chilean government were extreme but certainly not unique. The CIA has often been able to influence most Latin American countries without such drastic measures. For instance, Philip Agee, who spent twelve years in CIA operations work, reported that CIA agents in Ecuador served as that country's vice-president, as key labor officials, as important journalists, and even as student leaders. [182] In its latest attempt at Latin American intervention, however, the CIA has once against returned to direct confrontation, this time with the government of Nicaragua.

For most of the twentieth century, Nicaragua was ruled by the dictatorship of Anastasio Somoza and his two sons. Somoza was originally put into power in 1932 by the U.S. Marines who were occupying Nicaragua. Despite the Somozas' well-deserved reputation for intolerance and brutality, the American government continued its strong support of the Somoza dictatorship and its friendly policies toward multinational corporations. After nearly twenty years of struggle, the Somozas were overthrown by the Sandinista Front for National Liberation in 1979. The response of the Reagan administration, which came to power the next year, was much the same as Nixon's had been in Chile. Promised economic aid was cut back and then eliminated, economic and military support was provided to anti-Sandinista elements within Nicaragua, a network of bases was established in surrounding countries, and American agents trained and financed an army of Nicaraguan exiles (the Contras) who then invaded the country. And once again, acting under presidential orders alone, American agents violated both domestic and international law. The American government had Nicaraguan harbors mined and ignored the World Court decision that such actions were illegal. The CIA distributed a booklet to the Contras recommending the assassination of public officials who supported the Sandinistas, despite an Executive Order forbidding any American involvement in such activities. When Congress discovered these activities, a specific prohibition was written into the law that "no funds available to the Central Intelligence Agency, the Department of Defense, or any other agency or entity of the United States involved in intelligence activities may be. . .expended for the purpose. . .of supporting, directly or indirectly, military or paramilitary operation in Nicaragua. . ." [183] The Reagan administration's response was to set up an elaborate secret scheme to fund the Contras that involved numerous illegalities, including the use of military personnel to raise money from private sources and the diversion of profits from the secret sale of U.S. military equipment. [184]

NOTES

1. Marshall B. Clinard and Peter C. Yeager, *Corporate Crime* (New York: The Free Press, 1980), 22–23.
2. "The 500: The Fortune Directory of the Largest U.S. Industrial Corporations," *Fortune* 111 (April 27, 1987): 359–382.
3. Robert L. Heilbroner, "U.S. Inflation: What Goes Up. . .May Not Come Down," *Los Angeles Times*, 21 October 1979, X: 1 *passim*.
4. Ralph Nader, Mark Green, and Joel Seligman, *Taming the Giant Corporation* (New York: W. W. Norton, 1976), 211–212.
5. Samuel Richardson Reid, *The New Industrial Order* (New York: McGraw-Hill, 1976), 11–13.
6. Senate Committee on Governmental Affairs, *Voting Rights in Major Corporations* (Washington, D.C.: U.S. Government Printing Office, 1978).
7. Ivan Preston, *The Great American Blow Up: Puffery in Advertising and Selling* (Madison, Wis.: University of Wisconsin Press, 1975), 233–238.
8. David R. Simon and D. Stanley Eitzen, *Elite Deviance* (Boston: Allyn and Bacon, 1982), 87.
9. Lester Sobel, *Corruption in Business* (New York: Facts on File, 1977), 204–205.
10. August Bequai, *White-Collar Crime: A 20th Century Crisis* (Lexington, Mass.: Lexington Books, 1978), 55.
11. Christopher D. Stone, *Where the Law Ends: The Social Control of Corporate Behavior* (New York: Harper and Row, 1975), 175.
12. Ibid., 175–176.
13. Philip G. Schrag, *Counsel for the Deceived: Case Studies in Consumer Fraud* (New York: Pantheon Books, 1972).
14. Simon and Eitzen, *Elite Deviance*, 90.
15. William E. Blundell, "Equity Funding: 'I Did It for Jollies'," In John M. Johnson and Jack D. Douglas, eds., *Crime at the Top: Deviance in Business and the Professions* (Philadelphia: J. B. Lippincott, 1978), 153–185; Sobel, *Corruption in Business*, 172–174.
16. William N. Leonard and Marvin Glenn Weber, "Automakers and Dealers: A Study of Criminogenic Market Forces," *Law and Society Review* 4 (February 1976): 423.
17. Ibid., 407–424.
18. See, Ronald J. Ostrow, "Chrysler, 2 Executives Face Odometer Fraud Charges," *Los Angeles Times*, 25 June 1987, I: 1 & 25.
19. Simon and Eitzen, *Elite Deviance*, 89.
20. "How Billions are Wasted on Auto Repairs," *U.S. News & World Report*, 18 September 1978, 72.
21. Charles Vanick, "Corporate Tax Study, 1976," in the *Congressional Record*, Proceedings and Debates of the 94th Congress, Second Session, 122 (October 1, 1976): H12327-H12331. This figure was obtained by combining the companies listed in Table 2 that paid less than 1 percent of their income in tax with the companies listed in Table 1 that paid no taxes whatsoever.
22. Morton Mintz and Jerry Cohen, *Power Inc.: Public and Private Rulers and How to Make Them Accountable* (New York: Viking Press, 1976), 445; *Statistical Abstract of The United States, 1984* (Washington, D.C., 1984), 326.
23. See Ovid Demaris, *Dirty Business: The Corporate–Political Money-Power Game* (New York: Harper's Magazine Press, 1974), 99–122.
24. See "Multinational Corporations and Income Allocation Under Section 482 of the Internal Revenue Codes," *Harvard Law Review* 92 (April 1976): 1202–1238.
25. "IRS Not Set Up to Monitor Whether Interest and Dividend Income to Business is Being Reported, GAO Reports," *Corporate Crime Reporter* 1 (April 13, 1987), 5–6.
26. Sobel, *Corruption in Business*, 72.

27. Ibid., 151.

28. See Anthony Sampson, *The Seven Sisters: The Great Oil Companies and the World They Shaped* (New York: Bantam Books, 1975), 27–28.

29. See John M. Blair, *The Control of Oil* (New York: Random House, 1976), 246–251, for an explanation of the reasons for the vulnerability of the independents.

30. Blair, *The Control of Oil*, 235–260.

31. Judith Miller, "U.S. Aids Withheld Data on Oil, House Report Says," *The New York Times*, 4 January 1980.

32. Cited in Demaris, *Dirty Business*, 39.

33. Lester M. Salamon and John J. Siegfried, "Economic Power and Political Influence," *American Political Science Review* 71 (September 1977): 1026–1043.

34. Samuel Richardson Reid, *The New Industrial Order: Concentration, Regulation and Public Policy* (New York: McGraw-Hill, 1976). The figures are for the years 1947–1968, from Chart 5.1, p. 64.

35. Reid, *The New Industrial Order*, 152–153.

36. See Reid, *The New Industrial Order*, on this point.

37. Mark J. Green, Beverly L. Moore, and Bruce Wasserstein, *The Closed Enterprise System: Ralph Nader's Study Group Report on Antitrust Enforcement* (New York: Grossman, 1972), 149–150.

38. "The Frequency of Price Fixing: An Indication," *57 Northwestern Law Review* 151 (1962), as quoted in Green, Moore, and Wasserstein, *The Closed Enterprise System*, 150.

39. Marshall B. Clinard, Peter C. Yeager, Jeanne Brissette, David Petrashek, and Elizabeth Harries, *Illegal Corporate Behavior* (Washington, D.C.: U.S. Government Printing Office, 1979), 184.

40. The framers of the Achnacarry Agreement tried to skirt U.S. antitrust laws by nominally excluding the U.S. market from the agreement. But in practice, it was clearly impossible to exclude the United States, since at that time it was both the world's largest consumer and the world's largest producer of petroleum.

41. Blair, *The Control of Oil*, 60.

42. Quoted in Blair, *The Control of Oil*, 61.

43. Quoted in Blair, *The Control of Oil*, 60.

44. Quoted in Blair, *The Control of Oil*, 71.

45. Blair, *The Control of Oil*, 63.

46. Ralph Nader, "Introduction," in Green, Moore, and Wasserstein, *The Closed Enterprise System*, x.

47. Quoted in Jethro K. Lieberman, *Crisis at the Bar: Lawyers' Unethical Ethics and What to Do About It* (New York: W. W. Norton, 1978), 111.

48. See Lieberman, *Crisis at the Bar*, 110–113.

49. See Ed Cray, *In Failing Health: The Medical Crisis and the A.M.A.* (Indianapolis: Bobbs-Merrill, 1970), for a thorough examination of the American Medical Association's role in shaping the U.S. health care system.

50. Cray, *In Failing Health*, 182–199.

51. Lieberman, *Crisis at the Bar*, 79–87.

52. Richard T. Cooper and Paul E. Steiger, "Occupational Health Hazards—A National Crisis," *Los Angeles Times*, 27 June 1976, 1 *passim*.

53. Daniel M. Berman, *Death on the Job: Occupational Health and Safety in the United States* (New York: Monthly Review Press, 1978), 82–83; Brent Fisse and John Braithwaite, *The Impact of Publicity on Corporate Offenders* (Albany: State University of New York Press, 1983), 63–70.

54. Oliver S. Owen, *Natural Resource Conservation: An Ecological Approach*, 3rd ed. (New York: Macmillan, 1980), 522.

55. "10 Years After Kepone, Fishing Ban Remains," *San Luis Obispo (Calif.) Telegram-Tribune*, 29 July 1985.

56. Paul Brodeur, *Expendable Americans* (New York: Viking Press, 1974), 253–254.

57. Morton Mintz in the *Washington Post*, as reprinted in Brodeur, *Expendable Americans*, 271–272.

58. K. Lynch and W. Smith, "Pulmonary Asbestosis," *American Journal of Cancer* 24 (1935): 56.

59. R. Doll, *British Journal of Industrial Medicine* 12 (1955): 81.

60. Berman, *Death on the Job*, 85; John Coyners, "Corporate and White Collar Crime: A View by the Chairman of the House Subcommittee on Crime," *American Criminal Law Review* 17 (1980), 287–300; Henery Weinstein, "Did Asbestos Industry Suppress Data?" *Los Angeles Times*, 23 October 1978, 1 *passim*.

61. Stone, *Where the Law Ends*, 177.

62. Cooper and Steiger, "Occupational Health Hazards."

63. Joseph A. Page and Mary-Win O'Brien, *Bitter Wages: Ralph Nader's Study Group Report on Disease and Injury on the Job* (New York: Grossman, 1973), 22.

64. Melinda Beck, "The Toxic Waste Crisis," *Newsweek*, 7 March 1983, 20–24.

65. Quoted in Ellen Hume, "Firm Poisoned Wells with Waste, Kept State in Dark," *Los Angeles Times*, 19 June 1979; also see, Coyners, "Corporate and White-Collar Crime."

66. Grayson Mitchell, "Firm Knew of Peril in Love Canal Chemical Waste 20 Years Ago, Investigators Say," *Los Angeles Times*, 11 April 1979; Bill Richards, "Ex-Residents of Love Canal Area Bitter about Contamination Results," *Sacramento Bee*, 25 November 1979, A22; Stephen W. Bell, "Love Canal: The Chemicals and the Hard Feelings Linger," *San Luis Obispo (Calif.) Telegram-Tribune*, 15 November 1986, 1C.

67. Paul R. Ehrlich, Anne H. Ehrlich, and John P. Holdren, *Ecoscience: Population, Resources, Environment* (San Francisco: W. H. Freeman, 1977), 574.

68. Ibid., 574.

69. Quoted in Robert Hanley, "Mercury Polluting Meadowlands: Scientists Uncertain about Impact," *The New York Times*, 19 May 1978.

70. Robert Hanley, "Expert Tells of Excess Mercury in Woodridge Plant," *The New York Times*, 24 May 1978.

71. Robert D. McFadden, "Olin and 3 Ex-Aides Indicted on Dumping Mercury in Niagara," *The New York Times*, 30 January 1978; "Olin, Three Employees Sentenced in Mercury Dumping Case," *Environmental Reporter* 10 (December 21, 1979), 1675.

72. Andrew Szasz, "Corporations, Organized Crime, and the Disposal of Hazardous Waste: An Examination of the Making of a Criminogenic Regulatory Structure," *Criminology*, 24 (1986), 1–27.

73. Donald Janson, "Jersey Hunts Dumpers of Toxics," *The New York Times*, 30 January 1978.

74. Beck, "Toxic Waste Crisis."

75. Quoted in Mintz and Cohen, *Power, Inc.*, 110.

76. Jack Nelson, "Administration Hit for Health Cutbacks," *Los Angeles Times*, 8 May 1983, 1, 23–24.

77. Reginald Stuart, "U.S. Agency Suggests Ford Pintos Have a Fuel System Defect," *The New York Times*, 9 May 1978.

78. "Ford Pinto Scored in Coast Magazine on Peril from Fires," *The New York Times*, 11 August 1977; Jeffrey Mills, "Supplementary Material," *The New York Times*, 31 August 1978.

79. Mark Dowie, "Pinto Madness," in Jerome Skolnick and Elliott Currie, eds., *Crisis in American Institutions*, 4th ed. (Boston: Little-Brown, 1979), 26.

80. Reginald Stuart, "Ford Orders Recall of 1.5 Million Pintos for Safety Changes," *The New York Times*, 10 June 1978.

81. Stuart, "Ford Orders Recall—"; Fisse and Braithwaite, *Impact of Publicity*, 41–54.

82. "Internal Memo Reportedly Noted Firestone Tire Failures in 1972," *The New York Times*, 23 December 1978.

83. "Forewarnings of Fatal Flaws," *Time*, 25 June 1979, 58–60.

84. Jo Thomas, "Firestone Knew of Tire Defects 5 Years Before Recall, Papers Show," *The New York Times*, 24 December 1978.

85. "Analysts Discount the Impact of Firestone Memos," *The New York Times*, 26 December 1978; "Fatal Flaws," *Time*, 25 June 1979.

86. *The New York Times*, 28 March 1978, 63.

87. Steven Rattner, "Tire Tentatively Found Defective," *The New York Times*, 9 July 1978.

88. "Fatal Flaws," *Time*, 25 June 1979.

89. Quoted in Mintz and Cohen, *Power, Inc.*, 249.

90. Quoted in Stone, *Where the Law Ends*, 54.

91. Stanford J. Unger, "Get Away with What You Can," in Heilbroner, *In the Name of Profit*, 126.

92. Don C. Gibbons, "Crime and Punishment: A Study in Social Attitudes," *Social Forces* 47 (June 1969); 392.

93. Mintz and Cohen, *America, Inc.*, 268.

94. Nelson, "Health Safety Cutbacks;" Morton Mintz, "Lilly Official Knew of Deaths Before U.S. Approved Drug," *Washington Post*, 22 July 1983; Morton Mintz, "Lilly Chairman Decided to Sell Oraflex Despite Deaths," *Washington Post*, 13 November 1983.

95. Russell Mokhiber, "Greedy Corporations: Criminals by Any Other Name," *The Los Angeles Daily Journal*, 28 August 1986, 4; Philip Shenon, "Rehearing Sought Over Justice Aide," *New York Times*, 5 September 1985, B11.

96. Mark Dowie and Tracy Johnston, "A Case of Corporate Malpractice," *Mother Jones*, November 1976. Also, Barbara Ehrenreich, Mark Dowie, and Stephen Minkin, "The Charge: Genocide; The Accused: The U.S. Government," *Mother Jones* IV (November 1979): 28.

97. Barry Siegel, "One Man's Efforts to Tell Dalkon Story," *Los Angeles Times*, 22 August 1985, 1 *passim*.

98. Mokhiber, "Greedy Corporations."

99. Siegel, "One Man's Efforts."

100. Jonathan Peterson and Jesus Sanchez, "Merger May Clear Way to Settle Dalkon Shield Cases," *Los Angeles Times*, 4 July 1987, 1 *passim*.

101. Ehrenreich, Dowie, and Minkin, "The Charge: Genocide," 28–31.

102. Morton Mintz, "Upjohn's Shuck and Jive Routine," *Mother Jones* IV (November 1979): 31.

103. John Braithwaite, *Corporate Crime in the Pharmaceutical Industry* (London: Routledge and Kegan Paul, 1984), 260–261.

104. Morton Mintz, "If There Are No Side Effects, This Must Be Honduras," *Mother Jones* IV (November 1979): 32–33; also see, Braithwaite, *Corporate Crime in the Pharmaceutical Industry*, 247–256.

105. Braithwaite, *Corporate Crime in the Pharmaceutical Industry*, 250.

106. Yerachmiel Kugel and Gladys W. Gruenberg, *International Payoffs* (Lexington, Mass.: Lexington Books, 1977), 12.

107. "Commercial Bribery: Letter from the Federal Trade Commission," 15 May 1918, 66th Congress, 2nd session, Senate Document No. 258, 20 March 1920, 3.

108. See Clinard and Yeager, *Corporate Crime*, 186; *The New York Times*, 16 March 1976; W. Michael Reisman, *Folded Lies: Bribery, Crusades, and Reforms* (New York: The Free Press, 1979), 44.

109. Chamber of Commerce of the United States, *A Handbook on White Collar Crime* (Washington, D.C.: Chamber of Commerce of the United States, 1974).

110. Neil H. Jacoby, Peter Nehemkis, and Richard Eells, *Bribery and Corruption in World Business* (New York: Macmillan, 1977), 42.

111. Michael C. Jensen, "Companies' Payoffs in U.S. Come Under New Scrutiny," *The New York Times*, 16 March 1976, 1 *passim*.

112. Jacoby et al., *Bribery and Corruption*, 119.

113. Kugel and Gruenberg, *International Payoffs*, 61–63; Clinard and Yeager, *Corporate Crime*, 172.

114. Sobel, *Corruption in Business*, 153.

115. Ibid., 104.

116. Ibid., 104–105, 113–115; Kugel and Gruenberg, *International Payoffs*, 59–60.

117. Sobel, *Corruption in Business*, 106–112; Kugel and Gruenberg, *International Payoffs*, 59–60.

118. Karen Tumulty, "Kickbacks Common in Southland, Panel Told" *Los Angeles Times*, 28 February 1986, IV, 2.

119. *Corporate Crime Reporter* 1 (20 April 1987), 10–16; 1 (27 April 1987), 14–16.

120. Congressional Quarterly, *Congressional Ethics*, 2nd ed. (Washington, D.C.: Congressional Quarterly, 1980), 23.

121. See Richard Harris, "Annals of Politics: A Fundamental Hoax," *The New Yorker*, 17 August 1971, 50; Larry L. Berg, Harlan Hahn, John R. Schmidhauser, *Corruption in the American Political System* (Morristown, N.J.: General Learning Press, 1976), 88–107.

122. Quoted in Berg et. al., *Corruption in the American Political System*, 103.

123. Sobel, *Corruption in Business*, 28.

124. Sobel, *Corruption in Business*, 31; also see 16–32, and "Associated Milk Producers Fined $35,000 for Its Illegal Campaign Contributions," *The Wall Street Journal*, 2 August 1977, 7.

125. Sobel, *Corruption in Business*, 72–73.

126. Congressional Quarterly, *Congressional Ethics*, 22–23.

127. Sobel, *Corruption in Business*, 73.

128. See Kugel and Gruenberg, *International Payoffs*, 65–72; Sobel, *Corruption in Business*, 118–121, 125–127.

129. Sobel, *Corruption in Business*, 127–130; Kugel and Gruenberg, *International Payoffs*, 72–75.

130. Sobel, *Corruption in Business*, 121–125; Kugel and Gruenberg, *International Payoffs*, 75–78.

131. Ralph Nader, Mark Green, and Joel Seligman, *Taming the Giant Corporation* (New York: W. W. Norton, 1976), 23.

132. Dan Collins, "Free Enterprise Rushes to Fill a Delicate Need," *U.S. News and World Report*, 23 February 1987.

133. Quoted in S. Prakash Sethi, *Up Against the Corporate Wall*, 2nd ed. (Englewood Cliffs, N.J.: Prentice-Hall, 1974), 374.

134. Quoted in Sethi, *Up Against the Corporate Wall*, 376.

135. Quoted in Sethi, *Up Against the Corporate Wall*, 395.

136. Quoted in Sethi, *Up Against the Corporate Wall*, 398.

137. See Sethi, *Up Against the Corporate Wall*, 424–451.

138. Quoted in Norman Solomon, "Nuclear Big Brother," *The Progressive* 44 (January 1980): 9.

139. Solomon, "Nuclear Big Brother," 14–21; Vasil Pappas, "Some Utilities Generate Sparks by Keeping Close Eye on Critics," *The Wall Street Journal*, 11 January 1979, 1 & 32.

140. See Richard E. Morgan, *Domestic Intelligence; Monitoring Dissent in America* (Austin, Tex.: University of Texas Press, 1980), 15–36, for a review of the early history of domestic intelligence in the United States.

141. See Athan Theoharis, *Spying on Americans: Political Surveillance from Hoover to the Houston Plan* (Philadelphia: Temple University Press, 1978).

142. Gary T. Marx, "Thoughts on a Neglected Category of Social Movement Participant: The Agent Provocateur and the Informant," *American Journal of Sociology* 80 (September 1974): 402–442.

143. See Theoharis, *Spying on Americans*, 94–132.

144. Ronald J. Ostrow, "Electronic Surveillance Hits New Highs in War on Crime," *Los Angeles Times*, 18 December 1983, I: 4.

145. David Wise, *The American Police State: The Government Against the People* (New York: Random House, 1976), 141–182.

146. Julian Roebuck and Stanley C. Weeber, *Political Crime in the United States: Analyzing Crime by and Against Government* (New York: Praeger, 1978), 112.

147. Cathy Perkus, "Preface," in Nelson Blackstock, *COINTELPRO: The FBI's Secret War on Political Freedom* (New York: Vintage Books, 1975), ix.

148. Roebuck and Weeber, *Political Crime*, 111.

149. "FBI Behind Burglaries of Central American Agencies?" *San Luis Obispo (Calif.) Telegram-Tribune*, 21 February 1987, 14A; Eric Pianin, "Hill Told of FBI Drive on Foreign Policy Critics," *Washington Post*, 21 February 1987, A8.

150. Roebuck and Weeber, *Political Crime*, 111.

151. See Theoharis, *Spying on Americans*, 40–64.

152. Solomon, "Nuclear Big Brother"; Roebuck and Weeber, *Political Crime*, 114; Gene Blake, "New ACLU Suit Aims at Right-Wing Group," *Los Angeles Times*, 19 April 1984, III: 1.

153. Roebuck and Weeber, *Political Crime*, 107–110, 114–115.

154. See Noam Chomsky, "Introduction," in Blackstock, *COINTELPRO*, 7–8; Roebuck and Weeber, *Political Crime*, 29–31; David Wise, "The Campaign to Destroy Martin Luther King," *New York Review of Books* 23 (11 November 1976): 38–42.

155. Charles Nicodemus, "Anti-Dissent Techniques Varied Widely," *Los Angeles Times*, 22 August 1979, I-A: 4–6.

156. Chomsky, "Introduction," 9–11.

157. Nicodemus, "Anti-Dissent Techniques." See Blackstock, *COINTELPRO*, 34–35, 155, for copies of some of these cartoons.

158. Nicodemus, "Anti-Dissent Techniques."

159. Ibid.

160. John Kifner, "FBI Gave Chicago Police Plan of Slain Panther's Apartment," *The New York Times*, 24 May 1974; Chomsky, "Introduction," 12–13.

161. Nicholas Horrock, "Car Burnings and Assaults on Radicals Linked to FBI Agents in Last 5 Years," *The New York Times*, 11 July 1976, 20.

162. Chomsky, "Introduction," 15–16; Patrick Dillon, "San Diego Police Linked to 1972 Cover Up," *San Diego Union*, 2 June 1976.

163. Marx, "Social Movement Participant;" Dave Dellinger, *More Power Than We Know* (Garden City: Anchor Press, 1975), 65–66.

164. Andrew Karmen, "Agents Provocateur in the Contemporary U.S. Leftist Movement" in C. Reasons, ed., *The Criminologist: Crime and the Criminal* (Pacific Palisades, Cal.: Goodyear, 1974).

165. Charles Nicodemus, "Newly Opened Files Shed Added Light on FBI's 'War'," *Los Angeles Times*, 22 August 1979, IA: 3–4.

166. For a careful examination of the evidence concerning the attitude of the various presidents and attorney generals toward the FBI's illegal activities, see Theoharis, *Spying on Americans*.

167. Roebuck and Weeber, *Political Crime*, 35; Theoharis, *Spying on Americans*, 138.

168. See G. William Domhoff, *The Powers That Be: Processes of Ruling Class Domination in America* (New York: Vintage Books, 1978), for an excellent analysis of the process by which the major corporations shape U.S. foreign policy.

169. Morton H. Halperin, Jerry J. Berman, Robert L. Borosage, and Christine M. Marwick, *The Lawless State: The Crimes of the U.S. Intelligence Agencies* (Middlesex, England: Penguin, 1976), 147–148.

170. Select Committee to Study Government Operations with Respect to Intelligence, *Final Report, Book One: Foreign Military Intelligence and the Rights of Americans* (Washington, D.C.: U.S. Government Printing Office, 1976), 128.

171. Victor Marchetti and John Marks, *The CIA and the Cult of Intelligence* (New York: Dell, 1974), 95.

172. David Wise and Thomas B. Ross, *The Invisible Government* (New York: Random House, 1964), 165–183.

173. Ibid., 136–146.

174. Halperin et al., *Lawless State*, 42–44; Fred Branfman, "The Secret Wars of the CIA," in Howard Frazier, ed., *Uncloaking the CIA* (New York: Macmillan, 1978), 90–100.

175. Select Committee to Study Governmental Operations with Respect to Intelligence Activities, *Alleged Assassination Plots Involving Foreign Leaders* (Washington, D.C.: U.S. Government Printing Office, 18 November 1975).

176. Blair, *The Control of Oil*, 78–80.

177. Andrew Tully, *CIA: The Inside Story* (New York: William Morrow, 1962), 88–99; Wise and Ross, *Invisible Government*, 110–114; Blair, *The Control of Oil*, 78–80.

178. Select Committee to Study Governmental Operations with Respect to Intelligence Activities, United States Senate, *Covert Action in Chile: 1963–1973* (Washington, D.C.: U.S. Government Printing Office, 1975), 12.

179. Ibid., 33.

180. Ibid., 225.

181. The best source on the CIA's covert action in Chile is the Select Committee's *Covert Action in Chile*. For information on the plot against General Schneider, see Select

Committee, *Assassination Plots*, 225–254. Other sources include Harold R. Kerbo, "Foreign Involvement in the Preconditions for Political Violence: The World System and the Case of Chile," *Journal of Conflict Resolution* 22 (September 1978): 363–391; and Halperin et al., *Lawless State*, 15–29.

182. Philip Agee, *Inside the Company: CIA Diary* (New York: Stonehill, 1975).

183. Public Law 98-473 October 12, 1984, p. 1935.

184. See Richard Alan White, *The Morass: United States Intervention in Central America* (New York: Harper and Row, 1984); Steven Strasser, "The CIA's Harbor Warfare," *Newsweek*, 11 April 1984; Margaret Shapiro, "House Committee Rules CIA Manual was Illegal," *Denver Post*, 6 December 1984, 14A.

3

Occupational Crime

Ask the proverbial man in the street to name a white collar crime, and he will probably mention embezzlement or a high-tech computer crime—not one of the far more costly organizational crimes. Part of the reason is that the media give much more attention to occupational crimes than to the crimes of powerful corporate organizations.[1] Then too, organizational crimes are often complicated affairs, full of boring legal technicalities. But there is also a kind of romance about many occupational crimes that attracts public interest. Many people hold a grudging admiration for the embezzler or computer hacker who not only gets rich quick but does it while striking a blow at exploitive employers or a soulless bureaucracy. One suspects that there are more than a few law-abiding Walter Mittys who dream of making a fast million while settling the score with their boss. This image of the white collar criminal as Robin Hood hardly fits the facts of the crimes discussed below, but it nonetheless remains a significant part of the popular imagination of our times.

THE BUSINESS WORLD

Employee Theft

Losses from employee theft are believed to cost more than the losses from all street crimes put together.[2] "Inventory shrinkage" (loss from theft) is usually estimated to add about 2 percent to the cost of all retail goods, and some estimates put the figure as high as 4 percent.[3] The majority of this loss can be attributed to employee theft, not shoplifting, and it is therefore virtually impossible to make any purchase without paying a price for white collar crime. But the consumer is not the only loser: nearly a thousand businesses a year are believed to go bankrupt because of employee theft.[4]

Such numerical estimates help define the problem faced by contemporary business, but they can be terribly misleading. Even if they are correct—which is debatable—there is more to this kind of crime than meets the eye. Many managers see certain types of employee theft as a "fringe benefit" that helps make up for low wages or other occupational problems. Some of the alleged cost to the public may therefore be more illusory than real, because an end to employee theft might force employers to pay higher wages or make costly improvements in working conditions. Gerald Mars, a Cambridge sociologist who has published many studies on this subject, argues that employee theft actually has positive effects in that it increases job satisfaction, raises production, and makes for a healthier economy. It is doubtful, however, that Mars could get many owners of small businesses to accept his conclusions.

Any employee, from the president who signs the paychecks to the janitor who sweeps the floors, may steal from his or her employer. The popular conception that theft occurs mainly among lower-level employees is not supported by the evidence. Norman Jaspan, the head of a firm that specializes in the investigation of employee crime, found that 62 percent of the losses he encountered could be traced to thefts by company supervisors.[5] This doesn't mean that managerial personnel are more dishonest than others—only that their crimes result in higher losses. In the most extreme case, the directors of a firm may systematically drain off its assets, eventually leaving the stockholders with nothing but a worthless shell. Lower-level employees simply lack the power to commit such crimes.

In one of the best studies of employee theft to date, Hollinger and Clark found that about one-third of the more than nine thousand persons they interviewed admitted to stealing from their employer within the last year.[6] Much of this is petty crime that stems from the conflicting norms held by workers and employers. It has long been recognized that workers develop informal rules on the job that define not only the minimum amount of work expected of each employee but the maximum amount as well. Many eager young employees have been shocked when older workers demand they stop working so hard and making everyone else look bad. Similar rules usually govern stealing and other minor criminal offenses. In his study of a Midwestern television plant, Donald Horning found that the workers had a clear-cut idea about what kind of property they could and could not legitimately take home.[7] Power tools, heavy machinery, testing equipment, and other large, expensive items were defined as company property, and the theft of such property or of the personal property of other workers was clearly forbidden. But scraps, light tools, nails, screws, electrical tape, and the like were seen as being of uncertain ownership, and the workers viewed the theft of such things as a victimless crime that caused no real harm.

Of course, all work groups do not show such concern about their employer's interests—especially when they feel underpaid or abused by management. Under such circumstances, many employees may go well beyond the kinds of petty crimes just described. It is not unknown for the majority of employees in a plant or office to support, or at least ignore, a ring of criminals operating within the business. Such criminals often make considerably more money from the sale of stolen merchandise to professional "fences" or to their companies' legitimate customers than they do from their wages. Of course, some employees are willing to engage in criminal activities that violate their co-workers' code of fair play, but such crimes are more difficult to carry out, and the criminals run a substantially greater risk of detection.

Many of the biggest employee thefts are committed against stockbrokers and financial institutions that handle large amounts of expensive stocks and bonds. The enormous volume of stock transactions and the desire by brokerage houses to minimize paperwork have often led to surprisingly lax handling of valuable certificates. A security agent for one brokerage firm reported that investigators found missing stock certificates under desks and behind filing cabinets and water coolers. [8] Police have recovered stashes of pilfered stocks worth more than $1 million on several different occasions, and some raids have netted as much as $10 million. August Bequai has estimated that the cost of the theft of securities annually runs into billions of dollars. [9] Whatever the actual figure, it is clear that the lax scrutiny of many brokerage houses makes theft a relatively easy matter for knowledgeable employees. Although disposing of the stolen securities is a bit more difficult, it presents few serious problems for most thieves. In some cases they enlist the help of organized crime, while in others the professional criminals make the first move and actively seek out potential thieves. Because banks seldom question whether or not the holder of valuable stocks and bonds is actually the rightful owner, stolen certificates are often used as collateral for loans. Another approach is to pay an otherwise legitimate agent to transfer the ownership of stolen securities.

Money and property are not the only things taken from unwary businesses. The theft of confidential data or trade secrets has drawn increasing attention in recent years. In some cases, industrial espionage is carried on by specially hired agents using sophisticated electronic equipment and spy techniques that could be drawn straight from the pages of a pulp novel. Other times, valuable information is purchased directly from a double-dealing employee. Such activities are a crime in most states, but enforcement has been lax. In many states, ambiguities in the law make it difficult to win a guilty verdict, and as is often the case with embezzlers, employers are reluctant to prosecute for fear of the publicity. [10]

Embezzlement and Computer Crime

Embezzlers are the aristocrats of chiseling employees. They are, by definition, people who use a position of trust to appropriate someone else's assets for their own personal use. And because embezzlers often have goods jobs and high incomes, the reasons behind their crimes are not immediately apparent. In this respect the old saying about a man being led to ruin by "slow horses and fast women" may contain more than a grain of truth. Research has shown that many embezzlers turn to crime because they are living beyond their financial means.[11] In some cases the problem is gambling, in others a family emergency, heavy personal debt, or simply extravagant living. But that old homily is wrong in one respect, for an increasing number of convicted embezzlers are now women. This rapid increase in embezzlement by female employees probably reflects two things: their importance in bookkeeping and accounting jobs and the increasing pressure on all women to provide financial support for their families.

COMPUTER CRIME.   With computer-related businesses now employing over 2 million people, computer embezzlement has become the growth industry of contemporary crime. Whereas the average bank robbery amounts to only a few thousand dollars, the average computer crime nets about $400,000.[12]   Estimates of the total losses from computer crime range from $100 to $300 million a year.[13]   But those are really only educated guesses, and given the growing use of computer technology, they are probably far too low.

Such statistics have spurred the fear that computer crime may soon reach epidemic proportions as business continues to computerize and more people learn the skills necessary for such offenses. The potential losses are indeed high, for the amount of money involved in electronic fund transfers is enormous. In 1984 over 3 billion banking transactions were made on automatic teller machines—about three times the number made only four years before. And although consumer transactions greatly outnumber corporate transactions, the latter involve much greater sums of money. In 1984 the average transaction made on an automatic teller machine was about $14, whereas the average amount exchanged by wire transfers between corporations was around $2 million. The total amount involved in these corporate transfers is truly staggering—over $173 trillion a year.[14]   Still, many skeptics question the new fears about computer crime, arguing that the total losses are unlikely to exceed the losses that would have occurred if more traditional means had been used for those exchanges. A pilot study by the U.S. Department of Justice found that the average loss from the fraudulent use of automatic teller machines was only about $200, and even with the huge sums involved in wire transfers, the average loss per fraud was relatively insignificant—about $16,000.[15] However, the cost of some computer crimes does live up to public expectations. The biggest known computer embezzlement to date took place over a three-year period (1979–1981) at California's Wells Fargo Bank, where an employee used electronic fund transfers to deposit over $21 million in an account held by a group of boxing promoters. But defalcations of this size are difficult to conceal, and all the parties involved eventually were uncovered.[16]

The take from computer crimes may not compare with the organizational crimes discussed in the previous chapter. But the public is, nonetheless, fascinated with the popular image of the computer criminal as a young whiz-kid with a bedroom stuffed with exotic equipment and the ability to outsmart huge corporate bureaucracies with their legions of experts and specialists. Even the names given the techniques of computer crime have a humorous, offbeat ring. "Data diddling," for example, is the term applied to one of the easiest and most common computer crimes. The data diddler simply manipulates the information fed into the computer to his or her advantage. Funds that were intended to be deposited in one account may, for example, be credited to a different account controlled by the criminal. Another technique that is limited to skilled programmers is to place a "Trojan horse" in a program while it is being written. Once the program is installed on a computer, the criminal can activate the Trojan horse and give secret commands, unknown to the legitimate operators. The criminal might, for example, order the computer to make electronic fund transfers, erase personal debts, or reveal confidential data.[17]

Another approach to computer embezzlement is known as the "salami technique," because the criminals take "one thin slice at a time." Two computer programmers at a large New York garment firm instructed the company computer to increase each employee's income tax withholding by two cents a week and to deposit the money in the programmers' withholding accounts. At the end of the year, the embezzlers planned to receive their profits in the form of refund checks from the Internal Revenue Service. However, the disproportionate size of their refunds touched off an investigation that uncovered the crime.

Many computer crimes involve not the theft of money, but of information—an increasingly valuable commodity in modern society. In an operation sometimes known as "superzapping," computer operators use special programs that override security controls in order to reach confidential data. Some security-protected programs have a built-in "trap door" that allows the operator to bypass the safeguards and make changes in a program. Such trap doors are useful when removing bugs from the program, and they may inadvertently be left in the final version, or they may be placed there intentionally for use at a later time. Finally, a data thief may "piggy-back" on a legitimate user, tricking the computer into thinking that the criminal also has clearance to use the machine.[18]

Computer users and computer criminals are engaged in an increasingly sophisticated game of cat and mouse. An estimated $200 million a year is now being spent on computer safeguards. In many cases, users are required to give the computer a secret password before being given access to its files. But such security systems have an obvious fault—employees who work with those records must be given the password, which may then be used for illicit purposes. In order to prevent unwanted outsiders from tapping into their computer lines, a growing number of users are employing encryption systems that code computer transactions in such a way that they are extremely difficult to decipher without a special key. The equipment necessary for this system is expensive, however, and once again there is the danger that an unscrupulous employee will gain access to the code. It seems doubtful that any new innovation in computer security can do more than buy a little time until a way is found to defeat it, but such a delay may be well worth the price.

This growing concern about computer crime and the increasing number of cases in which "computer hackers" have broken into private computers to steal data or just to create havoc have lead to a host of new legislation. From 1975 to 1985, forty-six states and the federal government took legislative action to prevent the unauthorized use of computers. Yet a study by Erdwin Pfuhl found that enforcement agencies seldom actually charged anyone with these new crimes. Part of the reason is simply that many computer crimes are not reported, or no one can identify the offenders, put Pfuhl found that the stereotype of computer abuse as a kind of playful activity carried on by bright young men against anonymous corporations also played an important role in the lack of enforcement.[19]

EMBEZZLEMENT.   Despite the large sums taken by some computer embezzlers, they are still not playing for the biggest stakes in the world of occupational crime. Members of top management are usually the only ones in a position to pull off multimillion dollar crimes that can involve the looting of the assets of an entire corporation. For example, a West Coast financier, C. Arnholt Smith, illegally diverted millions of dollars from the U.S. National Bank of San Diego to finance other business ventures.[20] It was estimated that the debts from those operations constituted a large proportion of the $143 million in losses and uncollectible loans on U.S. National's books when it finally went bankrupt. The failure of U.S. National, which had sixty-nine branches and more than $1 billion in assets, was the largest bank failure in U.S. history up to that time.[21]

Out of a host of contenders, Robert L. Vesco appears to hold the crown as the nation's biggest embezzler and pillager of corporations. Vesco's exploits as the head of a far-flung financial empire first came to public light after he acquired control of a Swiss-based complex of mutual funds known as Investors Overseas Services. According to a subsequent complaint filed by the Securities and Exchange Commission, Vesco siphoned off $224 million in cash and securities from various IOS mutual funds. The money was then spirited away to Vesco-controlled banks in Luxembourg and the Bahamas. When Vesco got wind of the SEC investigation, he stuffed a black attache case with $200,000 worth of $100 bills and secretly donated the money to President Nixon's reelection campaign. Nevertheless, Vesco and his associates were the targets of an SEC suit filed in November 1972. After a New York grand jury also began investigating Vesco, this time on charges of criminal fraud, he moved to Costa Rica, where he had made over $25 million in investments. To make sure of his welcome, he also gave $300,000 to Costa Rican president José Figueres. Vesco seems to have chosen his friends wisely, for Costa Rica refused to extradite him on the grand jury's fraud charges. The same scenario was later repeated in the Bahamas—another center of Vesco's financial power, where yet another prime minister received substantial sums of money. On December 7, 1973, a Bahamian court refused to extradite Vesco, on the grounds that the sworn statements of the president, the accountant, and a former director of the defrauded company testifying to Vesco's fraud did not provide "sufficient evidence."[22]

Private businesses are not the only victims of such criminals; many unions suffer the same problem. The favorite targets of dishonest union officers are the pension funds upon which the financial security of so many millions of union members depends. The International Brotherhood of Teamsters, the largest single union in the United States, has had a particularly bad reputation in this regard. Investigators have found that organized criminals openly offered to arrange loans from the Teamsters' pension fund in exchange for a finder's fee. There is also substantial evidence that the fund financed numerous underworld projects, and several officials have been convicted of cheating the fund in various ways.[23] Two Teamster presidents, Dave Beck and Jimmy Hoffa, were sent to prison because of their conduct in office (Hoffa specifically for the misuse of pension funds), and a third Teamster president, Roy L. Williams, was elected while under indictment for allegedly attempting to bribe a U.S. senator, a charge on which he was convicted in December 1982.[24] In 1987, Williams admitted taking $1,500 a month in cash from organized criminals while he was a trustee of the Teamsters pension fund. He also said that their influence was critical to his election as president of the 1.7 million member union.[25] Williams's successor, Jackie Presser, and several associates are currently facing federal charges that they siphoned off $700,000 in union funds to pay "ghost employees" from organized crime who actually did no work.[26] Thus, it is hardly surprising that the Teamster Union has became notorious for its links to organized crime.

Commercial Bribery

Unlike most of the other crimes examined in these pages, a single act of bribery often involves both organizational and occupational crime. When, for example, the sales agent of one corporation pays off the purchasing agent of another, both kinds of crimes have been committed. The sales agent, in acting for his or her employer, commits an organizational crime, while the person who takes the bribe commits an occupational crime. This chapter will examine only the recipients of corrupt payments. Corporate involvement in bribery and corruption are discussed in more detail in chapter 2.

Commercial bribery is an extremely common crime that is estimated to involve more than $3 billion a year.[27] After the Lockheed bribery scandals focused attention on the problem, an offer of amnesty persuaded ninety-five major firms to publicly admit involvement in commercial bribery.[28] Moreover, a survey of businesspeople, lawyers, investigators, and accountants led *The New York Times* to conclude that commercial bribery is a common practice in a wide range of businesses at the wholesale, retail, and manufacturing levels.[29] The list of companies whose employees have been caught taking bribes is much too long to be reproduced here, but the products involved run the gamut of industrial production from chewing gum to bicycle speedometers.

It is doubtful that more than a tiny fraction of all commercial bribery ever comes to light. And when it does, prosecutors generally are much more inclined to go after the individual recipients of the kickbacks than the organizations that make the payments.[30] Prosecutions are usually based on the corrupt employees' failure to report the illegal payments as taxable income, even though similar tax evasion on the part of the corporate bribers is often ignored.

How much damage commercial bribery really causes employers is open to question. If a corrupt employee is persuaded to purchase an inferior product at an inflated price, the company may well suffer a serious loss. However, when the choice is among many more or less equal products at similar prices, the damage is less clear. In most cases the cost of the bribes is ultimately paid by the consumer. But because the size of the bribes is generally rather small in relation to the total value of the contracts involved, it is not even clear that consumers suffer a noticeable financial loss from commercial bribery.

Crimes against the Public

Up to this point we have dealt primarily with crimes against employers, but the general public is also victimized by occupational crime. One common example of such a crime is the short-changing of customers by sales clerks. Salespeople who knowingly lie in order to increase their commissions would fall into this same category, provided that they were not following official or unofficial company policies when carrying out such activities.

A particularly costly form of such crimes involves stockbrokers who make fraudulent statements about stocks in which they have a personal interest. Oftentimes these dishonest brokers are assisted by fellow conspirators who put out deceptive news releases, market analyses, and the like. According to government investigators, one victim of stock manipulators was told by his broker that his stock would be "the next IBM." Only after the victim had invested thousands of dollars was it discovered the firm involved was on the verge of bankruptcy, and that the broker wanted to unload the stock he and some friends owned before the firm went under. [31]

Another crime that vicitimizes unwary investors is known as churning. Because stockbrokers are paid on commission, their income depends on the volume of sales they make. As a result, some unscrupulous brokers take advantage of their clients' trust and "churn" their accounts, making the largest number of purchases and sales the client will allow, with little regard for the value or safety of the investments. This kind of offense is particularly common when a client grants a broker discretion to buy and sell stocks in response to market conditions. However, brokers will sometimes trade securities without permission from the client. If such offenses come to light, the broker usually claims to have received oral instructions from the client. Then, if the case ever comes to trial, it is only the client's word against the broker's. [32]

Insider trading, another common violation of securities law, was little known and little understood by the public until very recently.

This offense involves the use of privileged or "inside" information to gain a special advantage in securities dealings. Although this crime may not appear to be especially harmful, the laws against it were designed to preserve the public's confidence in the stock market as a viable investment for outsiders who aren't privy to confidential information.

The use of inside information to make a fast buck has been a part of Wall Street since its inception. But the feverish wave of mergers and take-overs in the 1980s seemed to have provided unprecedented opportunities for the unscrupulous trader, and the scandal that rocked Wall Street in 1986 proved there were many insiders ready and willing to take advantage of those opportunities. The affair started with Dennis Levine, a highly-placed merger and acquisitions specialist with the Wall Street firm of Drexel Burnham Lambert. Levine seemed to be a classic American success story—a middle class boy made good. At 33, he drove a red Ferrari, lived in a luxurious New York apartment, and had a million dollar a year compensation package from his employer. But his success story took an unexpected turn, when he was charged with using inside information to make $12 million dollars in illegal profits and was sentenced to a two-year prison term. [33]

The trail soon led investigators from Levine to Ivan F. Boesky, one of Wall Street's most successful stock traders of recent years. Boesky had apparently been making huge profits from the tips he had received from Levine and others and was fined a record $100 million for his offenses. [34] After Boesky, Securities and Exchange Commission investigators uncovered one crooked deal after another. By April of 1987, over sixty people had been indicted. An examination of the list of defendants reveals what can only be described as pervasive corruption among the top Wall Street firms. Among the defendants were a partner in Goldman Sachs; the Director of Kidder, Peabody; the head of risk arbitrage for Merrill Lynch; Vice Presidents from Paine Webber, E. F. Hutton, Kidder, Peabody, and Shearson Lehman Brothers, as well as numerous stock brokers and analysts. [35] It is clear that the major Wall Street firms were content to look to other way while top employees used their privileged positions to commit million dollar crimes and in some cases, the firms even shared directly in the take. [36]

CRIMES AGAINST GOVERNMENT

Because of the pressures of competition and the primacy of the profit motive, businesses are considerably more likely to engage in organizational crimes than are governments. But on the other hand, there appear to be proportionately greater opportunities for crimes against governments. Not only is government victimized by the same kind of pilferage and embezzlement that plagues private firms, but there are several crimes, such as tax evasion and election fraud, that affect only the government, and many others that pose more serious problems within the government than they do in the private sector. Although there is a growing concern about industrial espionage, for instance, no one doubts that the most serious espionage cases involve governments, not private enterprise. Even bribery and corruption, which are certainly common enough in the private sector, apparently are more often directed against public than private targets. While private firms give bribes as often as they are victimized by them, the government is almost always a victim rather than a perpetrator.

The problem of official corruption is probably as old as government itself, but that certainly does not mean that all governments are equally at fault. Each legislative body has its own traditions and its own subculture, and as with top corporate management, each presidential administration sets its own "ethical tone." The two most corrupt administrations in postwar America have certainly been those of Presidents Nixon and Reagan. The crimes that have come to be known as the Watergate scandal were by far the most serious, because they attacked the very heart of the democratic process. Yet corruption was much more widespread during the Reagan years. Well over one hundred members of the Reagan administration had serious ethical or legal charges raised against them,[37] and an 1987 estimate by the House Subcommittee on Civil Service put that number as high as 200.[38] As *Time* magazine put it: "While the Reagan administration's missteps may not have been as flagrant as the Teapot Dome scandal or as pernicious as Watergate, they seem more general, more pervasive and somehow more ingrained than those of any previous administration."[39] While the crimes of the Nixon administration were intended to perpetuate its power, President Reagan's appointees seemed unable to resist the temptation to enrich themselves at the public's expense.

Tax Evasion

Each occupation has its own structure of fraudulent opportunities, but almost all workers have a chance to commit one type of fraud—income tax evasion. Over 70 million Americans file income tax returns every year, and one estimate puts the annual loss from tax evasion at over $30 billion.[40] A survey of 1,698 Americans taken in the 1940s found that 57 percent of the men and 40 percent of the women admitted committing some type of tax evasion.[41] Interestingly, the survey found violations to be the most common among middle- and upper-income people, especially businessmen and lawyers. Prosecutions by the Internal Revenue Service are also concentrated in the higher social strata. There is evidence that millions of dollars a year are salted away in secret, overseas bank accounts by wealthy Americans seeking to avoid paying their taxes. [42]

Special investment schemes have been a very popular way to dodge taxes. Some of these manage to stay within the letter of the law, but many others do not, as witnessed by two huge fraud cases brought in 1987—the same year new tax laws were put into effect to try to stop the abuse of tax shelters. In one case, three well-known promoters created a tax shelter that generated $350 million in writeoffs by claiming losses on fraudulent government securities and interest expenses. Among the investors in this scheme were the head of CBS and the Postmaster General of the United States. [43] The second tax dodge involved the sale of limited partnerships in Transpac Drilling Venture, a firm that showed huge losses because of the fraudulent manipulation of its books. It is estimated that this scheme cost the U.S. government as much as $172 million dollars. [44] Although the investors in these tax dodges were not charged with criminal offenses, they did face huge bills for back taxes, interest, and penalties.

It is tempting to blame income tax evasion on the larceny that is said to be lurking in the hearts of even the most honest men and women. No doubt, there is some truth in this belief—if we were a nation of saints, there would be no tax evasion. But to understand this common crime, we must look to something other than universal human greed. The fact is that U.S. income tax laws could hardly provide more encouragement to would-be violators if they were intentionally designed for that purpose. The laws are so complex that even people who are willing to pay their taxes are often unable to figure out how much they owe. Income, deductions, depreciation, exemptions, and credits may be computed and manipulated in many different ways, and one person may pay lower taxes than another with the same income simply by being better at the "tax game." The obvious injustice of this situation encourages both contempt for the system of taxation and the attitude that paying taxes is not a responsibility of citizenship so much as a game that one wins or loses. If the percentage of income owed in taxes were determined entirely by accounting skills, the system might still claim some respectability. The tax laws, however, are replete with special advantages, loopholes, and benefits for those with the greatest political influence. Because every return cannot be audited, income tax collectors must rely upon the honesty of the individual taxpayers; yet the taxation system itself is so riddled with favoritism that it cannot claim the integrity it demands of its clients.

Power for Sale

Most forms of government corruption are occupational crimes, since they are obviously not intended to promote the government's organizational goals. However, this does not mean that all corrupt government employees are renegades without support or acceptance among their peers. There is strong evidence that many government agencies harbor deviant subcultures that encourage—or at a minimum, condone—various types of corruption. Such subcultures show considerable variation from one agency to another, but there is a fairly clear demarcation between elected officials on the one hand and government employees and bureaucrats on the other. The holders of elective office are in a unique position. Not only are they in constant contact with numerous groups and individuals who legitimately try to influence their decisions, but they are also dependent upon those same individuals to provide the campaign funds and support necessary to win reelection. The temptation to exchange political favors for financial support is a fact of political life, and the line between corruption and integrity is often blurred.

The structural position of government employees who do not have to stand for public election is more similar to the employees of large corporations. But despite the public attention focused upon corrupt politicians, the crimes of the bureaucrats are also important, for the government is much more than just the elected officials who head it. The workers who run the various government agencies may not be able to change the laws, but they can change the way the laws are carried out. And although most governmental bureaucrats and administrators lack the political influence of elected officials, they are further from the focus of public attention and therefore safer targets for corruption.

SELLING BUSINESS.   The history of the relationship between the meat packing industry and the U.S. military shows the way a tradition of corruption can develop in the commerce between business and government. As far back as the Spanish-American War, a general charged that "embalmed meat" was sold to the army by the big meat packing companies, and that their meat had killed more troops than the enemy's bullets. Teddy Roosevelt is reported to have said he would rather eat his hat than the canned meat given to soldiers during that war.[45] Over three-quarters of a century after those charges were made, government investigators found that meat packers, with the cooperation of corrupt inspectors, were still selling the military inferior meat at exorbitant prices. Testimony at a Senate hearing called to investigate the problem indicated that the military bought huge quantities of inferior meat, and that most of the meat purchased failed to meet the standards the manufacturers claimed for it. For example, one witness testified that knuckle meat normally priced at $1.85 a pound was substituted for sirloin valued at $3.85 a pound. And when auditors checked a 1.4 million-pound sample of meat sold to the military, they found that 66 percent of it failed to meet specifications. In some cases, unscrupulous meat packers may have been able simply to slip the low-grade meat past the inspectors, but the existence of a widespread network of corruption was apparent to the investigators. One civilian inspector testified that he received between $100 and $200 a week to "refrain from hassling the employees," and an army sergeant testified that he not only received cash payments but the services of a prostitute as well. At least sexual discrimination is one charge that cannot be leveled at the meat packers—one female inspector was given, along with free clothes and plane tickets, free weekend trips with a male company employee as an escort.

One source of corruption among the military inspectors was obviously the corruption in the meat packing industry itself. Fraudulent claims made by packers about inferior or even dangerous products have been recognized as a problem for at least eighty years. Upton Sinclair's turn-of-the-century novel *The Jungle* painted a vivid picture of the filth in the rat-infested Chicago stockyards and informed American homemakers that, in addition to meat, their breakfast sausage contained poisoned bread, dead rats, and dung.[46] The Meat Inspection Act of 1906, passed largely because of the furor surrounding Sinclair's novel, helped establish an official system of meat inspection. But by creating more inspectors that act, and the more comprehensive Meat Inspection Act of 1967, also created the potential for more government corruption. Periodic scandals involving bribed inspectors and inferior products have swept the industry throughout this century. Apparently "meat racketeering," which includes the bribery of buyers and union officials, is also a common practice, if the numerous bribery convictions involving the meat packing industry can be taken as a guide.

Of course, corruption in an industry does not guarantee that the government agencies that deal with that industry will also be corrupt. But in the case of the military meat inspectors, the indifference and ineptness of higher-ranking military officials played into the hands of corrupt elements in the meat-packing industry. According to the chairman of the Senate's Government Operations Subcommittee, an investigation "found that young kids recruited into the system were inadequately trained, unsupervised, and encouraged to steal meat." He added that "the kids also quickly learned to accept gratuities from the meat vendor they were supposed to be monitoring."[47] Thus, the incompetence of the military supervisors helped to create an environment in which a culture of corruption flourished, and crooked employees had little fear of punishment.

There is, unfortunately, nothing unique in the Department of Defense's relationship with the meat packers. DOD has a long history of corruption that goes far beyond any one industry. In September 1776, John Adams complained about a contract given the trading house of Willing, Morris & Company to supply gunpowder to the Continental Congress. Adams said that the supplier "without any risk at all, will make a clear profit of 12,000 pounds." But what bothered Adams the most was that both Mr. Willing and Mr. Morris were members of the congressional committee that had granted the contract. [48]

In more recent times, repeated public revelations about cost overruns and the failure of major weapon systems have lead to the Department of Defense's apparently well-earned reputation for corruption and inefficiency. In 1982 the General Accounting Office concluded that there was a 91 percent chance of a major cost overrun on the average military contract, and that fraud and waste cost the Department of Defense at least $15 billion a year. [49] Publicity about some of the more outrageous amounts the Department of Defense had paid for supplies, such as a $1,118.26 plastic cap for the leg of a stool, led to a coordinated effort among several government agencies to attack fraud in military procurement in 1986. Although "Operation DEFCON" was criticized for focusing too heavily on the small contractors, it did uncover a long list of crimes including fraud, kickbacks, and price fixing. [50]

Most state, local, and national governments have established systems of competitive bidding to minimize this kind of corruption. However, there are always exemptions to the bidding requirements that may provide opportunities for continued corruption. The Department of Defense, for example, awards more than half of its contracts without competitive bidding. [51] For one thing, bids are usually not required for small purchases. This rule facilitates "nickel-and-dime" corruption and allows unethical officials to avoid bidding requirements by splitting one lucrative contract into several smaller ones. Another common exemption is for emergency contracts—those that must be let too quickly for the slow-moving bidding process. This loophole can be exploited by bureaucrats who merely procrastinate until the need for the contract becomes an "emergency" and then award the contract to a cooperative firm without bidding. Finally, the purchase of professional services can often be made without competitive bidding. The theory behind this exemption is that it is necessary to hire the best-qualified and most competent professionals available, regardless of whether or not there is a lower bidder. But in practice, this exemption has opened the gates to corruption in the hiring of engineers, architects, auditors, and other professionals.[52]

Even without the exemptions, competitive bidding provides no guarantee against corruption. There are numerous dodges and tricks that crooked officials can use to ensure that the "right" bidder wins each contract. A common technique is to tailor the specifications sent out for bid to the product being offered by a favored bidder. One typical case from Atlantic City involved a local Ford salesman and Republican ward-healer who gave strong support to a political coalition that won control of city government. After the coalition's victory, he was allowed to write the specifications for some of the vehicles to be purchased by the public works department. Not surprisingly, they neatly described the Fords his automobile agency sold.[53]

A technique that is sometimes used when the "right" bid turns out to be higher than the others is to throw them all out on some technicality and start over. In another case from Atlantic City, the former public works director promised a contract for an air compressor to a particular company in exchange for a $1,200 kickback. Unfortunately for the director, its bid was the highest of the three received. His response was to reject all the bids on a minor technicality. Then, before new bids were solicited, the specifications were rewritten to require that the compressor have two reels. Since only the favored bidder's compressor had a second reel, it won the contract by default when all its competitors dropped out of the competition.[54]

SELLING IMMUNITY.   Only a few government employees have the power to hand out lucrative contracts, but those who work in law enforcement and regulatory agencies have something else to offer — immunity from the law. The history of police corruption in the United States is a long one. Reports dating from the time of the Civil War indicate that bribery was practically a universal phenomenon, and that "assaulting superior officers, refusing to go on patrol, releasing prisoners from the custody of policemen, drunkeness, extorting money from prisoners" were daily occurrences, often committed "under the protection of a political overlord."[55] Numerous investigative committees have described deep-rooted corruption in urban police departments. Since the turn of the century, New York City's policy force has been the subject of three major investigations: by the Lexow Committee in the 1890s, by the Seabury Committee a generation later, and by the Knapp Commission in the early 1970s.[56] Other official investigations of police misconduct include the Chicago City Council Commission on Crime in 1915, the Senate Committee to Investigate Crime in Interstate Commerce in the early 1950s, and the Pennsylvania Crime Commission, which published its report on the Philadelphia police department in 1974.[57] All of these investigations reached the same conclusion—that corruption in police ranks was a widespread and serious problem. Indeed, the pattern of corruption appears to be so pervasive that one highly regarded criminologist commented that "Federal and state investigating committees have revealed graft and corruption almost every time they have looked for them."[58]

The causes of this corruption are not difficult to find. Police officers simply have a lot of opportunities to receive bribes and payoffs. Not only can the police offer valuable services merely by being a little less vigilant, but they also are in constant contact with people who desire those services and have no compunctions about breaking the law to purchase them. Moreover, police work is carried out in a unique social environment that may easily come to encourage corruption. Polls show that, although the public respects police officers and wants their protection, there is nevertheless a considerable undercurrent of resentment toward those who wield the power of the badge, and even some fear about what the police are going to do with that power. Sensing the uneasiness so many of the rest of us feel in the presence of even an off-duty officer, those in police work tend to avoid social contact with the general public and to retreat into the company of other officers. As one criminologist put it, the police "separate themselves from the public, develop strong in-group attitudes, and control one another's conduct, making it conform to the interests of the group."[59] This sense of occupational solidarity is further reinforced by the dangers inherent in police work and by the need to depend upon one's fellow officers for help in difficult situations.[60] The occupational subculture that develops in such circumstances is an ideal vehicle for the transmission of a tradition of corruption. Even the most honest cops hesitate to report minor violations by their colleagues, and once such a custom becomes part of an occupational subculture, it can easily expand to include much more serious offenses.

Another factor underlying the problem of police corruption is the inadequacy of the laws the police are called upon to enforce. Criminologists have long recognized that the prohibition of such things as prostitution, gambling, and drug use creates a highly profitable black market that is soon exploited by organized criminals. While vastly stronger and more wealthy than individual criminals, organized crime is also more visible, and thus requires some measure of official protection. Considering the billions of dollars in annual earnings that such businesses generate, it would be surprising indeed if the racketeers were unable to find anyone willing to sell them protection. In fact, while the tolerance of corruption varies from one department to another, it is highly unlikely that there is a single major police department that is untouched by the influence of organized criminals. [61]

Police corruption is further encouraged by the fact that victimless crimes, such as gambling and prostitution, are not considered serious offenses. The idea that no one is being harmed by these crimes provides individual officers with an easy rationalization that allows them to continue to see themselves as "good cops" and still receive the financial rewards of corruption. As one officer put it when discussing this attitude toward gambling payoffs,

> Hell, everybody likes to place a bet once in a while. It's all part of the system. . . .Sure there are honest cops on the force, and more power to them. You take Captain —. Why, you can't buy him a cup of coffee. . . .But most of us are realistic. [62]

Although most police corruption stems from the attempts to legislate private morality, other ill-conceived laws also contribute to the problem. One such example is the maze of building ordinances regulating construction in New York City. As the chairman of the Building Trades Employers Association put it, "It is virtually impossible for a builder to erect a building within the city of New York and comply with every statute and ordinance in connection with the work." [63] A minimum of forty to fifty permits and licenses are required, and the number can run well over 130. The permits range in importance from the approval of the design of the building to the permission necessary when a tracked vehicle is moved across a sidewalk. In practice, builders seldom attempt the costly and time-consuming process necessary to secure all the required permits. Instead, they apply for a few of the most important ones and pay the police to ignore their other violations. For a small job, the Knapp Commission reported typical payoffs of between $50 and $150 a week, and on a larger job, they would be proportionately greater. Most contractors pay willingly, knowing that the cost of the bribes is much less than the cost of meeting the letter of the law. Even so, one study estimated that graft makes up about 5 percent of the total costs of construction in New York City. [64]

Powerful forces promoting police corruption are present in one form or another in all the major cities in the United States. But the degree of corruption within a department is also affected by the policies and personnel that guide it. In some cases, the roots of corruption can be traced to the highest levels of police administration and beyond to the elected officials who direct them. Police corruption and favoritism appear to be especially severe in departments that are under the direct political control of local officials. When the appointment of commissioners, the police chief, and even promotion through the ranks are controlled by politicians, the pressure to give special privileges to influential individuals is virtually irresistible, and the growth of one type of corruption soon leads to the growth of another.

In most of the major police scandals, top departmental officials were not actually involved in the corruption but were lax or indifferent to the struggle against it. The Philadelphia Police Department at the time of the Pennsylvania Crime Commission's investigation in the early 1970s provides a typical example. The Commission found that, although the top administrators were not corrupt, they repeatedly ignored the pervasive nature of the problem, insisting that it existed only in isolated, individual cases. This so-called "rotten apple" theory is often used by police administrators called upon to defend the integrity of their departments. But such attitudes are a major obstacle to reform, for it is extremely difficult to fight corruption in an organization whose leadership tries to pretend there really isn't much of a problem.

The most highly publicized investigation of police corruption in recent years came as a result of charges made by a whistle-blowing New York City policeman, Frank Serpico. The difficulty he and fellow officer David Durk had in winning a fair hearing for their charges illustrates the indifference top police administrators and elected officials often display toward the problem of corruption. When the two officers first began talking about the abuses they had seen, their colleagues told them to shut up and mind their own business. Serpico and Durk then took their complaints to higher and higher levels in the police administration, but they received an indifferent response. Time and again they were told that their charges were being fully investigated, but nothing was ever done. They were finally forced to bring their charges to the allegedly reform-minded mayor, John V. Lindsay, but once again no significant action was taken. It was not until they began talking to *The New York Times*, and the paper ran a series of articles on police corruption, that the Knapp Commission was appointed to investigate the problem. It is doubtful the reforms that resulted from the commission's findings did much to root out the long-standing tradition of corruption in the New York Police Department, but the commission did provide criminologists with one of the clearest and most comprehensive pictures of contemporary police corruption ever assembled.

Although the Knapp Commission found pervasive corruption in the NYPD, minor offenses were much more widespread than serious ones. The acceptance of small gratuities, special discounts, and similar favors were almost universal. The majority of those who accepted outright bribes did not actually seek out the payments but merely took advantage of offers from contractors, tow truck operators, and various criminals. These officers, known as "grass-eaters" in department slang, generally received only small individual payments ranging from $5 to $20, but taken together, those bribes could make a significant contribution to an officer's total income.

The subculture of corruption was so firmly established in the NYPD that loyalty to one's fellow officers actually became an important motivation to accept petty graft. Officers who refused were looked upon with suspicion by their colleagues, both because of the implied criticism of those who had taken bribes and because of the potential threat honest cops posed to the system of corruption. As the Knapp Commission put it: "Accepting payoff money is one way for an officer to prove that he is one of the boys and that he can be trusted. . . .these numerous but relatively small payoffs were a fact of life and those officers who made a point of refusing them were not accepted closely into the fellowship of policemen."[65]

Most corrupt officers apparently drew the line at petty graft and corruption and did not become involved in the big-time payoffs. However, it is also true that opportunities for big-time corruption were not available to all officers. Among the "meat-eaters"—officers who actively pursued corrupt income—the biggest sources of payoffs were the organized criminals who provided the public with various kinds of illegal goods and services. As a result, the officers who worked in such fields as gambling or drug enforcement raked in the largest profits. The part of town to which an officer was assigned also carried significant economic implications. Slum and ghetto areas with high concentrations of gambling and narcotics businesses were clearly the most lucrative for the willing officer. Harlem was not know as the Gold Coast in department slang because of its beaches or its mineral resources.

The detectives assigned to gambling enforcement devised the most sophisticated system to divide the spoils. Plainclothesmen in every precinct in New York City were involved in the "pad," a system in which regular payments were collected from gambling interests and then divided up among the officers. The Knapp Commission noted that this system for collecting payoffs from gamblers "has persisted virtually unchanged for years despite periodic scandals, department reorganizations, massive transfers in and out of the units involved, and the folding of some gambling operations and the establishment of new ones."[66]

The Knapp Commission found that most officers had much more negative attitudes toward narcotics than toward gambling. Many of those who took graft from other sources rejected narcotics payoffs as "dirty money." Perhaps for that reason, narcotics "scores"—one-time payments to individual officers—were the most lucrative form of graft in the NYPD. Single scores reportedly involved as much as $250,000. Despite the reluctance of many officers to accept "drug money," the commission concluded that there was still widespread corruption among narcotics officers.

The Knapp Commission left little doubt about the pervasive character of the corruption in the New York Police Department. Generations of administrators allowed the occupational subculture of the department to become so debased that it was the honest cops, not the crooked ones, who were the deviants. And if neither the top levels of the department's administration or the political leadership of the city were directly involved in the corruption, both clearly lacked the will to do anything about it. In this bottom-to-top pattern of corruption, rank-and-file officers are the principal source of corruption, while the upper administrative levels adopt a posture of passive indifference.

The Pennsylvania Crime Commission Report painted a remarkably similar picture of police corruption in Philadelphia. The system of payoffs, for instance, was almost identical to that found in New York. In both departments, "bagmen" made periodic rounds of illegal gambling operations to collect payoff money and then distributed it to participating officers. Like officers of the NYPD, the Philadelphia police considered narcotics money to be the dirtiest type of graft. But once again, those attitudes did not deter individual police officers from "scoring" suspected drug dealers for large payoffs. The crime commission heard reports that in 65 to 70 percent of narcotics arrests, a portion of the drugs seized were not turned in. These purloined drugs were used by the officers as "plants" to frame suspected narcotics dealers, sold on the black market, or diverted to personal use. The report indicated that some female addicts were forced to have sex with officers in order to avoid arrest, and that similar sexual harassment was directed at prostitutes as well. In a very different kind of offense, on-duty officers were apparently paid by local businesses to perform special services. In one case, a fast-food chain was found to have employed the equivalent of twenty-two full-time officers to act as private guards. The commission concluded that "police corruption in Philadelphia is ongoing, widespread, systematic and occurring at all levels of the Police Department. Corrupt practices were uncovered during the investigation in every police district and involved police officers ranging in rank from policeman to inspector."[67] As in New York, the top levels of the police administration were not directly implicated in the corruption, but they did their best to ignore it.

The opposite pattern of top-to-bottom corruption frequently develops in cities run by politicians with ties to organized crime. Typical of this pattern was the medium-sized Midwestern city studied by John A. Gardiner.[68] Wincanton, as Gardiner called this city, was caught up in the same pervasive corruption as New York, but the payoffs went primarily to the people at the top, not to the cops on the street. Vice in Wincanton was largely controlled by a single underworld boss, whom Gardiner dubbed Irving Stern. The Stern empire made large campaign contributions to most of the town's leading politicians and delivered regular monthly payoffs to a host of elected officials and city administrators. Gardiner estimated that only about ten of the 155 members of the Wincanton police force were actually on Stern's payroll, but that about half the department had accepted presents from him (usually turkeys or liquor). Stern did not have to pay off most officers because they knew that those who reported gambling or prostitution would be ignored or transferred to the graveyard shift.

Although it appears that there is a higher degree of corruption in police agencies than in other branches of the criminal justice system, no part of the system is immune. In most jurisdictions, the office of the prosecutor is a highly political one, and the decision whether or not to pursue a case is often influenced by extralegal considerations. The use of political influence usually stops far short of outright bribery, but criminal behavior by prosecutors is not altogether unusual, especially where organized crime is involved. The Kefauver Committee, which investigated organized crime in the 1950s, described the systematic dereliction of duties on the part of one district attorney of New York County, who was believed to have been on the payroll of organized crime:

> [He failed to take] effective action against the top echelons of the gambling, narcotics, waterfront, murder, or bookmaking rackets. His defense of public officials who were derelict in their duties and his actions in investigation of corruption and his failure to follow up concrete evidence of organized crime, particularly in the case of Murder, Inc., and the waterfront, have contributed to the growth of organized crime, racketeering, and gangsterism. [69]

Often the pressure to give immunity to certain criminals comes not from the prosecutor but from corrupt superiors. The famous antitrust suit against ITT provides a case in point. In 1970, ITT bought the Hartford Insurance Company, which proved to be a highly valuable acquisition. Hartford not only contributed its large cash reserves but earned one-quarter of ITT's profits in that first year. Thus, ITT was understandably worried when the U.S. Justice Department began looking into possible antitrust violations in the acquisition. An ITT subsidiary subsequently promised a $400,000 contribution to underwrite the Republican national convention proposed for San Diego, and almost immediately the Justice Department agreed to a consent decree allowing ITT to keep Hartford. [70] Although the appearance of impropriety was obvious in this case, it was not until a memo from ITT lobbyist Dita Beard was published by newspaper columnist Jack Anderson that the public saw the "smoking gun." The memo said, in part:

> Other than. . .John Mitchell, Ed Reinecke, Bob Halderman and Nixon *no one* has known from whom that 400 thousand commitment had come. . . .I am convinced that our noble commitment has gone a long way toward our negotiations on the mergers eventually coming out as Hal wants them. Certainly the President has told Mitchell to see that things are worked out fairly. . . .If it [the contribution] gets too much publicity, you can believe our negotiations with Justice will wind up shot down. Mitchell is definitely helping us, but cannot let it be known. Please destroy this, huh? [71]

Corruption of this kind rarely surfaces in the judiciary. [72] Whether this reflects the overall integrity of judges or their ability to use their influence to avoid prosecution is impossible to say. However, judicial corruption, especially in connection with organized crime, is certainly not known. Donald R. Cressey, a leading authority on organized crime, gave the following description of one congressional district under the control of organized criminals:

> In this district Cosa Nostra also "owns" both judges and the officials who assign criminal cases to judges. About 90 percent of the organized-crime defendants appear before the same few judges. It may properly be said that the entire political district is "owned" by the Cosa Nostra boss. [73]

One recent case of judicial corruption involved the indictment of Judge Harry E. Claiborne of the federal district court on charges of bribery, wire fraud, and filing false statements. The government's case was begun in response to the charge that Claiborne pressured a Nevada brothel owner, Joe Conforte, to pay him $130,000 in exchange for help in winning the reversal of a conviction for tax evasion. Investigation into the bribery allegation revealed Claiborne's failure to report more than $100,000 in income for 1979 and 1980. Claiborne's first trial ended in a deadlocked jury, and the government subsequently dropped the charges involving Conforte. At a second trial, on August 10, 1984, he was convicted by a federal jury of filing false income tax returns for 1979 and 1980. [74] Claiborne was impeached by the U.S. Senate and removed from his post in October 1986. [74]

SELLING INFLUENCE.   Up to this point we have examined only those instances of governmental corruption involving law enforcement or the administration of government regulations. These crimes certainly cost the taxpayers substantial amounts of money, but they pale in importance when compared with the offenses examined in this section. Police corruption, for example, certainly sets a shameful example for the rest of society, but it is not at all clear that its elimination would greatly reduce the victimless crimes that generate most payoff money. The higher up corruption reaches, however, the more serious a problem it becomes. Influence peddling and bribery among lawmakers is a profoundly antidemocratic activity that threatens to transform majority rule into rule by the highest bidder. All things considered, this may well be the central problem of modern democracy.

Despite the stakes involved, politicians who trade their influence for personal gain do not necessarily break the law. An elaborate system of regulations has been set up to limit both the sources and amounts of campaign contributions, but it is so full of loopholes that in actuality it does neither. But even without those loopholes, the current legislation governing campaign contributions reveals a curious kind of logic. If campaign contributions are used to buy influence, the logic of democracy wold dictate their prohibition and the creation of some other system of campaign financing. Even if the laws were changed to prevent contributors from side-stepping the current $1,000 limit, the new system would hardly be more democratic. The vast majority of campaign funds would still come from the wealthy who would still withhold their support from candidates who threaten their interests.[75]

Defenders of the current system argue that the contributions are simply gifts with no strings attached and do not influence the way elected officials perform their duties. But even if that highly unlikely contention were true, it ignores the role the big contributors' money plays in putting those with whom they already agree into office. Most politicians certainly believe they need great financial resources to have a reasonable chance to win elective office. A study by Ralph Nader's Congress Watch found that winners outspent losers by a margin of four to one in congressional races, and that Senate candidates who outspent their opponents won election 85 percent of the time.[76] Although some of this difference is probably due to the ability of the most popular candidates to attract more campaign contributions, that is only part of the explanation. After a careful statistical analysis of the variables that might affect the relationship between campaign spending and electoral success, Gary Jacobson concluded that "challengers and other nonincumbents do better the more money they spend, because their campaign expenditures purchase the attention of voters."[77]

The general laxity of the campaign financing laws might lead one to expect that they would seldom be violated, but that is not the case. Of all the members of Congress who were indicted for criminal offenses between 1941 and 1980, over 14 percent were charged with violating campaign financing laws.[78] Although the existing loopholes make it relatively easy for private individuals to spend as much as they want to help the candidates of their choice, the ban on direct contributions by corporations and unions makes it more difficult for such organizations to stay within the law. In order to maintain the appearance of legality, organizational contributors must persuade their employees, members, or stockholders to give money to political action committees that support their organizational interests. And though indictments are rare for such offenses, it is clear that corporations and unions often engage in fund-raising activities that violate not only the spirit of the law, but the letter as well. For example, although the law expressly forbids organizations to coerce employees to contribute, many employees still come under intense pressure to chip in to support their company's political interests. A recent report in the *Los Angeles Times* indicates that many large corporations actually have automatic deductions taken from the paychecks of "consenting" executives that are sent to company-controlled political actions committees (PACs).[79] Some companies have even given employees special bonuses with the expectation that they will be turned over to the appropriate PAC or encouraged employees to pad their expense accounts to reimburse themselves for their contributions.

One example of such illegal efforts to evade the campaign financing law can be seen in the activities of the American Shipbuilding Company. According to the charges brought by the special prosecutor for the Watergate case, that company gave bonuses to trusted employees that were then turned over to President Nixon's reelection campaign in 1972. Witnesses at the Senate Watergate hearings testified that the company paid bonuses worth $25,000 after taxes to eight different employees in 1972. Each recipient then wrote out a personal check that was sent to the president's personal attorney, who channeled the money into the Committee to Re-Elect the President. The witnesses testified that they had received other bonuses in 1970 and 1971 as well. As one witness revealed, "I knew from those conversations with the company secretary that the bonuses I was to receive were for political contributions and weren't bonuses at all."[80]

Although such blatant crimes only occasionally come to light, few successful politicians have remained untouched by charges of campaign irregularities. Some of the charges are undoubtedly groundless accusations made for political motives, but the ever-growing need for campaign funds puts pressure upon even the most principled politicians to accept questionable contributions. In 1986 successful candidates for the House of Representatives spent an average of $340,000 on their election campaign—four times more than only a decade before. In the Senate, expenditures averaged a staggering $3 million, about five times higher than in 1976.[81] One of the principal causes of the skyrocketing cost of election campaigns is the growing importance of television advertising. Another major factor is the professionalization of election campaigns. In the past, most campaign decisions were made by the candidate or a few close advisors, but today a candidate for major office is backed by myriad professional consultants, advertising agencies, and pollsters. The virtually universal belief that such costly services are essential to success puts tremendous pressure upon politicians to raise the money necessary to pay for them. The national finance chairman of the Democratic Party has estimated that some politicians spend up to half of their time seeking campaign funds. The late Senator Hubert Humphrey spoke for many politicians when he said, "Campaign financing is a curse. It's the most disgusting, demeaning, disenchanting, debilitating experience of a politician's life. . . .I just can't tell you how much I hate it."[82]

Despite the pressing financial need felt by most politicians, campaign contributions still have their limitations as a device to purchase political influence. For one thing, the most powerful and important political figures often have the easiest time raising funds and are therefore the least beholden to individual contributors. Then, too, the financial power of some special interests may be neutralized by opposing interests that also have large amounts of money to give away in the pursuit of their goals. Finally, presidential elections are now partially funded by federal funds, and so major party candidates are under less financial pressure than they were in previous years. As a result, many influence seekers attempt to curry favor by giving gifts, services, or money directly to government officials.

Because most politicians balk at accepting outright bribes, lobbyists often make small personal gifts that allegedly come with no strings attached. The most common inducements are small presents and gratuities—free meals at expensive restaurants, lavishly catered parties, free bottles of perfume, a case of soft drinks or another free sample of a company's product. At Christmas, General Electric has given away small deep-fat friers, Kraft Foods has handed out cheese packets, and 3M has distributed kits of cellophane tape.[83] A free bottle of perfume is obviously not enough to influence a senator's vote on a critical issue, but the hope of the growing army of Washington lobbyists is that the accumulation of small favors will create a sense of obligation that will ultimately be paid back in political favors. Former Senator Paul Douglas made this point well:

> The enticer does not generally pay money directly to the public representative. He tries instead by a series of favors to put public officials under such a feeling of personal obligation that [he] comes to feel that his first loyalties are to his private benefactors and patrons.[84]

Do such tactics work? The answer depends upon the individual official involved, but the growing number of Washington lobbyists who collectively spend $2 billion a year in the effort to win political influence apparently think so. And there are now over fifteen thousand lobbyists in Washington, or about thirty for each member of Congress. [85]

Outright bribery is certainly far less common than the more subtle forms of influence peddling. It is, however, the offense that is most likely to lead to criminal prosecution of political figures. Almost 42 percent of the criminal indictments lodged against congressional office-holders since 1940 involved some kind of bribery. [86] The services that influence peddlers attempt to buy run the gamut of political favors. If the charges brought against congressional officeholders can be taken as representative, the introduction of special bills and the right vote on a particular piece of legislation are the most sought after services. Over 30 percent of the bribery charges brought against congressional office-holders involved such favors. Help in winning government contracts, the second most sought after favor, was alleged in 27 percent of the charges. The use of congressional influence with the federal bureaucracy was involved in 15 percent of the charges. [87]

The most publicized bribery case in recent years was an FBI "string" operation known as ABSCAM. Agents working on this case posed as representatives of Kambir Abdul Rahman, a supposed Arab sheik in need of some Washington favors. Eight officials were persuaded to sponsor special bills or use their influence with the federal bureaucracy in exchange for cash payments and other rewards. One senator was given stock certificates in a bogus titanium mine in exchange for his help in winning government contracts. A representative was given $20,000 in cash for his services, and was videotaped stuffing the money into his pockets and then asking the FBI agents if any of it showed. The officials involved in ABSCAM were convicted of a variety of crimes and given fines and prison terms. A New Jersey state senator received the most severe sentence—six years in jail and a $40,000 fine. [88]

Despite the seriousness of the crimes involved, it is difficult to know what conclusions to draw from ABSCAM. Some observers have claimed that the ease with which the FBI unearthed crooked officials reflects the pervasive corruption among our elected officials. But others have held that the defendants were lured into crimes that they would not otherwise have committed, and that the government agents were actually creating crime, not preventing it.

The case of Daniel Flood, a U.S. representative from an impoverished coal region in northeastern Pennsylvania, is more typical, in that law enforcement agents played no part in his offenses. Flood, like many other powerful representatives, was very popular in his home district.

Through his position as chair of one of the subcommittees of the important House Appropriations Committee, he was able to funnel his own flood of federal funds into his home district. His constituents could be born at the Daniel J. Flood Rural Health Center, be educated at the Daniel J. Flood Elementary School, be employed in the Daniel J. Flood Industrial Park, and retire in the Daniel J. Flood Elderly Center. But Flood did not stop at promoting the interests of his constituents; he also used his legislative skills for personal profit.

Flood's undoing can be attributed to the testimony of his administrative assistant, Stephen Elko. Elko described how he served as the conduit for regular payments made by the Arlie Foundation to gain Flood's help in increasing the funding for the Agency for International Development's family planning program. Flood also was accused of taking a $5,000 bribe from a businessman trying to sell disaster relief housing to the government in the aftermath of Hurricane Agnes. And when a chain of California trade schools was about to lose its accreditation, and with it millions of dollars in federal grants, the company was alleged to have made a series of payments to Flood and Elko totaling $50,000; in exchange, Flood pressured the state commissioner of education to grant the school temporary accreditation. A New York rabbi testified that he gave Flood at least five $1,000 bribes in exchange for helping his small religious school obtain millions of dollars in federal grants. A banker said he gave Flood $4,000 worth of bank stock in exchange for using his influence to get the Treasury Department to approve a bank merger.

Despite strong testimony from such witnesses, Flood's first trial ended in a hung jury. The one holdout later said that he thought that seventy-five-year-old Flood had broken the law but he "would never vote guilty because Mr. Flood was too old [to go to jail]." Before a second trial got under way, Flood pleaded guilty as part of a plea bargaining deal. In exchange for a guilty plea to one misdemeanor charge, the prosecutor dropped eleven felony counts of conspiracy, bribery, and perjury, and Flood received one year's probation. [89]

Flood is a good example of a congressman who was determined to, in his own words, "Get all you can, while you can get it." [90] But many bribery cases have centered around powerful, well-financed groups reaching out to corrupt many different officials. One well-documented example can be found in the so-called Koreagate scandal, which raised, according to the *Washington Post*, "the most sweeping allegations of congressional corruption ever investigated by the federal government." [91] There is a good deal of hyperbole in that statement—the illegal payments made by the Gulf Oil Company, for example, far exceeded those involved in the Korean case (see chapter 2)—but it is true that Koreagate involved allegations against an exceptionally large number of officials and very substantial sums of money.

The Koreagate conspiracy apparently began when Representative Richard Hanna, a South Korean businessman named Tongsun Park, and the director of the Korean Central Intelligence Agency, Kim Hyung Wook, met to discuss methods of promoting South Korean interests on Capitol Hill. It was agreed to have Park appointed the South Korean government's exclusive agent for the purchase of rice in the United States and to use a portion of the $9 million Park was to earn from the deal to buy influence with the U.S. Congress. Some of the money was spent on lobbying and other forms of persuasion. Hanna, for instance, organized all-expense paid goodwill trips to South Korea for congressional officials, and Park became famous for his parties and lavish entertainment. But the conspirators' largess went far beyond entertainment and junkets. Park later testified that he had given $850,000 to thirty-one different members of Congress in order to advance his political interests. In his defense, Park said, "I thought I was taking part in the American political process. So far as I was concerned, I was helping congressional friends who were loyal to me."[92]

Although the public scandal centered on Park's activities, he was only one of the important South Korean figures involved. Leon Jaworski, the special counsel to the House Korean Lobbying Investigation, said that "Kim Don Jo [the Korean ambassador] is immeasurably more important to us than Tongsun Park. This whole thing was run right out of the Korean Embassy."[93] Jo invoked diplomatic immunity, but a Maryland businessman, Hancho Kim, was convicted of conspiracy to corrupt members of Congress and of lying to a grand jury about his part in another bribery scheme funded by the South Korean embassy. The investigation of the Koreagate scandal turned up some interesting information on other issues as well. Most significant was the discovery that U.S. corporations gave the ruling party in South Korea at least $8.5 million for its election campaign. It seems that the flow of corruption between South Korea and the United States was a two-way affair.[94]

Fraud, Embezzlement, and Conflict of Interest

Many of the crimes committed against the government by its employees are virtually identical to the offenses against business that we have already discussed. Employee pilferage and most types of embezzlement are, for example, substantially the same in both cases. However, some government employees—especially elected officials— have the opportunity to commit more unique types of offenses. Conflict of interest is, for instance, a problem of particular prominence among elected officials. Most such conflict fall into the gray area of behavior that is clearly recognized to be unethical but is not illegal. The Senate's code of ethics, for example, prohibits any member or employee from aiding the progress of legislation for the purpose of advancing his or her own financial interests, yet virtually every day members of Congress vote on bills that directly affect their personal finances. Seventeen of the forty-two members of the Senate Agriculture Committee, for instance, own farms or other farm-related interests.[95] *Congressional Quarterly* reported that in 1976, forty-four representatives had holdings in one or another of the top one hundred defense contractors, forty- eight had real estate interests, forty-one held gas or oil stock, and twenty were in pharmaceuticals.

Of course, the U.S. government is now so deeply involved in regulating the economy that it would be difficult for legislators to find any investments that would not be affected by their actions in one way or another. Senator Robert Kerr, a millionaire oilman who was often questioned about his conflicts of interest involving tax legislation for the oil industry, is reported to have responded, "Hell, I'm in everything."[96] However, there are two simple steps that even the wealthiest legislators can take to avoid conflicts of interest: to abstain from voting on any issue that might affect their financial interests and to place their holdings in a blind trust that is controlled by independent trustees. In 1980 *Congressional Quarterly* estimated that there were between twenty-one and thirty-one millionaires in the Senate and between twenty-five and thirty-three in the House and that "only a handful" of legislators lack any significant financial assets. Nevertheless, only three senators and two representatives had placed their holdings in a blind trust.[97]

In many cases, legislators have supported bills that were apparently designed specifically to promote their personal financial interests. The House of Representatives recently reprimanded Representatives Robert Sikes of Florida for failing to report his stock in Fairchild Industries in his annual financial disclosure statement. Moreover, Sikes had voted for a defense bill that contained a $73 million appropriation for an aircraft contract with Fairchild.[98]

The law practices of elected officials pose another common conflict of interest. Legislative bodies in the United States have historically been dominated by lawyers to an extent unknown in other nations. Thirty-one of the fifty-five members of the original Continental Congress came out of the law firms of the day, and lawyers still make up a majority of most Congresses.[99] There is nothing inherently wrong with so many lawyers going into politics; it can even be argued that lawyers can do a better job of writing laws because of their formal training. But serious problems arise when legislators continue to moonlight with their own law firms. In 1976, sixty-six members of Congress reported earning incomes of $1,000 or more from outside law practices, and in most cases their firms were not handling divorces or criminal cases but had clients with a direct financial interest in the way those members of Congress exercised their duties as elected officials. A survey of fifty law firms that had partners serving in Congress showed that their clients were generally powerful corporations with a huge stake in the way the country is governed. Forty of those firms represented banks, thirty-one represented insurance companies, eleven represented gas and oil companies, and ten represented real estate firms. The authors of the study concluded that "there is no doubt that the vested interests have sought out and systematically engaged the services of Congressmen who are lawyers."[100]

Because federal law expressly forbids members of Congress from taking on clients with direct claims before the federal government, some lawyer-legislators resort to an ingenious "two door" system for their law practices. Clients with claims before the government enter the law firm's offices through a door on which the legislator's name does not appear, and other clients go in a second door that includes names of all the partners. Representative Emanuel Celler of New York had one of the most notorious of these practices. The door to his law firm held two signs, one reading "Weisman, Celler, Allan, Spett, and Sheinberg," and the other without Celler's name. All cases dealing with the government were assigned to this second firm, but Celler nonetheless shared in the fees those clients paid."[101]   When a reporter told Celler that his double doors were a "notorious embarrassment" to Congress, Celler replied that "Your constituents are the final arbiter of any conflicts, and I'm always reelected." Apparently the arbiters changed their decision, because shortly thereafter Celler was defeated in the primary after fifty years in the House.[102]

Such conflicts of interests may be unethical, but most of them stop short of criminal behavior. There are, however, numerous ways for elected officials to profit from such illegal activities as fraud or embezzlement. Because most politicians control the expenditure of large amounts of campaign funds, there is always a temptation to convert some of those funds to personal use. Such an action clearly violates the statutes on criminal fraud, because the contributors gave money with the understanding that it was to be used for the politician's campaign and not for his or her personal expenses. Georgia Senator Herman Talmadge's former wife told a Senate committee that he kept a wad of cash, most of it in $100 bills, in the pocket of his overcoat. She testified that she often used the money, which on one occasion may have totaled as much as $45,000, for their daily living expenses.[103]   Also,

Talmadge's former aid Daniel Minchew testified that he was ordered to set up a bank account to convert campaign funds and fraudulent reimbursements from Senate funds to Talmadge's personal use. [104]

The personal staff each member of Congress is allowed to hire has provided another constant source of abuse. In 1979 each member of the House was allocated $288,156 to hire up to eighteen personal staffers, and each member of the Senate was given a much larger allocation—ranging from $508,221 to $1,021,127, depending on the size of the state represented. Moreover, the congressional staffs have been growing at a rapid pace, rising from a total of 10,700 employees in 1969 to 18,400 in 1979. The increasing number of staffers and the lax supervision exercised by the Congress combine to invite abuse. When members of Congress are not required to report how many hours their staffers work, or even what they do, embezzlement and fraud become easy matters. [105]

Nepotism, which had been a focus of complaints against federal legislators since they were first allowed to hire a staff at government expense, was not prohibited until 1967. Up to that time, well-known politicians commonly named their relatives to high-paying government positions. For example, Senator John F. Kennedy helped win his brother Robert a place on the staff of a very appropriate body—the Senate Select Committee on Improper Activities. And before he became president, Lyndon Johnson put both his brother and his brother's wife on the Senate payroll. However improper, those appointments did not violate any laws at the time, but a few members of Congress did engage in outright fraud by paying relatives who never actually worked for the government. For instance, New York Congressman Adam Clayton Powell, had his wife, Yvette, on the payroll of his congressional staff while she was living in Puerto Rico, over a thousand miles from the capital. [106]

There have been far fewer complaints about congressional nepotism since 1967, but that has not stopped congressional officials from abusing their hiring privileges in other ways. In 1976 the *Washington Post* charged that Representative Wayne L. Hays of Ohio kept his mistress, Elizabeth Ray, on the payroll of the House Administration Committee, which he chaired. [107] Hays later admitted to having a "personal relationship" with Ray but denied she was being paid to be his mistress. Ray, however, told the *Post* that, although she had been on the committee's payroll for two years, "I can't type, I can't file, I can't even answer the phone." [108]

While Hays might have been subject to fraud or embezzlement charges, no criminal action was taken against him. In fact, the only abuse of hiring privileges that seems to involve any significant risk of criminal prosecution is a payroll kickback scheme in which an office-holder receives part or all of the salary paid to staff members. Just over 10 percent of all the criminal charges brought against members of Congress in recent years involved payroll kickbacks. [109] One such case involved Representative Charles C. Diggs of Michigan, who was accused of taking kickbacks amounting to more than $60,000 from his congressional employees. Diggs allegedly arranged a raise for three members of his staff and then demanded that the extra money be given back to him. Apparently Diggs also placed two employees on his payroll who did not work at all and used their salaries to pay his personal bills. Another woman on his staff actually worked for Diggs's funeral home while being paid by the Congress. In October 1978, Diggs was convicted on twenty-nine felony counts in connection with these offenses; none-theless, he was reelected to the House the following November. [110]

CRIMES IN THE PROFESSIONS

The least researched and least understood of all white collar crimes are those that occur in the professions. While numerous works have been devoted to such specific offenses as embezzlement, antitrust vio-lations, employee theft, and political corruption, the illegal activities of professionals have received far less attention. The failure of criminolo-gists to give these serious offenses their due is, moreover, paralleled by the neglect shown by the police, prosecutors, and administrators.

Professional organizations often claim that greater outside supervi-sion would be nothing more than unnecessary meddling in their affairs, because the professions police themselves. And it is true that the asso-ciations of lawyers, physicians, and a few other professions do have great power to regulate their members, principally through control of professional licensing. But when the interest of the public clashes with that of the profession, this power has repeatedly been used to protect the profession and its individual practitioners. Professionals who vio-late their public trust—even those who violate criminal law—are seldom faced with sanctions from the agencies of self-regulation (see chapters 2 and 5).

Conflicts of interest between professionals and their clients are built into the very nature of the relationship, often straddling a fine line between the unethical and the illegal. One common source of conflict of interest for self-employed professionals lies in the financial relationship between practitioners, who try to maximize their profits, and clients, who must pay for their services. Most professionals have a direct financial interest in performing the greatest number of the most expensive services possible. On the other hand, the clients' interests are best served if the professional performs only those services that are clearly required and does so as inexpensively as possible. Although this conflict of interest exists in many occupations, it is most serious in the professions because clients are often unable to make an independent judgment about whether or not they actually need the services being recommended.

The greatest problem probably lies in the medical profession, because unnecessary medical procedures are not only costly but may pose a serious threat to the health and even the life of the patient. There is, moreover, ample evidence of large-scale "overdoctoring" of American patients. One study by Dr. Sidney Wolfe of the Health Research Group concluded that the antibiotics prescribed in American hospitals are unnecessary in a full 22 percent of all cases, and if that figure is accurate, those unnecessary antibiotics could be expected to produce approximately ten thousand potentially fatal adverse reactions. [111]   A 1981 study of the general medical service of a major university hospital found that more than one out of every three of its patients had some sort of iatrogenic (physician-caused) disease—most commonly, an adverse reaction to the medications they were given. [112]   But by all accounts, the most serious form of overdoctoring is unnecessary surgery. A Cornell University study found that in nearly one of every five cases in which a patient sought a second opinion, the second physician recommended against the proposed operation. Using such figures, a House subcommittee investigating the medical profession calculated that there were 2.4 million unnecessary surgical procedures a year, which cost the public $4 billion and resulted in the loss of 11,900 lives. [113]

International comparisons support his view. On a per capita basis, there are twice as many surgeons and anesthesiologists in the United States as in England and Wales, and on the average, they perform twice as many operations per person. The differences are especially pronounced in elective procedures such as appendectomies and hysterectomies. It may be that some of this difference is due to the "underdoctoring" of British citizens, but health statistics show that mortality rates in Britain are equal to or lower than those in the United States for all age categories. [114]   But the most persuasive evidence that U.S. physicians often allow their financial interests to override the interests of their clients comes from comparisons of different groups of patients within the United States. In research sponsored by the Department of Health, Education and Welfare, a group of government employees covered by Blue Cross health insurance, which pays physicians on a fee-for-service basis, was compared to a group belonging to a health maintenance organization that paid its physicians a flat salary, regardless of the number of procedures performed. The study found that the group covered by Blue Cross had twice as many surgical operations and that its subscribers lost considerably more work time. In addition, a similar study of Medicaid recipients also found that twice as many operations were performed on those who went to private physicians as on those who belonged to prepaid health plans. [115] The conclusion seems inescapable that the more money physicians make from a medical procedure, the more often they perform it. There is, moreover, a strong element of fraud in the behavior of many of the physicians who perform those unnecessary operations. Although they claim both explicitly and implicitly that their medical decisions are based exclusively on their best judgments about the welfare of patients, the evidence clearly shows that at least some practitioners actually give higher priority to financial considerations.

A more blatant conflict of interest occurs when a physician acquires a financial interest in firms that supply the medication and health services the physician prescribes. In hearings of the Senate Antitrust and Monopoly Subcommittee held in the 1960s, it was revealed that three thousand doctors owned pharmacies, twenty-five hundred ophthalmologists sold eyeglasses, and five thousand doctors owned stock in drug repackaging firms. Thus, over ten thousand of the nation's doctors were selling the products they prescribed. [116] The most brazenly exploitive of these enterprises were the drug repackaging firms, which bought drugs from other manufacturers, put on their own labels, and charged exorbitant markups. The owner-physicians then prescribed drugs carrying the brand name of their company, and the patients were forced to buy the medication they needed at a vastly inflated price. Not surprisingly, there is evidence that physicians who make a financial profit from products they prescribe are likely to prescribe them more often. For example, one comparison of a small group of Spokane, Wash., ophthalmologists found that those who sold glasses wrote 83 percent more prescriptions for glasses than the ophthalmologists who did not. [117] But the desire for a higher income is not the only source of these professional conflicts. Vivienne Walter's study of company doctors in Ontario, Canada, found that they experienced strong pressure from their employers to place the interests of the company ahead of those of their patients—for example, by minimizing the seriousness of injuries suffered on the job in their medical reports. [118]

The same kinds of conflicts of interest are found in the other professions as well, but fortunately, misconduct by lawyers and dentists is less likely to have the same life-threatening consequences. Whenever a professional is paid on a fee-for-service basis, the temptation to make extra profits by performing unnecessary procedures is always present. A clinical evaluation of thirteen hundred Medicaid dental patients in New York State found that 9 percent of the work involved outright fraud and that 25 percent of the amount billed to the state was for unnecessary work.[119]   Such abuses are somewhat more difficult for lawyers, since clients are likely to have a clearer idea of the services they actually need. Nevertheless, "overlawyering" is a growing problem. Clients may, for instance, be talked into suits or other legal actions that will provide the lawyer with lucrative fees but stand little chance of success. Lawyers can also try to make it appear that a relatively simple legal procedure, such as an uncontested divorce, requires special legal knowledge, when in fact most people can do it themselves at a fraction of the cost. Lawyers also lobby state and federal legislators to make their services legally mandatory for as many procedures as possible, thus guaranteeing themselves an exclusive market.

Similar problems exist among practitioners of criminal law, although in different forms. Critics of our criminal justice system, such as Abraham Blumberg, have long charged that some defense lawyers run "confidence games" on their clients. Blumberg has argued that, although a defense lawyer may pretend to be an independent professional who intends to do everything possible for the client, he or she is actually highly dependent on the goodwill of the prosecutor and the court. According to Blumberg, defense lawyers are often more concerned with an expeditious resolution of a case than with its outcome. Civil lawyers generally want to perform the longest and most costly procedures possible, but the criminal lawyer usually works with low-income clients and hopes "to limit its [the client's case] scope and duration rather than to do battle. Only in this way can cases be profitable."[120]   Not only does this approach maximize the number of clients the lawyer can handle, but it also helps maintain the defense lawyer's relationship with the judge and district attorney, who also want a quick resolution to criminal cases. Defense lawyers often try to appear to be expending every possible effort on their clients' behalf while actually seeking to convince them to plead guilty and bring their case to a quick conclusion.[121]

Although accountants seem to stand in the shadow of the more prestigious fields of law and medicine, they play a critical role in the corporate economy. Judicial precedents hold accountants responsible to provide accurate information about the firms they audit to a host of interested parties, such as stockholders, bankers, and potential investors. Federal laws passed after the disastrous stock market crash of 1929 not only make it a crime for a company to file a false financial statement, but also require that publicly owned corporations employ an outside auditor to examine those statements. Since a fraudulent statement can easily be used to inflate a firm's credit rating, enhance the value of its stock, or improve its image in the business community, it makes obvious sense to have an outside expert review them. [122] In actual practice, however, these supposedly independent auditors face a built-in conflict of interest, because they are being paid by the same firms they are supposed to be investigating. An accounting firm that gains a reputation for excessive zeal in its audits might find potential clients looking elsewhere for the services it provides.

One example of an independent auditor's complicity in the fraudulent schemes of its clients involved the now-defunct National Student Marketing Corporation. NSMC was launched with the aim of providing the burgeoning "youth market" with a network of campus representatives who would market products among students. The company was an immediate hit in the bull market of the times. Its stock originally went on sale at $6 a share, then soared to $80 a share in only six months, and peaked at $140 a share. NSMC quickly began acquiring other companies, including the cash-rich Interstate National Corporation. But it turned out that NSMC's success story was built upon fraud, misrepresentation, and deception. It was actually losing money when its financial reports claimed big profits. A partner and a former employee from Peat, Marwick, and Mitchell, one of the prestigious "big eight" accounting firms, were subsequently convicted of knowingly filing fraudulent statements with the Securities and Exchange Commission. Among other things, they filed reports showing profits for periods in which NSMC had none, and padded its accounts receivable and sales figures. One accountant was fined $10,000 and given sixty days in jail, and the other was fined $2,500 and given ten days in jail—the first time any employees of one of the big eight firms were ever sent to jail for professional misconduct. [123]

Of course, conflict of interest is not the only problem facing the professions. Some professionals engage in more blatant crimes, against which claims to the right of professional self-regulation are of little help. Lieberman cites the case of a lawyer who not only intentionally delayed the criminal case of his client so that he could charge for more court appearances, but also took $1,500 the client gave him to post bail and left him in jail. [124]

The corruption uncovered in the government-sponsored health care programs for the poor and the aged—Medicaid and Medicare—have been among the most publicized of all crimes in the professions. Medicaid and Medicare abuse has been estimated to cost the public over $1 billion a year, [125]   yet many enforcement agencies have been reluctant to bring criminal charges against the members of the powerful and esteemed medical profession. [126]

One major problem has been the growth of "Medicaid mills" — clinics in poor inner-city areas that specialize in providing quick, second-rate care to as large a volume of patients as possible. For instance, one Washington physician received hundreds of thousands of dollars in Medicaid payments a year while attempting to treat between fifty and sixty patients a day. [127] The Special Committee on Aging estimated that Medicaid mills receive 75 percent of the $3 billion the government spends on Medicaid each year. [128]

Although their activities are highly unethical, the providers of this shoddy medicine do not automatically break the law. Most of the outright crimes involve fraudulent claims for reimbursement. Pharmacies, for instance, commonly bill the government for larger numbers of pills than their customers actually receive, and medical laboratories often charge the government for tests that were never performed. [129] One Senate investigator posing as a Medicaid patient was told that her urine sample was normal, when in fact it was a mixture of soap and cleanser she concocted in the restroom of the clinic she was visiting. [130] Other government agents set up a bogus medical clinic in a poor neighborhood of Chicago and were soon besieged with propositions from thirteen medical laboratories seeking business. One laboratory offered a 50 percent kickback of all fees paid for medical testing, and others offered free tests for private patients, free x-ray equipment, and even free secretarial services. [131] The costs of all these inducements was to be made up by unnecessary tests the clinic was expected to order.

A study of California's medicaid and medicare program by Henry Pontell, Paul Jesilow, and Gilbert Geis concluded that "the very organization of the program invites fraud." They found that the fee-for-service delivery system "offers physicians the chance to amass considerable gain with little risk. Diagnostic tests that have not been performed can easily be billed to the state. . .[and] the professional background of the physician affords strong protection against discovery." And even if a physician is discovered, there is a "range of defensive tactics to safeguard against effective sanctions." [132]

The numerous reports of criminal activities in the professions, raise the question of whether or not they foster subcultures of corruption similar to those found among police officers and government inspectors. While it appears such subcultures may exist within some organizations or small groups of professionals, it is doubtful that a common subculture in any of the professions requires or directly encourages corruption, as occurred, for instance in the New York Police Department. If nothing else, the fact that a great deal of professional interaction is carried on in books, periodicals, and public meetings makes it unlikely that such attitudes could be shielded from public attention or that the numerous works on the professions would make no mention of such a subculture.

But if professional subcultures do not directly promote corruption, they do provide a sheltered environment in which it may flourish. A central element in all the subcultures examined here is a sense of common problems and goals, a feeling of occupational solidarity, and a belief that members should stand up and protect each other from outsiders. Such attitudes have not only led professional organizations to advocate social policies harmful to their clients, but they have encouraged those organizations to assist professionals in organizational crimes, such as price fixing, in order to maximize their income (see chapter 2). Moreover, serious cases of professional misconduct and fraud are commonly ignored or glossed over by the bodies charged with the regulation of the professions. These same attitudes have led individual practitioners to cover up the abuses of their colleagues, and even those who want to speak up come under strong pressure to go along with the system. Take, for example, the account of one dentist who was frustrated at hearing a patient's complaints about the high cost of correcting the dental problems caused by another dentist's shoddy workmanship. The dentist writes of his desire to inform the patient of the reason his bill was so high, but goes on to say that, "Of course I said no such thing, because I was mindful of the consequences to me of such a breach of so-called ethics. Dentists are not allowed to tell on one another."[133] Shoddy workmanship is not a crime, but the same attitudes that protect lazy or incompetent practitioners also protect the criminals. Thus, professional subcultures may not directly encourage or condone criminal activities, but they do provide a protective milieu in which occupational crimes are easily concealed.

NOTES

1. Sandra S. Evens and Richard Lundman, "Newspaper Coverage of Corporate Price-Fixing" *Criminology* 21 (November 1983): 529–541; A. Dershowitz, "Newspaper Publicity and the Electrical Conspiracy," *Yale Law Journal* 71 (December 1961): 288–289.

2. Norman Jaspan, *Mind Your Own Business* (Englewood Cliffs, N.J.: Prentice-Hall, 1974), 201; U.S. Congress, Joint Economic Committee, *The Cost of Crime in 1976* (Washington, D.C.: U.S. Government Printing Office, 1976), 8.

3. David McCintick, "Inside Jobs," in Editors of the *Wall Street Journal*, *Crime and Business* (Princeton, N.J.: Dow Jones Books, 1971), 16.

4. Charles H. McCaghy, *Deviant Behavior: Crime, Conflict and Interest Groups* (New York: Macmillan, 1976, 178.

5. Jaspan, *Mind Your Own Business*, v.

6. John P. Clark and Richard C. Hollinger, *Theft by Employees in Work Organizations* (Washington, D.C.: National Institute of Justice, September 1983); also see David L. Altheide, Patricia A. Adler, and Duane Altheide, "The Social Meaning of Employee Theft," in John M. Johnson and Jack D. Douglas, eds., *Crime at the Top: Deviance in Business and the Professions* (Philadelphia: Lippincott, 1978), 90.

7. Donald N. M. Horning, "Blue Collar Theft: Conceptions of Property Attitudes Toward Pilfering and Work Group Norms in a Modern Industrial Plant," in Erwin O. Smigel and H. Lawrence Ross, eds., *Crime Against Bureaucracy* (New York: Van Nostrand Reinhold, 1970).

8. Tim Metz, "Hot Stocks," in Editors of the *Wall Street Journal, Business and Crime*, 93.

9. August Bequai, *White Collar Crime: A 20th Century Crisis* (Lexington, Mass.: Lexington Books, 1978), 27.

10. Ibid., 89–90.

11. For some works on embezzlement, see Donald R. Cressey, *Other People's Money: A Study in the Social Psychology of Embezzlement* (Belmont, Cal.: Wadsworth, 1953), 1971; Virgil W. Peterson, "Why Honest People Steal," *Journal of Criminal Law and Criminology* 38 (July–August 1947): 94–103; Svend H. Riemer, "Embezzlement: Pathological Basis," *Journal of Criminal Law and Criminology* 32 (November–December 1941): 411–423; G. E. Levens, "101 British White Collar Criminals," *New Society*, 26 March 1964, 6–8.

12. Tim A. Schabeck, "Investigators Tackle Computer Crime," *Security World* (February 1977), 31.

13. "The Spreading Danger of Computer Crime," *Business Week*, 20, April 1981, 86–92; Irving J. Sloan, *The Computer and the Law* (London: Oceana Publications, 1984), v.

14. U.S. Department of Justice, *"Computer Crime: Electric Fund Transfer Systems and Crime*, NCJ-83736 (Washington, D.C.: U.S. Government Printing Office, 1982), v–vi; Bureau of Justice Statistics, *Electronic Fund Transfer Systems Fraud* (Washington, D.C.: U.S. Government Printing Office, April 1986).

15. Bureau of Justice Statistics, *Electronic Fund Transfers*.

16. "Danger of Computer Crime," *Business Week*; "Crackdown on Computer Crime," *Time*, 8 February 1982, 60–67.

17. Sloan, *Computer and the Law*, 9–10.

18. Ibid.

19.. Erdwin H. Pfuhl, Jr., "Computer Abuse: Problems of Instrumental Control," *Deviant Behavior* 8 (1987): 113–130.

20. Lester A. Sobel, ed., *Corruption in Business* (New York: Facts on File, 1977), 205.

21. Ovid Demaris, *Dirty Business: The Corporate-Political Money-Power Game* (New York: Harper's Magazine Press, 1974), 334–335.

22. There are many good descriptions of Vesco's exploits. See, for instance, Sobel, *Corruption in Business*, 51, 163–167.

23. Walter Sheridan, *The Fall and Rise of Jimmy Hoffa* (New York: Saturday Review Press, 1972), 531–532; Demaris, *Dirty Business*, 332; Robert W. Peterson, *Crime and the American Response*, (New York: Facts on File, 1973), 172; Rempel, "Teamster Chief Guilty."

24. William C. Rempel, "Teamster Chief, 4 Others Guilty, Jury Finds Plot to Cheat Fund, Bribe a Senator" *Los Angeles Times*, 16 December 1982, 1 & 16.

25. Robert L. Jackson, "Ex-Teamster Boss Tells of Mob Ties" *Los Angeles Times*, 2 June 1987, I: 9.

26. Ronald J. Ostrow and Robert L. Jackson, "U.S. Plans Suit to Get Control of Teamsters" *Los Angeles Times*, 10 June 1987, I: 1 & 17.

27. U.S. Chamber of Commerce, *White Collar Crime*.

28. Sobel, *Corruption in Business*, 151.

29. *The New York Times*, 16 March 1976.

30. See Marshall B. Clinard and Peter C. Yeager, *Corporate Crime* (New York: The Free Press, 1980), 166.

31. Bequai, *White Collar Crime*, 32.

32. Ibid., 25–26.

33. Susan Dentzer, "Greed on Wall Street" *Newsweek*, 26 May 1986; *Corporate Crime Reporter*, 1 (13 April 1987), 13.

34. Michael A. Hiltzk, "Inside Trader to Pay Penalty of $100 Million" *Los Angeles Times*, 15 November 1986, 1 & 30.

35. *Corporate Crime Reporter*, 1 (13 April 1987), 12–16.

36. Michael A. Hiltzik, "Kidder to Pay $25.3 Million as Insider Penalty," *Los Angeles Times*, 5 June 1987, 1 & 25; Michael A. Hiltzik, "Boesky is Expected to Plead Guilty to Fraud Charge" *Los Angeles Times*, 23 April 1987, IV: 1 *passim*; Michael A. Hiltzik, "SEC Charges Merrill Lynch Officer, Israeli" *Los Angeles Times*, 12 March 1987, I: 1 & 14; Annetta Miller, "The British Connection: The Insider-Trading Scandals Hit Merrill Lynch" *Newsweek*, 23 March 1987; Debra Whitefield and Tony Robinson, "3 Major Wall St. Figures Face 'Insider' Charges" *Los Angeles Times*, 13 February 1987, I: 1 & 27.

37. Richard Stengel, "Morality Among the Supply-Siders" *Time* May 25, 1987, pp. 18–20.

38. Associated Press, "Nofziger Just One of Many Indicted Ex-Reagan Aides" *San Luis Obispo (Calif.) Telegram-Tribune*, July 17, 1987, p. 8A.

39. Stengel, "Morality Among the Supply-Siders," p. 18.

40. Public Citizen Staff Report, *White Collar Crime* (Washington, D.C.: Congress Watch, 1974), 17–18.

41. James S. Wallerstein and Clemett S. Wyle, "Our Law-Abiding Law-Breakers," *National Probation* (March-April 1947): 107–112.

42. See Morton Mintz and Jerry Cohen, *America Inc.: Who Owns and Operates the United States* (New York: Dial Press, 1971), 273–275. For a discussion of tax fraud among landlords see Harold M. Groves, "An Empirical Study of Income Tax Compliance," *National Tax Journal* 11 (December 1958): 241–301.

43. Paul Richter, "Three Promoters of Big Tax Shelter Scheme Indicted," *Los Angeles Times*, 26 March 1987, I: 5; Arnold H. Hubasch, "3 Indicted in Huge Tax Fraud," *New York Times*, 26 March 1987, D1.

44. Paul Richter, "Del Mar Businessman, 6 Others Arrested in Massive Fraud," *Los Angeles Times*, 13 May 1987, IV: 1 & 6.

45. McCaghy, *Deviant Behavior*, 214.

46. Upton Sinclair, *The Jungle* (New York: Vangard Press, 1927).

47. See *Los Angeles Times*, 9 May 1976; Sobel, *Corruption in Business*, 96–97, 209.

48. Amick, *American Way of Graft*, 4.

49. David R. Simon and D. Stanley Eitzen, *Elite Deviance*, 2nd ed. (Boston: Allyn and Bacon, 1986), 138.

50. *Corporate Crime Reporter*, 1 (27 April 1987): 14–18.

51. Simon and Eitzen, *Elite Deviance*, 137.

52. See Amick, *American Way of Graft*, 40–41.

53. Amick, *American Way of Graft*, 22.

54. Ibid., 20–21.

55. Asher Byrnes, *Government Against the People* (New York: Dodd, Mead, 1946), 213.

56. New York Legislature,*Report and Proceedings of the Senate Commitee Appointed to Investigate the Police Department of the City of New York,(Lexow Committee)*(Albany: State Printing Office, 1895); New York Legislature, *Report of the Joint Committee on the Government of the City of New York, (Seabury Committee)* (Albany: State Printing Office, 1932); *The Knapp Commission Report on Police Corruption* (New York: George Braziller), 1972.

57. Special Committee to Investigate Organized Crime in Interstate Commerce, *Final Report*, U.S. Senate Report no. 307, 82nd Congress (Washington, D.C.: U.S. Government Printing Office, 1951); Chicago City Council, *Report of the Commission on Crime* (Chicago: Author, 1915); Pennsylvania Crime Commission, *Report on Police Corruption and the Quality of Law Enforcement in Philadelphia*, 1974.

58. Edwin H. Sutherland and Donald R. Cressey, *Criminology*, 10th ed. (Philadelphia, Lippincott, 1978), 402.

59. William A. Westley, *Violence and the Police* (Cambridge, Mass.: M.I.T. Press, 1970), 110.

60. On police subcultures see Westley, *Violence and Police*; and Jerome H. Skolnick, *Justice Without Trial: Law Enforcement in Democratic Society* (New York: John Wiley, 1966), 42–70.

61. For an excellent discussion of the effects of the legislation of morality, see Herbert L. Packer, *The Limits of the Criminal Sanction* (Palo Alto, Cal.: Stanford University Press, 1968); also see Edwin M. Schur, *Crimes Without Victims: Deviant Behavior and Public Policy* (Englewood Cliffs, N.J.: Prentice-Hall, 1965).

62. Skolnick, *Justice Without Trial*, 208.

63. *Knapp Commission Report*, 123.

64. National Advisory Committee on Criminal Justice Standards and Goals, *Community Crime Prevention* (Washington, D.C.: U.S. Government Printing Office), 255.

65. *Knapp Commission Report*, 65.

66. Ibid., 71.

67. Pennsylvania Crime Commission, *Police Corruption*, 5.

68. John A. Gardiner, *The Politics of Corruption; Organized Crime in an American City* (New York: Russell Sage, 1970).

69. Quoted in Donald R. Cressey, *Theft of the Nation: The Structure and Operations of Organized Crime* (New York: Harper and Row, 1969), 267.

70. Sobel, *Corruption in Business*, 5–15.

71. Quoted in Anthony Sampson, *The Sovereign State of I.T.T.* Harmondsworth, England: Penguin books, 1976, 180-181.

72. Jethro K. Lieberman, *How the Government Breaks the Law* (New York: Stein and Day, 1972), 214.

73. Cressey, *Theft of the Nation*, 252–253.

74. Robert Welkos, "Nevada Inquiry Becomes a Clash of Personalities," *Los Angeles Times*, 13 January 1984, I: 1 *passim*; Bob Secter, "House Unanimous in Vote to Impeach Judge Claiborne," *Los Angeles Times*, 23 July 1986, I: 1 *passim*. "U.S. Judge in Nevada Convicted of Filing False Income Tax Forms," *The New York Times*, 11 August 1984, p. 1; "Senate Impeaches Claiborne," *San Luis Obispo (Calif.) Telegram-Tribune*, 10 October 1986, 2A.

75. Gary C. Jacobson, *Money in Congressional Elections* (New Haven, Conn.: Yale University Press, 1980), 65.

76. Mark Green, *Who Runs Congress?*, 3rd ed. (New York: Bantam Books, 1979), 74.

77. Jacobson, *Congressional Elections*, 157.

78. This figure was calculated from data in Congressional Quarterly, *Congressional Ethics*, 2nd ed. (Washington, D.C.: Congressional Quarterly, 1980), 172–175, and in Green, *Who Runs Congress?*, 156–157.

79. Robert W. Stewart and Tracy Wood, "Political Giving: Corporate Contributions Buy Access" *Los Angeles Times* 26 October 1986, I: *passim* 1.

80. Lester A. Sobel, *Money and Politics: Contributions, Campaign Abuses and the Law* (New York: Facts on File, 1974), 156–157.

81. Mary Deibel, "Congress' Dilemma on Campaigns" *San Luis Obispo (Calif.) Telegram-Tribune*, February 14, 1987, p. 11B.

82. Quoted in Green, *Who Runs Congress?*, 3–4.

83. Green, *Who Runs Congress?*, 45.

84. Paul H. Douglas, *Ethics in Government* (Cambridge, Mass.: Harvard University Press, 1952), 44.

85. Green, *Who Runs Congress?*, 25.

86. See note 69.

87. See note 69.

88. "Congress Feels The Sting," *U.S. News & World Report*, 18 February 1980, 19–21; "Abscam's Toll," *Time*, 24 August 1981, 20; "End of a Sleazy Affair," *Newsweek*, 22 March 1982.

89. Green, *Who Runs Congress?*, 185–187; Congressional Quarterly, *Congressional Ethics*, 26–28.

90. Green, *Who Runs Congress?*, 186.

91. *Washington Post*, 24 October 1976.

92. "U.S. Drops Park Influence Case; Ends 'Koreagate'," *Los Angeles Times*, 17 August 1979.

93. Congressional Quarterly, *Congressional Ethics*, 39.

94. See Congressional Quarterly, *Congressional Ethics*, 36–47; Green, *Who Runs Congress?*, 191–194.

95. Congressional Quarterly, *Congressional Ethics*, 76.

96. See Drew Pearson and Jack Anderson, *The Case Against Congress* (New York: Simon and Schuster, 1968), 130–138.

97. Congressional Quarterly, *Congressional Ethics*, 76–78.

98. Ibid., 22.

99. Pearson and Anderson, *The Case Against Congress*, 116.

100. Ibid., 102.

101. Ibid., 118–119.

102. Green, *Who Runs Congress?*, 167–168.

103. Myra McPherson, "The Reluctant Witness—Betty Talmadge Testifies," *Washington Post* 13, June 1979, E1.

104. Congressional Quarterly, *Congressional Ethics*, 30–34; Bill Richards, "Panel Ends Talmadge Probe," *Washington Post* 13, July 1979, A2.

105. See Congressional Quarterly, *Congressional Ethics*, 89–103.

106. Pearson and Anderson, *The Case Against Congress*, 235–262.

107. *Washington Post*, 23 May 1976.

108. Quoted in Congressional Quarterly, *Congressional Ethics*, 94.

109. See note 69.

110. Congressional Quarterly, *Congressional Ethics*, 29-30.

111. Boyce Rensberger, "Thousands a Year Killed by Faulty Prescriptions," *The New York Times*, 28 January 1976, 1 *passim*.

112. K. Steel, P. M. Gertman, C. Crescenzi, and J. Anderson, "Iatrogenic Illness on a General Medical Service at a University Hospital,"*The New England Journal of Medicine* 304 (1981), 638–42.

113. Jane E. Brody, "Incompetent Surgery is Found Not Isolated," *The New York Times*, 27 January 1976, 1 *passim*; *Los Angeles Times*, 12 May 1976, 2.

114. Brody, "Incompetent Surgery."

115. Ibid.

116. Reported in "Doctors Who Profit from Prescriptions," *Consumer Reports*, May 1966, 234.

117. Reported in Mintz and Cohen, *Power, Inc.*, 180.

118. Vivienne Walters, "Company Doctors' Perceptions of and Response to Conflicting Pressures from Labor and Management" *Social Problems* 30 (October 1982), 1–12.

119. Herbert Denenberg, *A Shopper's Guide to Dentistry*, as quoted in Mintz and Cohen, *Power, Inc.*, 495–496.

120. Abraham S. Blumberg, "The Practice of Law as a Confidence Game: Organizational Cooptation of a Profession," *Law and Society Review* 1 (1967), 15–39.

121. Blumberg, "Law as a Confidence Game," and *Criminal Justice* (Chicago: Quadrangle Books, 1970).

122. James E. Sorenson, Hugh D. Grove, and Thomas L. Sorenson, "Detecting Management Fraud: The Role of the Independent Auditor," 221–251, in Gilbert Geis and Ezra Stotland, eds., *White-Collar Crime: Theory and Research* (Beverly Hills, Cal.: Sage, 1980).

123. Mintz and Cohen, *Power, Inc.*, 195–198; Sobel, *Corruption in Business*, 170–171; Lieberman, *Crisis at the Bar*, 147–153.

124. Lieberman, *Crisis at the Bar*, 200.

125. "Medical Overcharges up to 400% Reported," *Los Angeles Times*, 27 July 1976.

126. See, for example, Henry N. Pontell, Paul D. Jesilow, and Gilbert Geis, "Policing Physicians: Practitioner Fraud and Abuse in a Government Medical Program," *Social Problems* 30 (October 1982), 117–125.

127. "Medicaid Profiteer—or Pioneer," *Medical World News*, January 1974, 30–31.

128. Stuart Auerbach, "Medicaid Examiners Find Fraud Rampant," *Los Angeles Times*, 30 August 1976, 1 *passim*.

129. Stephen Rosenberg and James Posner, "Medicaid Surveillance and Utilization Review: A Description of the Medicaid Surveillance, Review and Enforcement Activities of the New York City Department of Health," in Allen Spiegel and Simon Podair, *Medicaid: Lessons for National Health Insurance* (Rockville, Md.: Aspen Systems Corporation, 1975), 93–100.

130. Auerbach, "Fraud Rampant."

131. "The Medicaid Scandal," *Time*, 23 February 1976, 37.

132. Pontell, Jesilow, and Geis, "Policing Physicians," 124.

133. "Paul Revere, D.D.S.," *Dentistry and Its Victims* (New York: St. Martin's Press, 1970), 19.

4

The Laws

Few people ever ask why murder, assault, or robbery are illegal. The social consensus condemning such acts is so strong that the answer appears self-evident, and virtually no one challenges that judgment. The legislation defining criminal behavior in the white collar occupations presents a stark contrast, for most of it arose in a climate of controversy and dissension that continued long after the enactment of the new laws. Indeed, the opposition has been so strong that many observers have been puzzled by the very existence of these laws, while others have argued that they represent nothing more than clever ruses intended to placate the public while carefully avoiding any real restrictions on the prerogatives of privileged individuals or powerful corporations.

To understand this issue, we must start with a broad sociological analysis of the origins of legal norms. Numerous theories have been proposed over the years, but most of the work in this area can be grouped in one of two broad schools. What might be called the consensus or functional theory sees the law as a reflection of widely held values and of the general consensus of public opinion.[1] According to this view, new laws result from the effort to apply society's "core values" to new situations and events, and those laws reflect the attitudes and needs of society as a whole.

The interest theory of law creation, on the other hand, sees the process of legislation as a struggle between competing groups striving to enact laws favorable to themselves. Thus, the law is seen to reflect the structure of power in a society, while its norms and values have only secondary importance. The advocates of this theory are divided, however, about which interests control the creation of new laws. The pluralists hold that constantly shifting alliances of different interest groups vary with each individual issue and that no single group holds a monopoly on power.[2] Accordingly, the efforts of these competing groups tend to cancel each other out, and the legislative process ultimately reflects the will of the people and the interest of society as a whole. The elitists, in contrast, hold that the government is controlled by a unified "power elite" or ruling class, composed primarily of those with great wealth and/or key positions in the corporate power structure.[3] This group wields such enormous power that legislative proposals that threaten its domination are never given serious attention. According to the elitists, the various laws creating white collar crimes are nothing more than symbolic gestures intended to placate public discontent without threatening the powers that be.

The proponents of these theories obviously cannot all be right. But before we attempt to evaluate the usefulness of these paradigms for the task at hand, we must first explore the historical context and development of the important pieces of white collar crime legislation.

PROTECTING BUSINESS: EMBEZZLEMENT AND PILFERAGE

Of all the laws examined here, the prohibition of theft is the most ancient. Indeed, the roots of this prohibition go too far back into legal history to concern us here. The nature of the early common law crime of larceny is important, however, because it provides the context in which the crimes of embezzlement, pilferage, and fraud were first defined. The most interesting thing about the crime of larceny was its extremely narrow definition. It originally included only the taking or carrying away of the property of another without the consent of the owner and with the intent to deprive him or her of its use. According to the strict style of legal interpretation followed by the early English courts, this meant that if someone were given a piece of fine clothing with instructions to have it cleaned, and the receiver absconded with it, no crime had been committed. At first glance this distinction may appear arbitrary and capricious, but closer examination of its social context reveals an inner logic. The fact that the common law prescribed the death sentence for anyone convicted of stealing any item valued at more than twelve pence makes such judicial nit-picking much more comprehensible. An extremely strict legal construction was one of the principal ways through which judges avoided imposing the harsh punishment demanded by common law tradition. Moreover, the misappropriation of another's property was still covered under civil law, and a victim could sue the offender for damages.[4]

This anomalous legal system worked well enough in the medieval English economy. Most people lived directly off the land, and the few consumer goods available were manufactured on a small scale and under strict guild control. But as commerce and the lucrative wool and textile trades grew, the increasingly influential mercantile class began pushing for a new legal approach. The result was the famous Carrier's case of 1473, in which a shipper was charged with breaking open a bale entrusted to him and stealing the contents. In a major breach of tradition, the defendant was found guilty on the grounds that, although the bales had been entrusted to him, their contents had not, and the appropriation of the latter therefore constituted larceny. As important as this expansion of the larceny law was, it appears to have made the legal system more rather than less illogical: after the new ruling, it was illegal to steal the contents of a package one had been entrusted with, but perfectly legal to steal the whole thing. [5]

A statute enacted in 1529 continued the legal trend begun in the Carrier's case by making a servant's theft of his or her master's property a felony. However, the courts of the day, deeply conditioned to strict legal interpretation, held that the master did not have technical possession of property entrusted to the servant by a third party, and thus its appropriation did not constitute a crime. This ruling was of only minor importance in governing the relationships between masters and servants, but the courts soon applied the new standards of larceny by servant to employees as well—a development of much greater significance. Whereas servants only occasionally received their masters' property from others, the acceptance of money or goods from third parties was an important part of the jobs of many clerks and employees. The court's response to the problem this ruling posed for the politically powerful merchant class was to steadily expand the definition of what constituted the "possession of the master." One of these interpretations held, for instance that if the servant placed money or goods received from another in a receptacle owned by the master, it was therefore in the master's possession. But there were limits beyond which these interpretations could not be stretched, and the growing power and importance of banks made the situation increasingly difficult. In 1742, John Waite, a cashier for the Bank of England (which had been established in 1694), stole six East Indian bonds with a value of over £13,000, yet he could not be convicted of any crime under the common law of that time. This case led to the enactment of the first embezzlement statute later that same year; however, it was very narrowly drawn and applied only to employees of the Bank of England. The first general embezzlement statute was passed in 1799, after a similar case involving another bank. Although that act applied only to servants and clerks, subsequent legislation applied criminal penalties to all persons who misappropriated property or money that had been entrusted to them. [6]

PROTECTING COMPETITION:
ANTITRUST LEGISLATION

Although some critics have pictured antitrust legislation as a radical form of economic experimentation, the opposition to monopoly actually is deeply rooted in the common law. If the courts have not always ruled in opposition to monopoly, that has been the general tenor of their decisions for more than five centuries. English records dating as far back as the twelfth century recount the efforts of kings and judges to prevent monopolistic practices at local fairs and markets. As commerce became more developed, opposition to the monopolistic practices of the trade guilds also grew. In later years, popular opposition helped stymie Queen Elizabeth I's efforts to grant national monopolies to court favorites, and even the great trading companies of a colonial era were eventually forced out of operation. There is, therefore, considerable evidence to support Franklin D. Jones's contention that the "history of Anglo-Saxon people discloses an undying hostility toward monopoly."[7]

Because of these inherited traditions, the laws of the American republic were opposed to monopoly from their very inception. Aside from the common law itself, several states wrote specific antimonopoly clauses into their constitutions. But if this legal foundation was more than sufficient to meet the problems of an agrarian economy with only small-scale cottage industry, it proved wholly unequal to the task of dealing with the problems of monopoly and the concentration of power that developed out of the industrial revolution. States with their own antitrust statutes found that they had great difficulty controlling the monopolistic practices of corporations that spanned the nation. The common law did cut across state boundaries and was thus more widely applicable, but the laws themselves were inadequate to regulate modern economic relations. The common law held agreements in restraint of trade to be null and void and allowed victims of such practices to sue to recover the losses they suffered, but there were no criminal penalties, and state prosecutors were unable to instigate cases on their own. When the victims of monopolistic practices did bring suit, they were almost always heavily outgunned by the legal firepower of the corporate giants they sought to restrain. The old approach to the control of monopolies and the preservation of fair competition thus proved increasingly impotent in the face of the growing concentration of corporate power.[8]

The federal government's first important piece of antitrust legislation was the Sherman Act of 1890, which remains the cornerstone of

U.S. antitrust policy to this day. The passage of the Sherman Act is generally regarded as a major victory for the nineteenth-century reformers who sought to curtail the growing power of the corporate giants. There are, however, many critics of this view. Often citing the ease with which the Sherman Act passed the "Fifty-first Congress"—nicknamed the Billion-Dollar Congress for its largess toward big business—these critics have argued that the Sherman Act was intentionally couched in vague, ambiguous terms in order to pacify the voters without materially affecting the interests of the major corporations.[9]

In order to understand the forces pushing for antitrust legislation, it is necessary to place them in the context of the profound social and economic changes that swept through the nation in the last part of the nineteenth century. The old middle class, composed principally of independent farmers and the owners of small-businesses, was in decline. Its traditional political power and its economic base were being eroded by an emerging corporate elite riding the wave of industrialization that was transforming the country.

The vast new plots of land available for cultivation in the West and the growth of railroad transportation transformed farmers into small capitalists growing cash crops for market. But for most of them, the 1880s and 1890s were hard times. As more and more land was put to the plow, farmers found that the prices their crops brought were declining. But the cost of the industrial commodities upon which they had come to depend was not going down. As economic conditions worsened on the farm, migration to urban centers drained away rural population, and agrarian discontent intensified. Although the farmers were often confused about the exact mechanisms involved, they recognized that they were being made to pay the price for the growth of industrial capitalism. High tariff barriers provided a sheltered environment for U.S. industry and kept it free from the international competition that would have meant lower prices for the manufactured goods farmers consumed. Since American goods were not competitive on the world market, the capital needed to purchase foreign technology and equipment was accumulated through the sale of cheap agricultural products on world markets.[10] Thus, as in virtually all industrializing countries, the surplus generated by American farmers was being used to finance the economic transformation that ultimately put them in a position of secondary social importance.

The first target of the farmers' discontent was the railroads, which charged exorbitant rates to ship the small farmers' grain to market but offered large rebates and other special favors to large corporations. Grain storage facilities (which were often owned by the railroads), along with grain buyers and middlemen, were also targets of the farmers' wrath. Several "Independent," "Reform," and "Antimonopoly" parties sprang up to press the farmers' cause. The most successful of these pressure groups was the Granger movement, which owed much of its popularity to the fact that it served both the social and the political needs of the farmers. The Grangers eventually forced a variety of regulatory legislation through the state legislatures, but the conservative courts threw most of it out. [11] As the frustration of the farmers grew, the focus of their discontent expanded to include the manufacturers of agricultural machinery and, ultimately, to monopolies, trusts, and big business in general. These disaffected agrarians ultimately came together under the banner of the Populist (or People's) Party. The preamble to the Populist platform of 1892 (two years after the passage of the Sherman Act) shows the depth of the feeling against big business and those in Washington who supported its interests.

> We meet in the midst of a nation brought to the verge of moral, political, and material ruin. Corruption dominates the ballot-box, the Legislatures, the Congress, and touches even the ermine of the bench. . . .The newspapers are largely subsidized, homes covered with mortgages, labor impoverished, and the land concentrated in the hands of capitalists. The urban workmen are denied the right to organize for self-protection; imported pauperized labor beats down their wages, a hireling standing army, unrecognized by our laws, is established to shoot them down, and they are rapidly degenerating into European conditions. The fruits of the toil of millions are boldly stolen to build up colossal fortunes for the few, unprecedented in the history of mankind; and the possessors of these, in turn, despise the Republic and endanger liberty. From the same prolific womb of governmental injustice we breed the two great classes—tramps and millionaires.

The Populists won almost 10 percent of the presidential vote that year and carried five Midwestern and Western states. They did not do as well in the South, but the Southern wing of the Democratic Party was deeply influenced by the Populist ideas of such men as William Jennings Bryan. The surprising success of this small, newly organized party competing in its first presidential election provides persuasive evidence of the strength of the public discontent with the growing economic and political dominance of big business.

Thus, there seems little doubt that the legislators of the Fifty-first Congress recognized the depth of the agrarian feelings about the need to limit the power of the trusts and feared the challenge of more Populist candidates if they openly opposed the final version of the Sherman Act. Not only did farmers still comprise well over half of the U.S. population in 1890, but antitrust, unlike the tariff question, was an issue on which urban workers and the petty bourgeoisie supported their rural counterparts. Moreover, the Sherman Act was very much in tune with the dominant ideology and the legal traditions of nineteenth-century America. The deep-seated American principles of individualism, free competition, and equality of opportunity could all be mustered to support the principles of antitrust. As Hans Thorelli pointed out, "Congress believed in competition. Most congressmen, indeed most Americans, would say in 1890 that antitrust legislation was but the projection of the philosophy of competition on the plane of policy." [12]

Thus, the evidence is persuasive that the passage of the Sherman Act was indeed a defeat for corporate interests at the hands of a popular mass movement. [13] But was that defeat merely symbolic—the passage of a piece of vague and useless legislation—or was it more substantive? The Sherman Act is certainly broad and general, but it is not, by most legislative standards, particularly vague. The first sentence of the first section specifically spells out its intention: "Every contract, combination in the form of trust or otherwise, or conspiracy in restraint of trade or commerce among the several states or with foreign nations is hereby declared to be illegal." Violation of this statute are declared to be a misdemeanor punishable by a $5,000 fine and/or up to one year in prison. Victims of antitrust violations are given the right to sue the monopolist for treble damages—that is, damages equal to three times the amount of the losses they actually suffered. It is true that the specific acts that constitute a restraint of trade are not spelled out, but the common law contained many precedents from which to draw, even if such precedents did not always fit the new realities of industrial capitalism.

Despite its promise, the Sherman Act proved ineffective because of the resistance of the Supreme Court and the failure of the executive branch to enforce it. For over a decade, no federal agency was established to investigate and prosecute antitrust violations. Then, in 1911, the Supreme Court invoked the "Rule of Reason," unmentioned in the original act, which limited federal prosecution to "bad" trusts that abused their dominant position in the market. Nevertheless, Presidents Theodore Roosevelt and William Howard Taft did eventually bring major antitrust actions that forced the breakup of such monopolies as Standard Oil and American Tobacco. The prodigious growth of holding companies, which bought up large chunks of stock in many competing firms, soon posed the same threat in a new form, however. Continued political pressure from the Progressives—the urban, middle-class successors to the Populists—and the repeated failure of the executive branch to enforce the Sherman Act, resulted in the passage of the Clayton Act of 1914. Aimed primarily at the holding companies, the Clayton Act prohibited corporate stock acquisitions that would substantially lessen competition, forbade the directors of one corporation to be directors of a competing corporation (interlocking directorates), and restricted several other anticompetitive practices. But where the

Sherman Act was broad, flexible, and at least a potentially powerful weapon against economic concentration, the Clayton Act had none of these attributes. It prohibited interlocking directorates but not interlocking management; it prohibited the acquisition of stock for monopolistic purposes but not the acquisition of assets. Thus, the Clayton Act failed to provide effective new weapons against the growth of economic concentration.

The Robinson-Patman Act, an amendment to the Clayton Act passed during the depths of the Great Depression, represented a response to the pressure from owners of small businesses seeking protection from what they saw as unfair corporate competition. The Robinson-Patman Act forbade firms to give their largest customers special discounts that were not justified by the cost reductions from a higher volume of sales and prohibited anticompetitive pricing practices. But it delineated those offenses with such specificity and in such turgid language that it often served to prevent firms from lowering prices in order to gain a legitimate market advantage—certainly not one of the goals of antitrust legislation. In many ways, the Robinson-Patman Act is more a piece of special-interest legislation than an antitrust bill, because it often served to restrict fair competition in order to protect a special class of businesses.

The last major antitrust act passed by Congress was the Celler-Kefauver Act of 1950, which was enacted in another period of strong public antagonism toward big business–this time touched off by reports of secret corporate dealings with German firms during World War II. This bill corrected several of the problems in the original Clayton Act but did nothing to untangle the snarl created by the Robinson-Patman Act. The Celler-Kefauver Act prohibited the acquisition of stock and the acquisition of assets when "the effect of such acquisition may be substantially to lessen competition or tend to create a monopoly." The inclusion of the prohibition on asset acquisition, as well as the use of the general term "may be" helped create new weapons against corporate concentration—weapons that were reinforced by the Supreme Court under Chief Justice Earl Warren, which held a more favorable attitude toward antitrust enforcement than its predecessors. [14]

The increasing concentration of corporate power associated with the growth of industrial capitalism spurred antitrust legislation in other English-speaking countries as well. Canada passed its Anti-Combines Act in 1889, one year before the Sherman Act. Like the Robinson-Patman Act, this bill was enacted largely as a result of pressure from small business. Large combines such as the Dominion Wholesale Grocer's Guild and the Canadian Packers Association were gaining control of the markets for many retail goods and threatening to wipe out smaller firms. However, big business interests were so successful in committee actions that the bill that was finally passed was unenforceable. As part of a general watering down of the language of the bill, the law was made to apply only to "unlawful" conspiracies that "unduly" restrained trade. Ten years later, however, the act was rewritten and the word "unlawful" dropped, and the bill became at least potentially enforceable. [15]

The Australian Industries Act of 1906, which prohibited combines that damaged the public interest, was a product of much the same social pressures as the Canadian act. Andrew Hopkins has argued that several recent bills designed to strengthen the original act had their origin in another problem caused by oligopolistic market control—inflation. Australian legislators apparently believed that they had to do something to reduce inflation in order to be reelected and that greater industrial competition would help achieve that end. [16]   Great Britain remained cool to antitrust legislation for a longer time, at first preferring to depend on the common law and later eliminating antitrust problems by nationalizing many key industries. However, Parliament did eventually enact an antitrust bill, the Monopolies and Restrictive Practices Act of 1948. [17]

PROTECTING DEMOCRACY: FAIR POLITICAL PRACTICES

The problem of government corruption is hardly a new one. Current laws against the bribery of public officials have deep roots in common law, but the earliest definitions of this crime were much narrower than they are today. The common law's greatest concern was not with the corruption of elected officials but with that of judges and other agents involved in the administration of justice. [18] Where the law did apply to officeholders, it focused on officials who bribed voters, and not the other way around. Since the list of eligible voters in the eighteenth century was restricted to a small group of landed gentry, it was easy for a politician to bribe his way into office—indeed, the voters in many boroughs expected to be rewarded for their support. In an effort to stop such abuses, Parliament passed an act in 1695–1696, forbidding candidates to give voters money, food, or entertainment before an election. In 1729, Parliament required voters to take an oath that they had received no such gratuities before they were allowed to enter the voting place, and voters who lied were subject to perjury charges. But by all accounts, these measures were of no avail, and the bribery of voters continued unabated. [19] Similar abuses also occurred in

America both before and after independence. George Washington, for example, was accused of campaign abuses in his 1757 race for the Virginia House of Burgesses for allegedly dispensing fifty gallons of rum, twenty-four gallons of wine, forty-six gallons of beer, and two gallons of cider. Since there were only 391 voters in his district, this represented an average outlay of over 1.5 quarts of spirits per voter. [20]

Over the years, the definition of bribery broadened as the number of voters grew and the general direction of bribery shifted. Today, bribery statutes generally apply only to officials who receive money from the public; those rarer instances in which candidates attempt to pay off voters are usually considered election fraud. Bribery is now defined as "the offering, giving, receiving, or soliciting of anything of value to influence action as an official or in the discharge of legal or public duty." [20] Moreover, the recent trend in judicial rulings has been to expand the definition of bribery to encompass agents of private firms as well as government employees and officials. In 1975, for instance, a federal appellate court held that it could "discern no reason why the Congress, in using the term 'bribery' intended that it be limited to the corruption of public officials." [21] Many individual states also have enacted specific "commercial bribery" laws to supplement the older statutes dealing with the corruption of public officials. The massive bribery scandal touched off by revelations that the Lockheed Corporation had paid off foreign officials in order to promote sales of its airplanes gave rise to another important piece of antibribery legislation—the Foreign Corrupt Practices Act of 1977. This act explicitly prohibited the bribery of the officials of foreign governments except in cases involving national security. [23]

Another perennial source of political corruption has been the need to generate campaign funds to pay for the cost of running for office. In some cases, large campaign contributions have become legal substitutes for bribery. In the early days of the Republic, the costs of political campaigns were low and were met largely from the candidate's own pocket or from "contributions" made by government employees subject to veiled (and sometimes not so veiled) threats to their jobs. As the cost of running for office grew, the old sources of funding proved inadequate, and politicians turned increasingly to the "spoils system"—handing out government jobs in exchange for campaign contributions. [24] Among the numerous legislative efforts to stop the extortion of money from public employees, the most significant was the Civil Service Reform Act of 1883, which protected employees against reprisals for failing to make campaign contributions and made it a crime for federal employees to solicit campaign funds from their co-workers. [25] But the sources of campaign funding had begun to change even before the passage of that act, as public employees were replaced by financiers and industrialists seeking government favors to protect their interests. [26]

The ability of corporations to buy offices for the candidates of their choice was never more apparent than in the presidential campaign of 1896. William Jennings Bryan, the Democratic candidate, had a total campaign fund of around $300,000, whereas his Republican opponent, William McKinley, received almost that much from the Standard Oil trust alone. Under the direction of master fundraiser and political manipulator Mark Hanna, McKinley raised a war chest that was estimated to contain anywhere from $3.5 to $10 million.

The specter of big business buying election after election inspired a movement to reform campaign financing. The National Publicity Law Association, an organization dedicated to campaign reform, counted many notable figures of the time as members—including Bryan himself—as well as a future Supreme Court justice and the presidents of the American Federation of Labor and Howard University. [27] Pressure from such organizations as well as the growing influence of the Progressive movement led to the passage of the Tillman Act of 1907, which prohibited corporations or banks from contributing campaign funds to anyone seeking federal office. Then, in 1910, Congress passed a law calling for disclosure of the names and addresses of all contributors who donated more than $100, and the following year campaign expenditures were limited to $5,000 for candidates for the House and $10,000 for candidates for the Senate.

The Federal Corrupt Practices Act of 1925 codified and revised the earlier legislation without making substantive changes. Although the Federal Corrupt Practices Act remained the principal law governing federal political campaigns for forty-seven years, it was notorious for its ineffectiveness. Lyndon Johnson called it "more loophole than law," and there were indeed numerous ways to evade it. [28] For one thing, it did not apply to primary campaigns, which in many parts of the country were more important than the final elections. Another problem was that campaign committees were required to report contributions only if they operated in more than one state, and few actually did. But the principal reason the act failed to achieve its ends was that enforcement was left up to the secretary of the Senate and the clerk of the House, who simply did not do the job. [29]

The Hatch Act of 1939, augmented by an amendment passed in 1940, prohibited federal employees from actively participating in national politics and forbade individuals or businesses working under contract to the government to make campaign contributions. The act also placed a $5,000 limit on the amount an individual could give in political contributions in a single year, but this provision was framed with so many glaring loopholes it was virtually meaningless. Later in the 1940s, the prohibition on corporate campaign contributions was extended to include labor unions as well. [30]

Despite repeated complaints from government officials, political scientists, and public interest organizations, nothing was done to plug the loopholes in the Federal Corrupt Practices Act until 1971. In that year, Congress passed the Federal Election Campaign Act, which set limits on the amount of money a candidate could spend on advertising or contribute to his or her own campaign from personal funds and required political committees and candidates to file itemized totals of their expenditures and report all contributions in excess of $100. Although this act represented a significant improvement over its predecessor, it, too, was filled with loopholes that allowed astute politicians to evade the intent of the law. Its most glaring inadequacy probably was the failure to establish an independent election commission to oversee electoral proceedings. Instead, enforcement was once again left up to the secretary of the Senate and the clerk of the House—the same offices that had failed to enforce the Federal Corrupt Practices Act. [31]

When the Watergate affair became a national scandal in the early 1970s, the unprecedented intensity of the media coverage created strong new demands for reform. In a series of amendments to the Federal Election Campaign Act, the existing system of campaign financing was completely overhauled. For the first time, spending limits were placed on both primaries and general elections, a system of public financing was created for presidential campaigns, and a Federal Election Commission was established to enforce the law. However, the sweeping new provisions of these amendments soon ran afoul of the Supreme Court. In a milestone 1976 decision, the Court held that the limitations on campaign spending, the limitations on the independent expenditure of personal funds, and the limitations on the use of personal funds for one's own campaign were unconstitutional. The Court also required that the Federal Election Commission be reconstituted so that all its members were appointed by the president, in order to avoid any mixing of the legislative and executive duties. The justices did approve some provisions of the act, including the limits on campaign contributions to candidates and political committees, the requirements for public disclosure of those contributions, and the public financing of presidential campaigns. This weakened version of the amended Federal Election Campaign Act, combined with a few procedural refinements passed in

1976 and 1979, now stands as the principal regulatory legislation for federal election campaigns.

Unfortunately, today's laws are little better than those of the past. Most of the various limits and restrictions in the law have been neutralized through the use of the Political Action Committee (PAC). For example, the maximum contribution an individual can make to a candidate is $1,000, while PACs are limited to $5,000. The problem is that there is no limit on the number of PACs representing the same interests, so wealthy contributors channel their money into many different PACs which can all contribute to the same candidate. In the congressional races of 1986, PACs spent more than $130 million to elect their favorite candidates. [32] Moreover, the vast majority of the PACs are controlled by the same interest group—big business. Between January 1, 1985 and June 30, 1986, about two-thirds of the contributions from PACS came from corporations and their trade associations. [33]

Although not directly related to campaign finance, the Ethics Bill of 1978 was also of considerable importance. This act gave the force of law to provisions in the new Senate and House codes of ethics that required public financial disclosures by all federal legislators and high officials in the executive branch. It also placed some restrictions on the so-called "revolving door" through which federal employees move directly from government positions to jobs in the same industries that they had regulated. In an attempt to curtail the use of lucrative job offers as a lure to gain special favors from government regulators, the bill imposed a two-year waiting period on government employees seeking to make such a move. The Ethics Bill also provided for the creation of an Office of Government Ethics to help administer the law, and set forth civil penalties for violators of the disclosure provisions and criminal penalties for those government employees who ignored the restrictions on their future employment. [34]

PROTECTING THE PUBLIC: CONSUMERS, WORKERS, AND THE ENVIRONMENT

The earliest consumer protection laws in Great Britain go back to the common law crime of "cheating"—that is, fraud by use of false weights and measures. But a crime was considered to have occurred only when ordinary prudence would not have been sufficient to safeguard the victim. A statute passed in 1541 expanded the law of criminal fraud somewhat, but still required that some device such as a false letter or seal be employed in the commission of the crime. Other types of fraud were not included in the criminal law for over two centuries.

Following the ancient axiom of *caveat emptor* ("Let the buyer beware"), the responsibility for preventing fraud was placed on the consumer.

But as in the case of larceny, the early common law doctrines proved inadequate to meet the needs of the modern era. The problem was that the growth of mass production and nationwide marketing greatly weakened the traditional restraints on commercial behavior that develop when buyers and sellers live and work in the same small communities. The explosive increase in the volume of trade also multiplied the opportunities for fraudulent gain. The tonnage of shipping leaving English ports, for instance, increased over 300 percent during the eighteenth century, as commerce began to take center stage in British life.[35] As the problem of commercial fraud grew, it became increasingly obvious that something had to be done.

The modern law of criminal fraud began during the reign of King George II, with the passage of a 1757 statute that declared, "Whereas divers ill-disposed persons, to support their profligate way of life, have by various subtle strategems, threats and devices, fraudulently obtained divers sums of money. . . all persons who knowingly and designedly, by false pretense or pretences, shall obtain from any person or persons, money, goods, wares, or merchandises, with intent to cheat or defraud any person or persons of the same. . . shall be deemed offenders."[36] As its wording makes clear, this statute was intended to restrain the practices of charlatans and confidence men, not "legitimate" business people. Subsequent judicial interpretations, however, steadily expanded its scope until the crime of false pretenses came to fill the gap left between the larceny and the embezzlement laws—that is, crimes in which the thief acquires the property of another through fraud and thus receives it voluntarily but without rightful possession in the legal sense. Today, fraud is one of the most universally recognized crimes against consumers, although as we shall see in the following chapter, enforcement agencies have failed to apply the broad legal principles contained in the fraud statutes to many types of white collar crime.

Although the problem of fraud is as old as commerce itself, a multitude of new problems for consumers, workers, and the general public sprang from the growth of industrial capitalism. Of these, the first to win widespread public interest was the problem of monopoly and the ever-increasing concentration of economic and political power in the hands of the industrial corporations. But as the battle for effective antitrust action against the monopolists dragged slowly on, other abuses of the new economic order came to the fore. Improved technology in printing and paper production made possible the growth of cheap mass-market magazines, and editors soon discovered that "muckraking" exposés sold magazines. A new breed of investigative reporter sprang up, and began exploring the seamy side of urban life and government misconduct. But the primary target of these muckrakers was big business, which many of them saw as the root cause of a pervasive national corruption.[37]

From a legislative standpoint, the muckrakers were most successful in attacking the abuses of the food processing industry, which was just putting together the first nationwide food distribution network. Much of the credit for the passage of the Pure Food and Drug Act and the Meat Inspection Act of 1906 must go to the efforts of a host of crusading reformers. Harvey W. Wiley, head of the Department of Agriculture's Bureau of Chemistry, did much to publicize the problem of unsafe food with his famous experiments on a group of volunteer subjects known as the Poison Squad.[38] Even more important was Upton Sinclair's muckraking classic, *The Jungle*, which shocked the nation with its graphic descriptions of the foul conditions found in Chicago's packing houses:

> These rats were nuisances, and the packers would put poisoned bread out for them, and they would die; and then rats, bread, and meat would go into the hoppers together. . . .Men, who worked in the tank rooms full of steam. . .fell into the vats; and when they were fished out, there was never enough of them to be worth exhibiting—sometimes they would be overlooked for days, till all but the bones of them had gone out to the world as Durham's Pure Beef Lard![39]

Despite the public outcry, the system of federal inspectors established by the Pure Food Act might never have been put into place if Sinclair's revelations had not triggered a 50 percent drop in sales and threatened the packers with the loss of their lucrative European markets.[40] As Gabriel Kolko pointed out in his study of the Progressive Era, these events forced the large meat-packing firms to become supporters of regulatory legislation. Not only did meat inspection offer the best way to restore public confidence in the product, but the costs of maintaining adequate sanitation were a much greater burden on small meat-packing firms and thus helped the large corporations to consolidate their control over the market.[41]

The muckrakers were also concerned about the growing toll of deaths and injuries among industrial workers. But with the coming of World War I and the ensuing economic boom of the 1920s, the muckrakers passed from the American scene without winning any significant victories in the battle for industrial safety. Theoretically, injured workers and their families always had the right to sue employers under the provisions of the common law, but in actuality, employers were provided with such generous legal defenses that victims had little chance to win their cases. If the employee had caused the accident in whole or in part, if he or she had voluntarily chosen to work at the hazardous job, or even if another employee was responsible for the accident, the employer could escape liability. [42]

The increasing number of industrial accidents and mounting pressures from workers led many states to pass employer-liability laws that greatly reduced the defenses allowed under common law. Judges, more and more often faced with destitute complainants who had been crippled or maimed in industrial accidents, also began formulating new interpretations that held employers more strictly accountable. As a result, there was a flood of lawsuits from injured workers, and employers began reevaluating their opposition to proposals for a workman's compensation plan. As Lawrence M. Friedman and Jack Ladinsky put it, "The existing tort system crossed an invisible line and thereafter. . . represented on balance a net loss to the industrial establishment. From that point on, the success of a movement for change in the system was certain." [43] The result of those reforms was the state run workman's compensation system that developed in the first quarter of this century. The new statutes were a trade-off between workers and employers. The employers agreed to pay for injuries and deaths arising in the course of employment, and the workers agreed to a legal limit on the amount of damages for which the employer would be liable.

Despite serious flaws in this system—occupational disease, for instance, was not covered at all—it represented a major step toward just compensation for injured workers. But except for a prohibition on the production of white phosphorous matches and a few railroad safety acts, little was done at the federal or state level to actually improve worker safety. The Gauley Bridge disaster of 1930–1931 brought the problem of worker safety back to public attention. In this tragedy, almost five hundred workers were killed by the silica dust churned up during tunneling work for a hydroelectric plant. Most of the fatalities occurred well after the project had been completed, although 169 black workers literally dropped dead during construction and were buried two or three to a grave in a nearby field. Despite the national attention the Gauley Bridge disaster received, no significant legislative action was taken to improve worker safety during the Great Depression. [44]

Although the economic crisis of the 1930s paralyzed the effort to win greater protection for workers, hard times did stimulate a new concern among consumers that their purchases bring the best possible value per dollar. The beginning of the consumer movement is often dated to the 1927 publication of Stuart Chase and F.J. Schlink's *Your Money's Worth*. [45] This pioneering work vehemently attacked deceptive advertising and high-pressure sales techniques and called for the scientific testing of consumer goods to make more accurate information available to the public. The book received such a strong public response that in 1929 Schlink established Consumer's Research, Inc., to carry on scientific consumer research, and he soon began publishing *Consumer's Bulletin* in order to publicize its findings. The legislative achievements of the fledgling consumer protection movement were meager, however. Kallett and Schlink's attack on the pharmaceutical industry, *100,000,000 Guinea Pigs*, won national publicity, but it was not until 1938, in the wake of the Elixir Sulfanilamide tragedy, that a bill tightening governmental regulation of the drug industry was finally passed.[46] This "elixir" was a sulfa drug mixed in an entirely untested solvent, diethylene glycol. It was not until the drug was put onto the market, and over one hundred people had died, that the manufacturers discovered that the solvent was toxic. The consumer movement was also able to win representation on several of the new government agencies set up to stimulate economic recovery during the Great Depression, but these representatives were usually overwhelmed by powerful and well-financed business opposition.[47]

The outbreak of World War II eclipsed public concern about the protection of consumers and workers, and there was little change in this attitude in the conservative climate that prevailed in the early postwar years. By the mid-1950s, however, there was new interest in social reform that led to the activism of the 1960s and early 1970s. This era of social concern and political involvement produced breakthroughs in consumer protection and occupational safety, as well as in environmental protection. One major cause of this new activism was the example set by the civil rights movement. Not only were reformers encouraged by the struggle to abolish the segregation system, but many of them also gained first-hand experience with the techniques of grass-roots political organization. At the same time, the ever-growing size of industrial and marketing concerns and the beginnings of the computer revolution left the public facing a marketplace that was more complex, more dangerous, and more depersonalized than ever before. The unprecedented affluence of this era also played a role in the growth of these movements, by encouraging higher expectations and the belief that social problems could be solved through collective action.

The issue of consumer protection was the first to reemerge. Works such as Vance Packard's *The Hidden Persuaders* began calling attention to consumer problems toward the end of the 1950s,[48] but an equally important factor was the political appeal of the issue. Because everyone is a consumer, consumer protection bills tended to draw broad-based support. Moreover, consumer protection was much cheaper to implement than were the other major social programs of the 1960s. As the war in Vietnam became an increasingly heavy financial burden, the political appeal of consumer protection grew stronger and stronger. [49]

The first important piece of consumer protection legislation to come out of this era was the Pure Food and Drug Act of 1962. Originally begun as an effort to limit price gouging and other abuses in the drug industry, in its final form the bill dealt exclusively with improvements in drug safety and effectiveness. The major reason for the transformation and eventual passage of this bill was the Thalidomide tragedy and those horrible pictures of the deformed babies born to mothers who had taken the drug. [50]

Automobile safety was another consumer issue that had received sporadic attention for years until a dramatic incident finally brought matters to a head. Congress had been holding periodic hearings on auto safety since 1956, but only a few minor pieces of legislation had resulted. The 1966 Senate hearings on auto safety might well have had the same result if the chairman had not called for testimony from a young lawyer who had just written a book on auto safety. It was not so much what Ralph Nader said at those hearings—although he did provide a damning account of corporate irresponsibility—but what General Motors did to try to discredit him (see chapter 2) that spurred congressional action. The scandal that broke when GM's efforts at harassment and intimidation came to public light made Ralph Nader's name a household word and assured the passage of the National Traffic and Motor Vehicle Safety Act of 1966. Among other things, this act authorized the National Traffic Safety Commission to set safety standards for the automobile industry and to require that manufacturers recall defective vehicles. [51]

The political influence of organized consumer groups continued to grow throughout the 1960s and into the 1970s, when they won what some observers consider to be the single most important piece of consumer legislation of the contemporary era—the Consumer Product Safety Act of 1972. [52] This act established a commission that was given broad powers to set safety standards, recall or ban hazardous products, and institute criminal proceedings against companies that disobeyed its orders. Several other pieces of consumer protection legislation were also passed during the 1960s and 1970s. The rapid expansion in the use of consumer credit led to the enactment of regulations governing truth in lending, the fair reporting of credit information, equal opportunity for credit regardless of gender or ethnic group, and unfair or deceptive banking practices. Other acts set standards for product warranties and established controls on lead paint and other toxic substances. [53]

Like many of the other social movements we have been discussing, the environmental movement can trace its origins to the turn of this century. But unlike present-day environmentalists, the early "conservationists" such as Theodore Roosevelt were primarily concerned with managing the natural environment for the maximum economic benefit and paid less attention to environmental protection itself. The conservation movement sprang in large measure from the realization that the frontier, which had played such an important part in American history, was finally gone, and the concomitant fear that the nation was squandering the resources upon which its economic survival depended. The modern environmental movement was born in an era of much greater industrial development. It was in large measure a response to the endless miles of new highways, to urban sprawl, to the threat to animal species, to the frightening increase in pollution—in sum, to the nagging fear that the environment might eventually become unfit for human life.

Although local problems created serious concern in many parts of the nation, the environment barely existed as a national political issue in 1960. But the increasing severity of environmental problems, combined with greater media attention, created a tremendous upsurge of interest in the last part of that decade. Between 1969 and 1971, environmental issues jumped from tenth to fifth in the ranks of public concerns.[54] One of the major causes of this change was the increasing size and militance of the organized environmental groups. On April 22, 1970, these groups came together to celebrate "Earth Day" in nationwide observances that attracted millions of people and focused public attention upon environmental issues. In an hour-long television special, Walter Cronkite of CBS-TV described the crowds as "predominantly white, predominantly young, and predominantly anti-Nixon,"[55] and more of those young, well-educated, middle-class Americans soon flocked to environmental organizations. Between 1970 and 1971, the membership in the five largest organizations increased by 33 percent. Such groups as the Sierra Club, the National Wildlife Federation, the Friends of Earth, and the Environmental Defense Fund grew increasingly militant during the 1970s, openly supporting and opposing candidates, lobbying legislators, launching numerous lawsuits, and staging marches and mass demonstrations.[56] But as the environmentalists became increasingly organized and assertive, so did their opponents—especially the manufacturers and developers who saw environmentalism as a threat to their profits.

Water pollution was one of the first environmental problems to receive the attention of the government, probably because it was so clearly linked to the transmission of contagious disease. The first water pollution laws were enacted at the state level, but those early statutes were ineffective, both because of lax enforcement and because of the lack of jurisdiction over pollution carried downstream from other states.

The history of federal legislation goes back to an 1899 act forbidding the dumping of debris in navigable water, but the first significant federal water pollution legislation wasn't passed until 1948. Over the following two decades, the federal government slowly expanded its involvement in water purity regulation and began providing financial assistance for the construction of local water treatment plants. The publicity surrounding the 1967 sinking of the giant oil tanker *Torrey Canyon* and the massive oil spills from the offshore drilling near Santa Barbara, Cal., led to the passage of a bill to increase private liability for the cost of cleaning up oil spills and repairing the damage they cause. The toughest water pollution bill to date was passed in 1972; it set a five-year deadline for polluting industries to adopt the "best practicable" control technology and another deadline four years after that for the installation of the "best available" pollution control devices. The bill also gave the Environmental Protection Agency, which had been created in 1970 to bring the federal government's environment programs under a single bureaucratic roof, authority to initiate legal action against polluters.[57]

The government was much slower to respond to the problem of air pollution, which had been growing progressively worse since the end of World War II. The frightening siege of air pollution in Donora, Pa., in 1948, which killed twenty people and sickened half of the town's population of twelve thousand, failed to stimulate any new legislation. Fierce opposition from the automobile industry delayed the first federal effort to regulate auto emissions until 1965, and a timetable requiring significant reductions in emissions from new cars and the creation of national standards for stationary emissions was not adopted until 1970.

Numerous other pieces of environmental legislation were passed in the 1970s. Many were trivial, but others were of considerable long-term importance. Particularly significant were the measures that gave the Environmental Protection Agency authority to seek a court order to ban the sale of any dangerous chemical, authorized the EPA to regulate the sales of pesticides, and placed controls on the environmental damage caused by strip mining.

Environmental and consumer protection were only two of the many social issues to gain public attention during the 1960s. The new spirit of activism soon spilled over into the effort to protect the health and safety of the American work force—a problem that is, after all, intimately related to environmental protection, for the same pollutants spewed out by factories also poison the workers who labor inside.

It was the workers in one of the world's most dangerous occupations—coal mining—who pushed through the first new occupational safety legislation. In the mid-1960s, coal miners began a concerted effort to persuade the states to include black lung disease (an often fatal ailment caused by the inhalation of coal dust) in workman's compensation programs. After encountering considerable opposition from the leadership of the United Mine Workers Union, angry miners formed independent organizations—the Black Lung Association and the Association of Disabled Miners and Widows. The drive for new legislation gained impetus from a Farmington, W. Va., mine disaster that claimed the lives of seventy-eight miners in November 1968. In February 1969, West Virginia coal miners went out on a three-week wildcat strike and staged a march on the state capital in order to press their demands for workman's compensation for black lung disease. Later that year, they finally won federal assistance with the passage of the Coal Mine Safety Act.[58]

Faced with the indifference of union leadership to the problem of occupational safety, workers in other industries also took independent action. In June 1965, twelve thousand Teamsters walked off the job in Philadelphia to protest the firing of four employees for refusing to work under dangerous conditions. Jimmy Hoffa, the president of the Teamsters, called the strike illegal and ordered the workers back to the job, but they refused. Similar wildcat actions were taken by the members of other unions. In July 1966, nine thousand members of the United Automobile Workers walked off the job at three Ford plants, citing a long list of grievances centered around health and safety issues. In February 1967, the members of a UAW local struck a General Motors plant in Ohio because of the firing of two workers for refusing to carry out hazardous work. Rank-and-file discontent over health and safety issues also cropped up in the International Longshoremen's and Warehousemen's Union, the International Association of Machinists, the International Union of Electrical Workers, and the United Steelworkers of America.

This grass-roots activism finally forced union leadership to take up the issue of worker safety. President Johnson, faced with deep party division over his conduct of the war in Vietnam and anxious to solidify his union support, submitted a worker safety bill early in 1968. The bill won widespread union support but was nonetheless defeated in Congress. The same motivation led Johnson's successor, Richard Nixon, to propose another worker protection act. Although weaker than the previous bill, the Occupational Safety and Health Act of 1970 remains the most significant piece of worker safety legislation enacted to date. This act requires employers to provide a workplace "free from recognized physical hazards that are likely to cause death or serious physical harm to employees" and to meet the standards promulgated by the Occupational Safety and Health Administration. It also gives OSHA the power to shut down any operation that places workers in "immediate danger" and grants workers the right to make complaints directly to OSHA with a guarantee of anonymity and protection from employer reprisals.[59]

CORPORATE CRIMINAL RESPONSIBILITY: WHO CAN COMMIT A CRIME?

Although an examination of the origins of the laws against such traditional crimes as murder, assault, or robbery would take us too far afield, we need to consider the question of whether or not a corporation can commit such offenses. The primary concern of the law has always been the regulation of relations between persons, but as far back as the twelfth century, other entities began to be recognized as "persons" for legal purposes. The origins of this concept lay in the efforts of the medieval clergy to free itself from the control of local lords. In the early medieval era, churches were considered to be the property of the regional landowner, but as the clergy began to assert its independence, it rejected claims of outside ownership. But if the lord did not own the church, who did? At various times it was said that the church was owned by its "four walls" or its patron saint, but ultimately the collective body known as "the church" was recognized as the legal owner. Later, as the capitalist economic system grew, the corporation also won recognition as a "juristic person." This development proved a great boon to corporations, who enjoyed as juristic persons many of the legal rights and protections of real persons.[60]

There was, however, a price to be paid, for the logic of the law ultimately required that new responsibilities accompany the new privileges. There is some dispute about exactly when these new "persons" were first held civilly liable for their actions, but it certainly occurred soon after the inception of the concept. Criminal liability was much slower to develop. The first application of the criminal law to a corporate entity was based on the ancient common law doctrine that a master was criminally responsible if a servant threw something out of the master's house onto a street or highway and thereby caused a public nuisance. The corporations involved in the earliest cases were cities that failed to maintain safe roads and waterways; later, the same law was applied to railroads and other private corporations. This precedent was slowly expanded on a case-by-case basis, until corporations came to be held liable for all criminal offenses that did not require criminal intent.

But the doctrine that corporations were unable to form criminal intent was no more legally defensible than the earlier restrictions on corporate liability, and it was rejected in a 1908 case involving railroad rebates. In this ruling, the judge cited the language of the specific statute at issue and went on to point out the obvious contradiction involved in holding that a corporation could act through its agents but could not form a criminal intent through them. It is now common for corporations to be charged with criminal violations of the regulatory statutes as well as more serious offenses such as fraud and perjury. The most recent legal development in the centuries-long expansion of corporate responsibility came in an Indiana case in which the Ford Motor Company was charged with reckless homicide in connection with the gas tank problems of the Ford Pinto (see chapter 2). Although the company was ultimately acquitted, the court ruled that the Indiana homicide statute was applicable to corporations as well as to individuals.[61] Prosecutors were more successful in a 1985 case in Illinois, where a far smaller firm, Film Recovery Systems, was found guilty of involuntary manslaughter for causing the death of one of its workers (see chapter 5).[62] In 1987, a Texas construction company and its president both pleaded *nolo contendere* (no contest) to charges of negligent homicide in the death of a worker who was crushed when an excavation ditch collapsed.[63] At the time of this writing, involuntary manslaughter charges are also pending against several other firms for similar offenses.[64]

ORIGINS OF THE LAWS

Having examined the historical development of the laws creating white collar crimes, we can now return to the theoretical issue posed at the beginning of this chapter: Are those laws a reflection of society's normative consensus, a product of a pluralist struggle among many more or less equal groups, or are they merely symbolic acts designed to placate social protesters and protect the privileges of the ruling elite?

The weakness of consensus theory is immediately apparent from the historical evidence. Most of the numerous antitrust, consumer protection, campaign financing, environmental protection, and worker safety laws were controversial issues at the time of their enactment. Many powerful interest groups tried to influence the content of those bills and worked to prevent or promote their ratification. Only a handful of the laws in question can be said to have reflected an uncontested normative consensus. Even those laws, for example, the prohibitions on larceny, embezzlement, and pilferage, can be explained as the products of pressure from specific interest groups, albeit with little significant opposition.[65] Equally damaging to the consensus theory is the fact that many activities that violate society's "core values" are not prohibited by criminal law. For example, the acceptance of the doctrine of *caveat emptor* meant that the unethical and deceptive practices used by merchants were perfectly legal, despite the fact that they clearly violated both social and religious standards. The inadequacies of consensus theory should not, however, lead us to conclude that society's norms and values played no part in the genesis of these laws. To the contrary, there is little doubt that an appeal to the public's sense of justice and fair play is one of the reformers' most powerful weapons in their battle to restrain the abuses of the elite. In the end, however, pressure from special interest groups appears to have been the *sine qua non* of legislative action.

But if the interest theory provides the best explanation of the creation of the "white collar laws," which version of it are we to accept— the pluralist or the elitist? The immediate temptation is to say that the pluralists have the better case, since the mere existence of laws restricting the activities of the corporate elite indicates that no single group controls all facets of the legislative process. However, the elitists argue persuasively that many of these so-called reforms were of little practical import, and that in other cases the final results of the legislative struggle have actually benefited the ruling elite. More careful analysis shows both sides to be needlessly polemic. Although the elitists can rightfully claim that many legislative reforms appeared to be much more substantive than they actually were, there is no doubt that this network of legislation contains many provisions that were strongly opposed by significant segments of the corporate elite.[66] By the same token, the pluralist claim that the legislative process has been controlled by shifting alliances of groups that ultimately balance each other out, so that the "will of the people" has prevailed, comes much closer to ideology than to empirical fact. Although various reformist groups and defenders of the status quo have indeed shifted alliances from time to time and from issue to issue, there can be no doubt that the corporate elite controls a vast concentration of political and economic power that dwarfs its opposition.

In order to understand the origins of the "white collar" legislation, we must look beyond the dynamics of interest group politics to the social and economic forces that lie at the heart of the system of industrial capitalism. The social movements that led to the reforms discussed here arose out of the dislocations and conflicts caused by development of that economic system. In many cases, traditional segments of society threatened by new economic developments still had considerable political power to muster in their defense. For instance, both the antitrust movement and the more general populist movement, of which it was a part, represented an attempt by small farmers and businesspeople to strike back at the corporations that were choking off their means of subsistence. The early reforms prohibiting political contributions by corporations also sprang from the same sources.

The demand for legislation to protect workers, consumers, and the environment was stimulated by other facets of the process of industrialization. Traditionally, producers and consumers lived together in the same small towns, and there was little need for formal consumer protection legislation. If a local merchant or craftsman used shady techniques to exploit consumers, complaints spread quickly through the community, and various informal controls could easily be brought to bear. With the growth of big cities and mass marketing, the relationship between producers and consumers was fundamentally altered. The consumer's movement was part of an effort to find an effective substitute for the informal controls of the small town. The growth of industrial capitalism also brought about fundamental changes in the techniques of production. As new technologies and methods of production sprang up, a frightening array of poisons and pollutants were soon being spewn out into the environment. The environmental movement stemmed from the desire of people to protect themselves from the new hazards created by industrial technology and to preserve the quality of the environment.

Thus, conflicts and contradictions in the political economy of industrial capitalism provided the original impetus for the social movements that agitated for new legislation. The conflicts between producers and consumers, labor and business, small farmers and corporations, are inherent in industrial capitalism, and any changes in the delicate balance between those conflicting groups may spur appeals for legislative intervention. Other problems, such as environmental pollution, stem directly from industrial technology, whether the system of economic organization is capitalistic or socialistic. But although such general problems may ultimately lead to new legislation, the dynamics of the process of law creation soon transform them into a struggle between specific interest groups, some battling to change, and others to defend the status quo.

Few, if any, of the antitrust, fair campaign practice, environmental, or consumer protection laws examined here would have been passed if large-scale, grass-roots movements had not pushed for their enactment. In most cases, one version or another of these laws was under consideration for years, slowly shuffling from committee to committee until the popular pressure grew great enough to force reluctant legislators to vote against the desires of the economic elite—to which most of them were tied with both economic and political bonds.

Because reformers are usually outspent and outmaneuvered by their more highly placed opposition, the chances for significant reforms are slim as long as the public remains apathetic. But hardships created by the failures and contradictions of the political economy can arouse the public from its lethargy. The emergence of effective leadership has proven to be a key factor in transforming popular discontent into the kind of social movements necessary to force reforms. These "moral entrepreneurs," as Becker called them, work to bring disaffected people together in political organizations and to spread public awareness of social problems.[67] The media attention focused on a dramatic disaster or scandal often has provided an important rallying point for reform. Deadly pharmaceuticals, mine disasters, oil spills, the revelations of the muckrakers, Watergate, and numerous other scandals have galvanized the forces of reform and cut the ground out from under their opposition. Yet it is a reciprocal relationship: without the efforts of an organized social movement, even such a dramatic incident as the Gauley Bridge disaster failed to stimulate meaningful reform.

The legislative history of many successful reforms follows a similar pattern. The original efforts of reformers are met with strong resistance from the elite interest, effectively blocking any legislative action. But if the reformers gain strength and continue pushing for action, the elite may come to accept the idea that some reform is necessary. Elite interests then begin working to reshape the reformers' proposals in order to minimize their negative impact and/or to win some compensatory benefits. The final shape of the reforms often emerges from intense political infighting about issues of which the public has little knowledge or awareness.

The power of elite interests can be seen in the fact that most proposed reforms, including many needed to deal with urgent social problems, are never enacted. Moreover, many of the reform bills that have been passed were gutted of any real content or rewritten to actually benefit elite interests. On the other hand, even nations in the advanced stages of capitalist development retain some degree of economic decentralization, and successful reform movements often benefit from divisions within the ruling elite. For example, the insurance industry has often supported automobile safety legislation, even though the automobile industry has been vehemently against it. A similar split between Eastern high-sulfur coal producers and Western low-sulfur producers occurred in the battle over the enactment of emission regulations for coal-fired power plants.[68]

The ratification of a new law, even if it is a strong one, is not the end of a successful reform movement. As we shall see in the next chapter, the enforcement process plays a critical role in determining whether or not the reforms remain symbolic or result in significant social change. This is particularly true because of the tendency of many politicians to avoid tough decisions that are likely to offend either the organized reformers or the entrenched elites. As a result, many of the lawmakers' most difficult problems are, as Neal Shover put it, "transformed into administrative problems to be worked out between regulators and the industry."[69] And it is the result of this administrative struggle that often decides the success or failure of a reform movement.

NOTES

1. Many social theorists of the first half of this century accepted this position. For example, see Emile Durkheim, *The Division of Labor in Society*, trans. George Simpson (Glencoe, Ill.: The Free Press, 1947); Pitirim A. Sorokin, *Society, Culture, and Personality* (New York: Harper, 1947). For a more recent version of this theory, see W. Friedmann, *Law in a Changing Society* (London: Ballantine, 1971).

2. Influential pluralist works include David Reisman, *The Lonely Crowd* (New York: Doubleday Anchor, 1953); Arnold M. Rose, *The Power Structure: Political Process in American Society* (London: Oxford University Press, 1967). For a recent study that focuses more exclusively on the sociology of law, see Lawrence M. Friedman, *Law and Society* (Englewood Cliffs, N.J.: Prentice-Hall, 1977).

3. The elitist position is the dominant one in contemporary sociology. For examples, see William J. Chambliss, "Sociological Analysis of the Law of Vagrancy," *Social Problems* 12 (1964): 67–77; Richard Quinney, *Critique of Legal Order: Crime Control in Capitalist Society* (Boston: Little Brown, 1974); Austin Turk, "Law as a Weapon in Social Conflict," *Social Problems* 23 (1976): 276–291; and Neil Gunningham, *Pollution, Social Interest, and the Law* (London: Martin Robertson & Co., 1974).

4. Allen Z. Gammage and Charles F. Hemphill, Jr., *Basic Criminal Law*, 2nd ed. (New York: McGraw-Hill, 1979), 226–227.

5. Jerome Hall, *Theft, Law and Society*, 2nd ed. (Indianapolis: Bobbs-Merrill, 1952), 3–33.

6. Ibid., pp. 35–40, 62–66.

7. Franklin D. Jones, "Historical Development of the Law of Business Competition," *Yale Law Journal* 35 (June 1926): 905.

8. Hans B. Thorelli, *The Federal Antitrust Policy* (Baltimore: Johns Hopkins Press, 1955), 9–53; also Jones, "Law of Business Competition."

9. Among the numerous authors who have taken this position are Charles Beard and Mary Beard, *The Rise of American Civilization*, rev. ed. (New York, Macmillan, 1930), 327; Samuel E. Morison and Henry Steele Commager, *The Growth of the American Republic*, 4th ed. (New York: Oxford University Press, 1951), 144; Carl Solberg, *Oil Power* (New York: Mason/Charter, 1976), 48–49.

10. For a concise analysis of the relationship between agriculture and industrial development in nineteenth-century America, see C. Wright Mills, *White Collar* (London: Oxford University Press, 1951), 13–33.

11. Harold Faulkner, *Politics, Reform and Expansion: 1890–1900* (New York: Harper & Brothers, 1959), 67; also Thorelli, *Antitrust Policy*, 58–59.

12. Thorelli, *Antitrust Policy*, 226–227.

13. On this point, see Albert E. McCormick, Jr., "Dominant Class Interests and the Emergence of Antitrust Legislation," *Contemporary Crises* 3 (1979): 399–417.

14. See Mark J. Green, Beverly C. Moore, Jr., and Bruce Wasserstein, *The Closed Enterprise System* (New York: Grossman, 1972), 47–60, 298–412; A. D. Neale, *The Antitrust Laws of the United States of America* (New York: Cambridge University Press, 1960).

15. Colin H. Goff and Charles E. Reasons, *Corporate Crime in Canada: A Critical Analysis of Anti-Combines Legislation* (Scarborough, Ont.: Prentice-Hall of Canada, 1978), 41–49.

16. Andrew Hopkins, *Crime and Business: The Sociological Sources of Australian Monopoly Law* (Canberra: Australian Institute of Criminology, 1978).

17. Charles E. Reasons and Colin H. Goff, "Corporate Crime: A Cross-National Analysis," in Gilbert Geis and Ezra Stotland, eds., *White-Collar Crime: Theory and Research* (Beverly Hills, Ca.: Sage, 1980), 126–141.

18. Gammage and Hemphill, Jr., *Criminal Law*, 314.

19. William Holdsworth, *A History of English Law* (London: Sweet and Maxwell, 1938), X: 573–577.

20. Congressional Quarterly, *Congressional Ethics*, 2nd ed. (Washington, D.C.: Congressional Quarterly Press, 1980), 193.

21. *Allen v. State*, 72 P.2d 516, 63 Okla. Crim. 16.

22. *U.S. v. Pamponio* 511 R2d 953 (1975).

23. See W. Michael Reisman, *Folded Lies: Bribery, Crusades, and Reforms* (New York: The Free Press, 1979), 151–166, 176–177.

24. Herbert E. Alexander, *Financing Politics: Money, Elections, and Political Reform*, 2nd ed. (Washington, D.C.: Congressional Quarterly Press, 1980), 45–46.

25. Congressional Quarterly, *Congressional Ethics*, 194.

26. Alexander, *Financing Politics*, 46–47.

27. Ibid., 26.

28. Mark Green, *Who Runs Congress?*, 3rd ed. (New York: Bantam Books, 1979), 17.

29. Ibid., 17–18; Congressional Quarterly, *Congressional Ethics*, 194–195; Alexander, *Financing Politics*, 26–27.

30. *Congressional Ethics*, 194–195; Alexander, *Financing Politics*, 26–27.

31. *Congressional Ethics*, 197–198.

32. Mary Deibel, "Congress' Dilemma on Campaigns: If PACs Don't Pay, Who Will?" *San Luis Obispo (Calif.) Telegram-Tribune*, 14 February 1987, 11B.

33. Computed from data in Robert W. Stewart and Tracy Wood, "Political Giving: Corporate Contributions Buy Access," *Los Angeles Times*, 26 October 1986, 1 *passim*.

34. *Congressional Ethics*, 48–56, 182–188.

35. Hall, *Theft, Law and Society*, 77.

36. Quoted in Hall, *Theft, Law and Society*, 40.

37. For a comprehensive account of the activities of the muckrakers, see C. C. Reigier, *The Era of Muckrakers* (Chapel Hill, N.C.: University of North Carolina Press, 1932).

38. James S. Turner, *The Chemical Feast* (New York: Grossman, 1970), 107–137.

39. Upton Sinclair, *The Jungle* (New York: Vangard Press, 1927).

40. Robert O. Herrmann, "The Consumer Movement in Historical Perspective," in David A. Aaker and George S. Day, *Consumerism: Search for the Consumer Interest* (New York: The Free Press, 1971), 10–22; Mark V. Nadel, *The Politics of Consumer Protection* (Indianapolis: Bobbs-Merrill, 1971), 7–19.

41. Gabriel Kolko, *The Triumph of Conservatism* (New York: The Free Press, 1963).

42. Joseph A. Page and Mary-Win O'Brien, *Bitter Wages: Ralph Nader's Study Group Report on Disease and Injury on the Job* (New York: Grossman Publishers, 1973), 49–50.

43. See Lawrence M. Friedman and Jack Ladinsky, "Social Change and the Law of Industrial Accidents," *Columbia Law Review* 67 (January 1967): 50–82; Neal Shover, "The Criminalization of Corporate Behavior: Federal Surface Coal Mining," in Geis and Stotland, *White Collar Crime*, 98–125; Elliott Currie, "Sociology of Law: The Unasked Questions," *Yale Law Journal* 81 (November 1971): 134–137.

44. Page and O'Brien, *Bitter Wages*, 59–63; Daniel M. Berman, *Death on the Job: Occupational Health and Safety Struggles in the United States* (New York: Monthly Review Press, 1978), 27–28.

45. Stuart Chase and F. J. Schlink, *Your Money's Worth* (New York: Macmillan, 1927).

46. Arthur Kallett and F. J. Schlink, *100,000,000 Guinea Pigs* (New York: Vangard Press, 1933).

47. Lucy Black Creighton, *Pretenders to the Throne: The Consumer Movement in the United States* (Lexington, Mass.: Lexington Books, 1976), 19–29, 113; Nadel, *Politics of Consumer Protection*, 36–43; Herrmann, "The Consumer Movement in Historical Perspective," 12–14.

48. Vance Packard, *The Hidden Persuaders* (New York: McKay, 1957).

49. Nadel, *Politics of Consumer Protection*, 121–139.

50. See Nadel, *Politics of Consumer Protection*, 36–43.

51. S. Prakash Sethi, *Up Against the Corporate Wall: Modern Corporations and Social Issues of the Seventies*, 2nd ed. (Englewood Cliffs, N.J.: Prentice-Hall, 1974), 373–398; Nadel, *Politics of Consumer Protection*, 137–143; Creighton, *Pretenders to the Throne*, 52–55.

52. Creighton, *Pretenders to the Throne*, 38–39.

53. Joel R. Evans, *Consumerism in the United States* (New York: Praeger, 1980), 391–439; Creighton, *Pretenders to the Throne*; Nadel, *Politics of Consumer Protection*.

54. John C. Whitaker, *Striking a Balance: Environment and Natural Resources Policy in the Nixon-Ford Years* (Washington, D.C.: American Enterprise Institute for Public Policy Research, 1976), 9.

55. Ibid., 2–7.

56. Walter A. Rosenbaum, *The Politics of Environmental Concern* (New York: Praeger, 1973), 53–91.

57. J. Clarence Davies III and Barbara S. Davies, *The Politics of Pollution*, 2nd ed. (Indianapolis: Bobbs-Merrill, 1975), 27–44.

58. Page and O'Brien, *Bitter Wages*, 143–144; Berman, *Death on the Job*, 31–32.

59. Page and O'Brien, *Bitter Wages*, 167–189; Patrick G. Donnelly, "The Origins of the Occupational Safety and Health Act of 1970," *Social Problems* 30 (October 1980): 13–25.

60. James S. Coleman, *Power and the Structure of Society* (New York: W. W. Norton, 1974), 13–31.

61. Thomas J. Bernard, "The Historical Development of Corporate Criminal Liability," *Criminology* 22 (February 1984): 3–17.

62. Barbara J. Hayler, "Criminal Prosecution of Corporate Crime: The Illinois Corporate Murder Case," presented at the Western Political Science Association, March 20-22, 1986, Eugene, Oregon; Larry Green, "3 Officials Guilty of Murder in Cyanide Death at Plant," *Los Angeles Times*, 15 June 1985, 1 & 5; Ray Gibson and Charles Mount, "3 Former Executives Guilty in Cyanide Death," *Chicago Tribune*, 15 June 1985, 1: 1 & 5.

63. "Texas Construction Company and President Plead Guilty to Negligent Homicide in Connection with Work Related Death," *Corporate Crime Reporter* 1 (20 April 1987): 4–5; Barry Siegel, "Murder Case a Corporate Landmark," *Los Angeles Times*, 15 September 1985, 1: 1 *passim*.

64. "Orkin and Two of its Employees Charged with Involuntary Manslaughter," *Corporate Crime Reporter* 1 (April 20, 1987): 1–2; "General Dynamics Involuntary Manslaughter Case in Michigan Heads for Appellate Decision," *Corporate Crime Reporter* 1 (April 13, 1987): 3–4; "Long Delay in Connecticut Corporate Homicide Case," *Corporate Crime Reporter* 1 (April 20, 1987): 5–6.

65. For an excellent discussion of the social and economic forces that reshaped the common law crime of larceny, see Hall, *Theft, Law and Society*, 13–14, 62–79.

66. Clinard and Yeager comment that "there is little recognition by radical or Marxist thinkers that even the largest corporations are increasingly being subjected to severer restrictions, heavier penalties, and stronger governmental control, largely in response to the activities of the consumer, environmental, and other groups." Marshall B. Clinard and Peter C. Yeager, *Corporate Crime* (New York: The Free Press, 1980), 75.

67. See Howard S. Becker, *Outsiders: Studies in the Sociology of Deviance* (New York: The Free Press, 1963), 147–164.

68. See Bruce A. Ackerman and William T. Hassler, *Clean Coal/Dirty Air* (New Haven: Yale University Press, 1981).

69. Shover, "Criminalization of Corporate Behavior," 120.

5

Enforcement

Although most people recognize the importance of the struggle to enact new legislation, the public is surprisingly naive about the enforcement process. It is commonly assumed that once a new law is enacted, it is more or less automatically enforced. Law enforcement agencies are seen to be mere servants of the law, carrying out the dictates of the people as codified by their legislators. But criminologists have long recognized that such agencies do not merely enforce the law–they create it as well. When resources are allocated to one sort of enforcement and not to another, the law as it actually affects the man or woman on the street is changed. If enforcement agencies decide that they will not prosecute a certain kind of offense, in effect they cancel whatever sanctions the law may contain.

This question of discretionary enforcement is critical to all criminal justice, but especially for the white collar crimes. The power and influence of the offenders often make the decision to prosecute a major corporate crime as political as the legislative process that created the original law. Even when the enforcement process is less overtly political, the huge scale and complexity of many white collar offenses, and the chronic shortage of resources for investigation and prosecution, may require many difficult decisions about which cases to pursue and which to ignore.

The complexity of so many white collar offenses seems to require a much more elaborate enforcement bureaucracy than is necessary for common street crimes. Local police and prosecutors handle many occupational crimes, but they are hopelessly outmatched by big-time organizational criminals. The FBI is the only traditional law enforcement agency in the United States with the resources to deal with major offenders, but its primary focus is still on occupational crime. The principal responsibility for the enforcement of the laws regulating corporate behavior rests with specially created regulatory agencies as the Federal

Trade Commission and the Environmental Protection Agency. In addition, a third kind of bureaucratic structure has developed as the professions have attempted to free themselves from the threat of outside control, and it is to this professional self-regulation that we first turn our attention.

PROFESSIONAL SELF-REGULATION

Physicians, lawyers, and other professional groups generally have succeeded in keeping the criminal offenses of their members out of the criminal justice system. By their very nature, the occupational duties of most professionals are complex and difficult for the outsider to understand. Thus, even in the best of circumstances a criminologist or police investigator might have considerable difficulty in determining if the self-serving actions of a particular practitioner were simply bad judgement or outright fraud. To add to this problem, many professionals have intentionally sought to create an aura of mystery about their work and generate a sense of awe in the public mind. This professional mystification has helped not only to insulate professionals from the outside "meddling" of the criminal justice system, but from the complaints of their customers as well.

A related problem is the spirit of camaraderie and mutual support that exists in most professions. Although at first glance such a normal communal spirit hardly seems dangerous, it has contributed to the professionals' reticence to report abuses by their colleagues or give legal testimony against them. As one expert on discipline in the medical profession put it, "There's a great reluctance on the part of doctors to interfere with another doctor's reputation and a means of livelihood. The philosophy apparently is that a man's reputation is more important than the welfare of his patients."[1] The same attitudes are present in the legal profession. As Garbus and Seligman noted, "Attorneys and judges generally refuse to report instances of professional misconduct. They will not testify against each other. There is a strong tendency to treat serious misconduct complaints as private disputes between attorney and client."[2] Aside from the obvious harm such attitudes cause the clients of the professional system, they also make it much harder to investigate criminal activities.

Compared with other workers, professionals enjoy a high degree of individual autonomy. Indeed, some sociologists have come to see autonomy as the defining characteristic of a profession. Eliot Freidson holds that "a profession is distinct from the other occupations in that it has been given the right to control its own work. . . only the profession has the recognized right to declare. . . 'outside' evaluations illegitimate and intolerable."[3]   Many professional groups have won the legal right of self-regulation, including the control of licensing and disciplinary proceedings. Self-regulation has many advantages for the professionals, but few for the general public. The boards and agencies charged with controlling professional misconduct deflect criminal complaints away from the justice system, thus protecting fellow professionals from prosecution. Although the agencies of self-regulation have strong sanctions at their disposal, their members have generally shown great leniency toward their fellows—perhaps on the assumption that they might someday be on the other side of the consumer complaint.

The principal responsibility for the regulation of the medical profession lies with each state's board of medical examiners. The boards are composed of physicians (in some states a few other medical professionals are included), who are usually appointed by the governor upon the recommendation of the state medical society. The main power of these boards lies in their control of medical licensure. Most of their time is devoted to granting licenses to new physicians, but they are also charged with taking disciplinary actions against incompetent or unethical practitioners. Medical examiners generally maintain high standards for the granting of a medical license; once a license is issued, however, it is rarely revoked. Once admitted to the fellowship of physicians, incompetent or even criminal practitioners are apt to be given the protection of their fellows. Of the approximately 320,000 physicians in the United States, 16,000 are believed to be incompetent or unfit, but on the average only seventy-two licenses are revoked each year.[4]   It is clear from the miniscule number of revocations that only the most serious kinds of offenses, committed in a blatant and public fashion, result in the loss of a medical license. For instance, the single most common cause for revocation of a license for disciplinary reasons is not fraud or malpractice, but narcotic law violations, which usually involve either an addicted physician or one who supplies drugs to addicts.[5]

The legal profession regulates itself in much the same manner. In most jurisdictions, the local bar association is responsible for processing complaints and initiating investigations of misconduct, but the ultimate responsibility usually rests with the courts. Disciplinary proceedings are often prosecuted by a local grievance committee and tried by a court-appointed referee. State bar associations seldom provide adequate funding for disciplinary agencies, and almost all place complicated procedural obstacles in their way. Consequently, few complaints result in disciplinary action. Moreover, such actions are extremely time-consuming, sometimes taking more than five years from start to finish.[6] The California State Bar, for example, received approximately five thousand complaints against lawyers in 1975-1976, but fewer than one thousand of them were actually investigated. And of those investigated, only eleven cases resulted in permanent disbarment, while the licenses of forty-two other offenders were temporarily suspended.[7] This small number of disciplinary actions in a state with approximately fifty thousand practicing lawyers clearly shows the inadequacy of this system of professional self-regulation.

Even the American Bar Association itself recognizes the problem, although it has not taken any effective steps to deal with it. The ABA's Special Committee on Evaluation of Disciplinary Enforcement, chaired by former Supreme Court Justice Tom Clark, called the failure of the legal profession's disciplinary mechanisms a "scandalous situation" and went on to note, "With few exceptions the prevailing attitude of lawyers toward disciplinary enforcement ranges from apathy to outright hostility. Disciplinary action is practically non-existent in many jurisdictions; practices and procedures are antiquated; many disciplinary agencies have little power to take effective steps against malefactors."[8] A similar committee formed by the Bar of the City of New York, after finding that well-placed, influential lawyers largely escaped disciplinary action for misconduct, conduced that "the system catches only the small fish."[9]

Ironically, the same professional organizations that claim to be watching out for the public's best interest have themselves been involved in repeated criminal activities. As pointed out in chapter 2, medical and bar associations have often committed antitrust violations such as price fixing and restraint of trade. Together with lax enforcement practices, these repeated criminal activities clearly indicate that the agencies of professional self-regulation are primarily concerned with the interests of professionals, not with those of the public, and cannot be considered important agents for the control of white collar crime.

GOVERNMENT REGULATION

The government bureaucracies set up to regulate various aspects of economic behavior have a far greater impact on the problem of white collar crime than the attempts at professional self-regulation. Regulatory agencies have been established to do everything from maintaining free competition to protecting the health and safety of the public. Indeed, these agencies, not the traditional criminal justice system, shoulder most of the burden of bringing organizational offenders to justice.

From the legislator's standpoint, regulatory agencies have two important advantages over the criminal justice system. For one thing, they make the lawmaker's job easier by taking over the responsibility for the formulation of specific rules, standards, and guidelines. In the case of environmental pollution, for example, pollutants must be identified, their effects on the public's health must be determined, and safe exposure levels must be set. In addition, numerous other issues, concerning the specific techniques to be used to achieve these goals and the economic costs involved, must be decided. Although a legislative body could handle such questions, it would be an extremely time-consuming task involving matters well beyond the expertise of most legislators. But the availability of such expertise is not the only advantage legislators have seen in the creation of regulatory agencies. Such agencies also provide a convenient place to pass the buck when politicians want to avoid making decisions that are likely to be unpopular with an important constituency.

Regulatory Agencies

FEDERAL AGENCIES.   The primary responsibility for dealing with organizational crime rests with a diverse group of federal regulatory agencies. Most of the older agencies, such as the Interstate Commerce Commission, the Federal Trade Commission, and the Securities and Exchange Commission, are organized as independent units under the direction of a group of commissioners appointed by the president. The original idea was to put the responsibility for regulatory problems in the hands of a group of experts and then to insulate them as much as possible from political interference. But on the whole, this approach has failed to live up to its promise. The commissions were never really insulated from politics, and many of them became "captives" of the industries they were supposed to control.

A new generation of reformers, concerned with such issues as environmental pollution and consumer protection, argued that a different organizational structure was needed. As a result, the newer regulatory agencies, such as the Environmental Protection Agency, are usually headed by a single administrator with a staff of assistants who are under much tighter legal restraints than they were under the older commissions. [10] For example, in order to give the FTC maximum flexibility to do its job, Congress intentionally refrained from defining the "unfair methods of the competition" it was supposed to prevent. But the Clean Air Act of 1970 not only mandated that the EPA administrator set specific clean air targets to "protect public health," but it also required that those targets be met no later than 1977. [11] Moreover, it gave "any citizen" the right to sue the EPA if it failed to carry out the act's requirements. [12] But as Lynxwiller, Shover, and Clelland showed in their study of the regulation of surface mining, even the most specific legislative mandates cannot eliminate the discretionary power of individual employees.[13] Another important difference between the commissions and the new agencies is that the former have much greater freedom from presidential control. Commissioners are appointed for a fixed term and are subject to early removal only via congressional impeachment. Administrators, on the other hand, serve at the pleasure of the president and may be removed whenever the chief executive decides to do so.[14]

Space does not allow for a review of all the regulatory bodies that play a role in controlling white collar crime, but we will examine the most important agencies, one of which is certainly the Federal Trade Commission. When it was created in 1915, the FTC was charged with preventing unfair competition, anticompetitive mergers, and interlocking directorates. But over the years, it took on responsibility for controlling a much wider variety of unfair trading practices, including false advertising, commercial bribery, and price discrimination. The FTC's responsibilities in the antitrust field are broadly defined. For example, the law calls on the agency to prevent "unfair methods of competition" and stop mergers whose "effect may be to substantially lessen competition or tend to create a monopoly." Such general language is obviously subject to many different interpretations, and FTC policy has tended to make wide swings back and forth as the political climate and the agency's commissioners changed.

Because the Antitrust Division of the Justice Department handles many of the same kinds of antitrust cases as the FTC, there is considerable duplication of effort. The principal difference between the two organizations lies in their techniques of enforcement. The FTC is limited to civil and administrative action; if it decides to pursue a case after it conducts an investigation, it will either initiate a hearing before an administrative law judge or bring an action in civil court. The Antitrust Division of the Justice Department, in contrast, has jurisdiction over all criminal cases. Should the FTC decide that one of its cases warrants criminal action, it can recommend such action to the Justice Department, but the final decision rests with the attorney general, not an independent commission, and is thus more subject to direct political influence. In other regards, however, the two agencies are quite similar.[15]

The Securities and Exchange Commission was created after the stock market crash of 1929 in an attempt to restore public confidence in the securities market. Although the SEC's responsibilities have expanded over the years, its overall objectives have remained unchanged. It is the SEC's job to prevent misrepresentation in corporate financial statements and in the sale or exchange of securities. It also regulates procedures for the solicitation of proxies, enforces restrictions on "insider trading," and supervises other aspects of securities transactions. The commission has the power to take a wide range of administrative actions. After an administrative hearing and a possible court appeal, the commissioners can expel members from stock exchanges, revoke the registration of brokers and dealers, or censure individuals for misconduct. If the facts warrant, they can also recommend criminal prosecution to the Justice Department.

A 1977 report of the House Commerce Subcommittee rated the SEC as one of the government's three most effective regulatory agencies.[16] This success in large measure reflects the business community's recognition that such regulation is essential to maintain public trust in the stock market. Thus, the SEC has not had to battle against as many powerful interest groups as have most other regulatory agencies.

The Food and Drug Administration operates under a very different kind of mandate. Rather than economic regulation, the health and safety of the public is its main concern. When it was created in 1906, the FDA made only spot checks on food and drugs to detect adulteration or mislabeling. But like other regulatory agencies, the FDA found its powers and responsibilities growing over the years, usually as a result of the public outcry about the deaths from some dangerous new drug. After the Sulfanilamide tragedy, the FDA was empowered to take steps to ensure new drugs were safe *before* they were out on the market. And after the Thalidomide case, the FDA was charged with ensuring that drugs were not only safe, but also effective (see chapter 4 for the details of these cases).[17]

In approving a new drug, the FDA has the difficult task of weighing its benefits against its possible dangers. The mere fact that a new drug has hazardous side effects is not sufficient to ban its use, because it may, for example, be the only effective treatment for a serious disease. Before permitting a drug to be put on the market, the FDA requires the manufacturer to conduct extensive tests, first on laboratory animals and then on a small group of patients under carefully controlled conditions; finally, the drug is released to a limited number of physicians to see how safe it is in ordinary medical use. Although they appear to be careful and cautious, these procedures are seriously flawed by the fact that the manufacturer, not the FDA, conducts the tests. Because drug companies often have an enormous financial stake in the drugs they test, there is a strong motivation to bias the testing procedures or even falsify the data (see chapter 2). Without undertaking its own tests, the FDA has no way of detecting such deception. Another serious weakness is the FDA's lack of authority over physicians. The misuse of prescription drugs accounts for numerous deaths and injuries that could be prevented by more careful control of the way in which drugs are prescribed. [18]

The Consumer Product Safety Commission, a much newer agency than the FDA, was created to handle all consumer safety problems not already being dealt with by other government organizations. (Outside the CPSC's realm are food and drugs, which are the responsibilities of the FDA, and automobiles and tires, which are handled by the National Highway Traffic Safety Administration.) The CPSC has the responsibility to promulgate regulations protecting the public from unsafe products and to enforce both those standards and others created directly by legislative mandate. But unlike the FDA, the CPSC has no power to prevent dangerous new products from reaching the market; in most cases, it can act only after injuries and deaths have already occurred.

The Environmental Protection Agency's original mandate was to deal with the air and water pollution, but in recent years many other tasks have been added to its list of responsibilities, including the authority to regulate solid wastes, pesticides, noise pollution, and toxic substances. The EPA was given some very specific congressional mandates, but the effectiveness of this approach is a matter of debate. On the positive side, the mandates have forced the EPA to make controversial decisions it might otherwise have avoided and to act more expeditiously than many other regulatory agencies. The mandates have also proven to be an effective bargaining chip in its attempts to win industry cooperation. On the negative side, the deadlines set by Congress may occasionally have forced the EPA to act too hastily. Specific legislative mandates reduce the EPA's flexibility and, in some cases, have precluded the use of the most effective means of dealing with a particular environmental problem. [19] They have also made the EPA more vulnerable to time-consuming legal challenges from both environmentalists and polluters. [20]

Another factor that sets the EPA apart from most other regulatory agencies is its political environment. In addition to a powerful lobby that attempts to obstruct its regulatory mission (a common problem for most such agencies), the EPA must reckon with powerful groups demanding that the agency carry out its statutory goals. This environmental lobby is well organized and well financed—attributes of which few other citizen groups can boast.

The Occupational Safety and Health Administration was set up "to assure so far as possible every working man and woman in the nation safe and healthful working conditions." Its specific duties are to create safety regulations for the workplace and to carry out periodic inspections to make sure the regulations are being followed. Although a reading of the Occupational Safety and Health Act of 1970 (the legislation that created OSHA) would lead one to assume that the primary issue facing the agency concerns technological feasibility of different pollution control techniques, the real issue has turned out to be cost. The agency's principal objective has often seemed to be to balance the safety of the workers against the cost of providing safe conditions. Not surprisingly, its decisions have been highly controversial, and few other agencies have been subject to so great a barrage of criticism.

THE ROLE OF THE STATES.   Even though the lion's share of the responsibility rests with the federal government, the states play a significant role in the effort to control organizational crime. In some cases the states conduct separate operations that run parallel to those of the federal agencies; in others, state and federal efforts are coordinated to achieve maximum efficiency. Some states are also paid by the federal government to perform specific enforcement duties. For example, the EPA has agreements with twenty-eight states to help enforce its regulations in exchange for a 50 percent federal subsidy.[21]

The states also have their own white collar crime legislation that often parallels the federal statutes. Most states have their own antitrust laws—fifteen of which actually preceded the Sherman Act.[22]   Every state except Alabama has enacted what are known as "little FTC" laws, which cover unfair, deceptive, or anticompetitive business practices. And although federal preemption remains a problem, many states have enacted environmental or consumer protection laws that significantly strengthen national legislation. Organizationally, most states have followed the advice of the National Association of Attorneys General and given their own attorney general the responsibility for enforcing those laws.

In comparison to the states, the federal government obviously has greater resources and broader jurisdiction—and oftentimes, tougher laws as well. Because the states lack both authority over interstate commerce and the financial means to handle complex large cases, they have tended to concentrate on smaller violations. However, the states have on occasion combined forces against major offenders. In one case involving General Motors, for example, forty-six states undertook a joint effort to stop the automaker's practice of putting the engines built by one division in cars bearing the name of another.[23] Another problem for the states is that they are more vulnerable to threats by corporate criminals to move to another jurisdiction if the law is too vigorously enforced. The states do enjoy some advantages over the federal government, however. State enforcement agencies usually stay in better touch with local conditions, and they can often move much faster than can the cumbersome federal bureaucracy.[24]

The Regulatory Process

RULE MAKING.   Unlike traditional law enforcement, many regulatory agencies not only enforce the rules but also create them. An appraisal of the effectiveness of such agencies thus becomes a difficult task, for we must evaluate not only how well they enforce the rules, but also the rules themselves. Even the strongest enforcement effort obviously will have little impact if the regulations themselves are inadequate. Although the particulars vary from agency to agency, the process of formal rule making is a complex and time-consuming job that usually involves numerous staff and research reports, public hearings, and administrative procedures. The objective of such lengthy procedural requirements is to make sure that rule makers explore all sides of the issue at hand and arrive at a carefully considered judgment. When powerful interest groups utilize obstructionist tactics, however, the final result of this process is often a bureaucratic paralysis that frustrates the goals the agency presumably was established to achieve.

Some of the worst problems of this kind have cropped up at the Occupational Safety and Health Administration. Despite the rapidly growing list of potentially hazardous substances, OSHA has promulgated fewer than two new exposure standards a year.[25] This failure of the rule-making process obviously has made it impossible for OSHA to ensure the level of occupational safety mandated by its enabling legislation.

The FDA has had similar difficulties. The Food Additives Amendment requires that "potentially unsafe substances" be tested before being used as food additives, and the DeLaney Amendment forbids the marketing of any substance shown to cause cancer in laboratory animals. However, the FDA has repeatedly dodged these requirements by putting potentially hazardous substances in its list of additives that are "Generally Recognized As Safe" (GRAS). For example, the artificial sweeteners known collectively as cyclamates were not removed from the GRAS list until fifteen years after they were found to cause cancer in animals,[26] and the makers of another artificial sweetener, saccharin, won a special legislative exemption shielding their product from the requirements of the law. Numerous other additives have also been placed on the GRAS list even though serious safety questions have been raised about them.[27]

The rule-making efforts of the federal regulatory agencies have not all been as dismal as the examples cited above might suggest. The EPA, equipped with a strict legislative mandate and prodded by an active environmental lobby, has done a somewhat better job, and even OSHA and the FDA have promulgated standards restricting some of the most obvious threats to health and safety. But the fact remains that in most cases the rules made by regulatory agencies have fallen far short of the legislative standards they were expected to meet.

INVESTIGATION AND CASE SELECTION.   Once the rules and the standards are in place, the next step is to uncover the violators. Compared to traditional street crime, the task of unmasking white collar criminals is a difficult one indeed. For one thing, the wealth and influence of many offenders enable them to do a much more effective job of concealing their crimes. And the crimes themselves often involve a complex web of economic interactions that require a great deal of investigative work to reconstruct. A classic example of this problem can be found in the antitrust case the FTC brought against the oil industry in the early 1970s. The so-called Exxon case consumed 12 to 14 percent of the agency's entire antitrust budget,[28] and yet after eight years of investigations and proceedings the case was dropped because of its "length and complexity."[29]

Another difficulty encountered by regulatory agencies is that the victims of organizational crimes often do not know they have been victimized or where to direct their complaints when they discover their problem. People who eat food with carcinogenic ingredients, buy short-weighted products, or breathe contaminated air seldom know with any degree of certainty that they have been the victims of a crime. Still, the regulatory agencies receive a large volume of complaints from businesses, special-interest groups, and the general public. The problem is that those complaints tend to be concentrated in a few narrow areas where the harm is most obvious, and many of the most serious types of white collar crimes fail to spur public response.

In order to uncover these hidden offenses, regulatory agencies must conduct their own investigations—a costly and time-consuming chore for these chronically underfunded organizations. In a few industries, such as meat packing, in which the law requires constant inspections, this problem has been resolved by requiring that each firm pay the cost of full-time inspectors. This system has obvious financial benefits for the government, but it is also conducive to corruption. A common problem is that inspectors often come to see the firms they work with day in and day out as their real employer and neglect the public interest (see chapter 3). Most often, however, inspectors are full-time employees of an enforcement division within a regulatory agency; accordingly, they examine many different firms and are less likely to identify with any single company. The problem here is that the enforcement agencies are grossly understaffed. In 1980, OSHA had only twenty-eight hundred inspectors to cover over 4 million workplaces, and the number has declined significantly since then. [30] As one commentator put it, "The typical establishment will see an OSHA inspector about as often as we see Halley's Comet." [31] OSHA naturally attempts to maximize its effectiveness by concentrating on the firms that are most likely to have safety problems. But even this kind of effort to maximize hopelessly inadequate resources can have serious drawbacks. In 1981 OSHA decided that if a review of a company's log of occupational injuries showed that its injury rates were below average, the firm would be exempt from a full "wall to wall" inspection. Many companies responded exactly as they should have been expected to—they falsified their records. An OSHA crackdown against such offenders in 1986 and 1987 resulted in charges against Union Carbide, Chrysler, Caterpillar Tractor, Ford, General Dynamics, Shell, and other major corporations. [32]

The enforcement of the Fair Packaging and Labeling Act of 1967 provides another example of the same problem. Although the act covers all the myriad packaged goods sold in the United States, only *two* people were assigned to enforce it. [33] The FDA's inspection program for insecticide contamination is given a much higher priority by the agency, and yet Ralph Nader's investigative team reported that less than 1 percent of food shipments were actually checked for pesticide contamination. [34]

Despite such meager investigatory resources, the regulatory agencies uncover or are made aware of many more violations than they can actually prosecute. Regulators are therefore faced with a dilemma: Do they go after the important, time-consuming cases and risk possible political reprisals from powerful corporate offenders, or do they pursue the less important cases that can be quickly resolved, thus producing the maximum number of convictions to impress congressional oversight committees? Even though it subverts the official goals of regulation, the latter approach has proven to have a powerful appeal to self-interested bureaucrats. A 1970 Ralph Nader report on the FDA made a convincing case that the agency was pursuing just this kind of policy. According to the report, the FDA mounted a strong enforcement effort against so-called quacks, such as the Church of Scientology and some health food advocates, but showed little interest in the criminal activities of the large food processors. [35]

Similarly, a Nader report on antitrust enforcement charged that the FTC and the Antitrust Division of the Justice Department concentrated on small-time antitrust offenders and avoided challenging multinationals that pose the real threat to competitive markets. [36] This criticism was strengthened by an American Bar Association report that reached similar conclusions. [37] Such attacks, combined with the reformist spirit stimulated by the Watergate scandals, led to a revitalization of the FTC, which was given new leadership, new programs, and new enforcement powers. [38] The commission then began to pursue more "structural" cases that directly attacked the oligopolistic control of major markets. In the early 1980's, however, the FTC came under intense pressure from the Reagan administration and its supporters in Congress to back off from its aggressive enforcement policy, and none of the structural cases were resolved in a manner that can be expected to provide real benefits for the consumer. [39]

At best, the FTC's enforcement efforts have been meager, but in the 1980s there has been a virtual administrative paralysis. From 1977 to 1981, the FTC filed an average of eight antitrust complaints a year and agreed to about twenty-five more consent orders in which violators promise to stop their criminal activities. In the 1981–1983 period, in contrast, the number of complaints fell to only three per year, and consent orders declined to eleven per year—a drop of over 50 percent. The hopeless inadequacy of the FTC's efforts is even more obvious in the area of mergers. Of the 2,533 corporate mergers reported in 1983, the FTC investigated only thirty, and it sought a total of just six injunctions. [40]

REGULATORY ENFORCEMENT.   Once a regulatory agency has decided to pursue a particular case, three courses of action are open to it. One option is an *administrative action,* which usually involves an official agency hearing before an administrative judge. Representatives of the agency and the accused present their cases, and the judge makes a ruling that is subject to an appeal to a regular court. The second option is to take *civil action* by bringing suit against the offender in federal court. Finally, the agency can recommend that a *criminal action* be taken by the Justice Department or, in some cases, by a federal district prosecutor. Here, as noted above, the final decision rests with the Justice Department or the individual prosecutor.

Oftentimes an agency will initiate enforcement action by issuing a warning that further action will be taken unless illegal behavior stops. The agency may also enter into negotiations with the offenders, often in conjunction with other civil or administrative actions against them. Successful negotiations typically end with corporate offenders agreeing to administrative or court decrees banning future violations but not admitting their guilt (an important factor in any future civil actions). Corporations that violate consent decrees are then subject to civil action by the agency or a contempt citation from the court. Unfortunately, regulatory agencies seldom devote sufficient resources to police the consent decrees, and most violations go undetected. In cases involving faulty products, regulatory agencies commonly seek a recall order under which the corporation will agree to repair the defective merchandise. Administrative agencies sometimes issue unilateral orders requiring either that remedial action be taken to correct past harm or that the offender cease and desist from further illegal actions. An agency may also seek a federal court injunction, which is backed by the power of contempt. Finally, many kinds of violations may result in fines handed down through administrative, civil, or criminal channels, and prison sentences may be given to individual offenders by the criminal court.

Given all these possible responses, the choice of sanctions obviously plays an important role in determining whether or not justice is ultimately done. And unlike the decision whether or not to pursue a case, the choice of sanction is a matter of public record that is easily available to criminologists. Far and away the most comprehensive study of this important issue was conducted by a research team headed by Marshall Clinard at the University of Wisconsin. Working with one of the few large government grants ever given for research into white collar crime, the Wisconsin study concluded that corporations were not subjected to the "full force of the law."[41] The data amassed by the researchers showed the legal response to be so feeble that, in the vast majority of cases, the government was satisfied when the offending corporation merely agreed to stop breaking the law. Few actual punishments were handed out, even for serious corporate crimes. The study examined 1,529 sanctions given to 477 of the largest manufacturing firms in the United States in 1975 and 1976. Almost one-half (44.2 percent) of the "sanctions" involved only warnings, one-fourth (24.6 percent) were "future effect orders" (usually requiring the corporation to stop its illegal activities), and 7 percent were retroactive orders requiring the offenders to take some action to rectify the harm their crimes had caused. Thus, over three-fourths (75.8 percent) of the cases involved no actual penalties. Of the remainder, 21 percent were civil fines, and only 2.4 percent involved criminal fines. [42]

As low as they are, these figures still overestimate the percentage of firms that actually are punished. Although in theory fines do constitute a type of punitive action, corporate fines seldom even equaled the amount of profit made from the illegal actions. Four-fifths of the fines in the Clinard study were for less than $5,000. [43] Moreover, the study found that the size of the fines did not increase with the size of the offender. The median fine against the smallest firms in the study was $750; for the medium-sized firms, $1,650; and for the largest firms, $1,000. A $1,000 fine against a multibillion dollar corporation cannot be said to constitute a punishment in any realistic sense of the word. Some observers have argued that the stigma of a criminal conviction is in itself enough punishment, but this argument has rarely been applied to the lower-class men and women who commit most street crimes, and it holds even less weight when the offender is a large, impersonal organization.

Of course, regulatory agencies can ask the Justice Department to prosecute individual executives, but such requests are relatively rare and seldom result in actual prison sentences. The Wisconsin study found only fifty-six cases over two years in which executives had been convicted of criminal offenses because of their involvement in organizational crimes, and only sixteen of them served any time in jail.[44] A study of the antitrust cases brought from 1890 to 1969 reached similar conclusions. Despite explicit criminal sanctions in the Sherman Act, the study found less than half (44.7 percent) of the 1,551 cases brought during that period involved criminal charges. And even after a criminal conviction, the chance of imprisonment was less than one in twenty (4.9 percent).[45]

A survey of the legal actions against major corporations conducted by *The New York Times* provided evidence of this double standard of justice at work in another government agency. According to the *Times*, of the 3,360 criminal tax cases brought by the Internal Revenue Service in a two-year period, only nine involved major corporations. Moreover, the IRS devoted only 2.5 percent of its investigation time to examination of the tax returns of major corporations.[46]

THE CRIMINAL JUSTICE SYSTEM

Although the regulatory bureaucracy now shoulders most of the responsibility for dealing with organizational crimes, the traditional criminal justice system still plays an important role in the effort to control white collar crime. Police and prosecutors at the local, state, and national level bear the primary responsibility for taking action against most occupational criminals, and the criminal justice system takes over responsibility for corporate crimes when the regulatory agencies come to the Justice Department to request criminal prosecution.

Local police, who are the front line in the struggle against street crime, have much less impact on the problem of the white collar crime.

For one thing, most local police departments are too small and ill-prepared to deal with the complexities of the white collar crime. U.S. counties, for example, operate more than seventeen thousand different police departments, but over 60 percent of those departments have fewer than ten full-time employees.[47] Even large urban departments with much greater resources devote surprisingly little effort to white collar crime. Most urban police departments don't have even a fraud unit, and those that do exist tend to be underfunded and understaffed. For example, even after the District of Columbia added a Consumer Fraud unit to its Check Fraud section, its activities still accounted for less than 1 percent of all arrests in the District of Columbia.[48] Finally, apart from small size and inadequate resources, local police play so small a role in the battle against white collar crime because most major white collar crimes transcend local and even state boundaries, thus leaving primary jurisdiction to the federal government.

A number of federal enforcement agencies exercise jurisdiction over specific kinds of white collar crime (e.g., the Postal Inspection Service and the Customs Service), but the Federal Bureau of Investigation is the only national agency with broad police powers in this area. The FBI has traditionally focused its attention on those "street" crimes that come under its jurisdiction, such as bank robbery and auto theft. After the Watergate scandals and the appointment of William Webster as director, the FBI directed new attention to white collar crime. In 1980, the FBI allocated 22 percent of its force of special agents and 15 percent of its budget to the investigation of white collar crime.[49] More recently, however, the FBI seems to be backing away from that policy and returning to its more traditional concerns.

The FBI's primary focus in the area of white collar crime has always been on occupational offenses and the role organized criminals play in corrupting legitimate businesses. It would be helpful if the FBI would give more attention to major corporate offenders, but at least it has directed its efforts toward one of the most harmful occupational crimes—the corruption of government, labor, and business officials.

At the local level, most of the investigory work for white collar cases is handled by the prosecutor's office, not the police. But once again the evidence shows that the justice system is ill-prepared to meet the challenge. To cite a few examples, in the middle 1970, Akron, Ohio, had only one attorney and six investigators on its consumer fraud unit, Baltimore had three attorneys and six investigators, Boston had only one attorney, Buffalo had two attorneys, and Dallas had none. There was not a single full-time attorney assigned to white collar crime cases in the entire state of Texas.[50] Los Angeles, with the largest white collar crime unit in the country, still had only twenty attorneys and nine auditors.[51] The response to a short-term grant given by the Law Enforcement Assistance Administration in improve the enforcement effort in this area showed how great the need actually is. The grant money allowed local district attorneys to hire a total of 149 investigators to work in special white collar crime units, and they were inundated by 157,000 inquiries and 43,000 complaints in a single year.[52]

This dismal picture is much the same at the state level. A 1975 survey of state attorneys general offices found that only thirty of the fifty states had consumer fraud units and that those units had to make do with meager resources.[53] As a result, the volume of state cases against white collar criminals has been very light, and most of the charges have involved minor occupational offenders. Even joint efforts, in which the resources of many local prosecutors were pooled, have proven inadequate to deal with major cases. A joint antitrust investigation of the oil industry mounted by the district attorneys of Los Angeles, Brooklyn, Houston and Denver was such a case. As one Los Angeles official put it, the oil companies "were too big. . . we had to throw in the towel."[54] Bequai summarized the situation well when he wrote, "The prosecutorial machinery at the local, county, city and state levels is too small, ill equipped and politicized to act decisively against major white collar crime cases."[55]

A survey of California district attorneys conducted by Benson, Maakestad, Cullen, and Geis in 1987 lends support to these conclusions.[56] For one thing, they found that, although all the district attorneys' offices considered the prosecution of corporate crimes to be within their jurisdiction, they actually spent very little of their effort on this kind of work. Sixty-two percent of the offices that responded prosecuted fewer than ten corporate financial offenses a year, and 81 percent prosecuted fewer than ten environmental offenses a year. The most common limit on the prosecution of such cases mentioned by the district attorneys was the lack of sufficient staff and resources. As the authors of this study put it: "It is unlikely that district attorneys forgo prosecuting many serious street crimes because the effort is judged to be too costly or time consuming. In corporate cases, administrative costs seem to take precedence over the traditional symbolic function of the law to maintain moral boundaries."[57] The district attorneys surveyed were naturally reluctant to admit that they allowed political considerations to influence their prosecutorial judgment, but a surprising 25 percent did admit that they allowed local economic considerations to influence their decisions.

The inadequacy of the enforcement effort is reflected in the tiny proportion of the criminal justice system's resources devoted to white collar crime. But the true picture is even worse than it seems, for compared to street crimes, white collar crimes are much more difficult to uncover and prosecute, and effective enforcement therefore requires that far greater resources be devoted to each white collar offense. The criminal justice system, like the regulatory agencies, receives few complaints from the victims of white collar crime and must therefore pursue "a proactive" enforcement strategy. In other words, enforcement agencies cannot simply react to the complaints they receive but must actively seek to uncover offenses. Obviously, this is another difficult and time-consuming task.[58]

Kenneth Mann's excellent study of attorneys who defend white collar cases shows how differently the criminal justice system operates when dealing with white collar and street criminals.[59] In theory, the law provides a strict system of procedural safeguards that protects the defendant from the vast power of the state. The defendant is supposed to be represented by an independent attorney, who battles the prosecutor under the impartial eye of the presiding judge. But a large body of evidence shows that for most street criminals, the justice system actually functions more like an assembly line than a legal obstacle course. Since most of their clients have only limited means, defense attorneys have a strong interest in processing each case quickly and going to the next client. The criminal attorney is also under strong pressure from the prosecutor and the court to move legal proceedings along as rapidly as the overburdened system will permit. The vast majority of cases against street criminals never come to trial but are settled by a negotiated agreement in a process that has come to be known as "plea bargaining."

The operation of "white collar justice" presents a startling contrast. As Mann shows, the white collar criminal's attorney is intensely adversarial from the moment he or she first makes contact with the enforcement agency. While the common criminal's counsel is likely to be extremely limited in the amount of time and money that can be devoted to the client, good white collar attorneys prepare their cases with painstaking attention to detail, often employing the services of private investigators and hired professionals. One of the most important differences is that the white collar criminal's attorney gets involved much earlier. While street criminals seldom get an attorney until they are arrested and charged with a crime, white collar criminals know about the allegations and hire an attorney at a much earlier stage in the legal process. Thus, attorneys for white collar criminals spend most of their effort in preventing charges from being filed. Indeed, the white collar attorneys interviewed by Mann considered a case to be a failure if their client was charged with an offense, even if he or she was later found not guilty. The key to this process is what Mann calls *informa-*

tion management—the attempt to conceal incriminating evidence from the prosecutor. Not only do the attorneys try to place legal obstacles in the way of the government's efforts to gather evidence, but they also tell their clients exactly which kinds of evidence still in their control would be most damaging if revealed. Although it is illegal for attorneys to advise their clients to destroy such evidence, the intelligent and well-educated defendants typical of white collar cases hardly need such explicit instructions.

The impact of the criminal courts on the problem of white collar crime is limited by the action or inaction of the enforcement agencies. But the courts do play an important symbolic role in deciding what kind of punishment will be meted out in the few cases that end in convictions. One frequent criticism of the courts concerns the common use of the *nolo contendere* ("no contest") plea. The legal consequence of this plea are similar to those of a guilty plea, except that the defendants do not officially admit their guilt, and their plea therefore cannot be used as evidence in subsequent civil cases. While this may appear to be a minor difference, it is actually of great importance, because the criminal penalties handed down for white collar crimes are usually much less severe than the civil liabilities such crimes create. The *nolo* plea deprives the victims of white collar criminals of the benefit of using the government's investigatory efforts in their civil cases. Moreover, the fact that the defendants are never forced to admit their guilt tends to reduce the stigma otherwise attached to a criminal conviction. Many observers have also charged that judges often make a subtle distinction between a defendant who enters a plea of *nolo contendere* and one who pleads guilty, and that the former will receive a lighter sentence. [60]

Despite these problems, prosecutors have continued to accept *nolo contendere* pleas as part of plea bargaining arrangements designed to avoid time-consuming trials. Between 1890 and 1970, 73 percent of all anti-trust convictions came on *nolo* pleas. And even when the prosecutors object to those pleas, they are usually overruled by the judge. Between 1960 and 1970, the courts accepted pleas of *nolo contendere*[61] in 95 percent of the antitrust cases in which the prosecutor objected; between 1970 and 1976, the government objected to forty-seven *nolo contendere* pleas in antitrust cases, only to be overruled in all but one case. [62]

Sentencing is another area in which judges have often been accused of favoritism toward offenders of high socioeconomic status. [63] However, criminological research has produced mixed results on this point. A 1982 study by Wheeler, Weisburd, and Bode found that higher-status defendants charged with white collar crimes were more likely to receive jail sentences than were lower-status defendants.[64] The researchers suggested three possible explanations for this unexpected finding: (1) because most cases against very high-status defendants were never prosecuted, the few cases that were prosecuted were especially compelling; (2) the research was conducted shortly after the Watergate scandals, when judges may have been especially sensitive to the problem of elite criminality; (3) judges felt that 'crimes of greed" by the wealthy were more blameworthy than "crimes of need" by others.

More recent studies provide supporting evidence for the first two explanations. Hagan and Palloni's examination of the records of one federal district court showed that judges were tougher on white collar offenders in 1975 (after the Watergate scandal) than they were in 1973 (before Watergate).[65] One of the best studies to date is Hagan and Parker's analysis of securities violations that occurred during a seventeen-year period in Ontario, Canada.[66] By measuring social class by structural position rather than occupational prestige and including data on the prosecutor's decision about which charge to bring, they discovered significant differences in sentencing among different groups of high status offenders. The employers (those who own a business and hold authority over others) at the top of the structural hierarchy received significantly more lenient sentences than other white collar offenders. This was primarily because employers were charged with less serious offenses than other criminals who had committed crimes of equal severity. In contrast, managers (those who hold authority over others but do not own the business), received more severe punishment than others. This study also found that the prosecution of securities offenders increased significantly in the post-Watergate era and concluded that managers had been the primary scapegoats for the public's demand to crack down on white collar criminals. Finally, Susan Shapiro's study of the Securities and Exchange Commission found that lower-status offenders were less likely to have legal action brought against them for minor offenses but more likely to be criminally prosecuted for serious offenses. And although high-status defendants charged with criminal offenses had, on the average, committed more serious crimes, they were no more likely to receive a jail sentence than lower-status offenders.[67]

Whatever the attributes of the individual offenders, it is clear that those charged with white collar crimes receive much more lenient sentences than other offenders. A study of the sentencing practices of federal courts in 1971 showed that, whereas 71 percent of the defendants convicted of auto theft received jail sentences with an average term of thirty-six months, only 22 percent of those convicted of embezzlement were sent to jail, and those sentences averaged only twenty months.

Further, only 16 percent of those convicted of securities fraud were sentenced to prison, and those sentences averaged less than a year.[68] Similar disparities were uncovered in a study of the sentences handed out in the Southern District of New York from May to October of 1972 and in all federal courts during the fiscal year ending June 30, 1972. In both cases, those charged with white collar crimes were less likely to go to prison and more likely to receive short sentences if they were imprisoned. For example, an individual convicted of a white collar crime in southern New York stood a 36 percent chance of going to prison, whereas defendants convicted of comparable nonviolent "street" crimes went to prison 56 percent of the time.[69] A federal study of felony cases resolved in 1983 found higher rates of incarceration for all groups than the earlier studies, but white collar offenders were still the least likely to go to jail. A person arrested for a white collar offense in the eight states and one territory included in the study had a 60 percent chance of being sentenced to prison, while 65 percent of other property offenders and 67 percent of the violent offenders were given jail sentences. Moreover, white collar offenders were given significantly shorter sentences. Only 18 percent of the white collar offenders were sentenced to more than one year in prison, while 26 pecent of the property offenders and 39 percent of the violent offenders were given more than a year.[70] One problem with this study is that it defined all persons committing forgery/counterfeiting, fraud, or embezzlement as white collar offenders regardless of whether their crime was committed in the course of a legitimate occupation or as part of a criminal career. It appears that the majority of these offenders would not have been considered white collar criminals by most definitions. Had the definition been more restrictive, one suspects the study would have found an even greater disparity between white collar and "street" offenders.

The Wisconsin study found that only 4 percent of the sanctions handed out for corporate crimes involved criminal cases against individual executives. Of the convicted executives, 62.5 percent received probation, 21.4 percent had their sentences suspended, and only about one in four (28.6 percent) received short jail sentences. The average sentence was just over a month (37.1 days). Moreover, excluding a single case in which two 6-month sentences were handed out, the remaining fourteen defendants received sentences averaging only nine days.[71] As mentioned earlier, McCormick's study found that less than one in twenty of those convicted on criminal antitrust charges was sent to jail.[72] Most ironic of all, however, was the fact that the first eleven men sent to prison under the Sherman Act were all *labor*, not business, leaders, even though the clear intent of Congress was to restrain big business, not the unions. [73] The first business executive was not sent to prison under the Sherman Act until 1961— seventy-one years after its enactment.

Not only do white collar criminals in general receive more lenient sentences than are given to those charged with other offenses, but organizational criminals receive lighter sentences than occupational criminals. Wheeler, Weisburd, and Bode's study of the sentencing of white collar offenders found that, whereas antitrust violators were seldom sent to prison, convictions for tax evasion or violation of SEC laws (both usually occupational crimes) were much more likely to result in incarceration. [74] Further evidence for this conclusion can be found at the prosecutorial level. The Wisconsin study found that only fifty-six persons were convicted of corporate crimes in 1975 and 1976. During those same two years, however, the federal government alone convicted 357 persons for just one occupational crime—government corruption. And if all the other prosecutions of occupational crimes were added in, the total obviously would be vastly greater. [75]

An important precedent for the criminal prosecution of white collar criminals was set in June 1985, when three officials of Film Recovery System Inc. were found guilty of murder for the death of an employee. The victim was Stefan Golab, a Polish immigrant who worked around vats of sodium cyanide (used to remove silver from old film) in a poorly ventilated factory that violated numerous health and safety codes. He repeatedly complained about headaches, nausea, and vomiting, and requested to be transferred to another part of the plant. While working near a chemical vat on June 10, 1983, Golab began shaking and foaming at the mouth, and after being helped outside, he collapsed and died. The executives, who had heard numerous complaints from sick workers and knew of the safety violations, were found guilty of murder and sentenced to twenty-five years in prison and a $10,000 fine. [76]

CIVIL SUITS

Civil suits brought by the victims of street crimes are never considered to be part of the criminal justice process. But with the repeated failures of the government's enforcement efforts, such suits have become a significant factor in the control of white collar crime. Indeed, the framers of some regulatory legislation (e.g., the Sherman Act) actually saw private suits as an important technique of enforcement.

The lawsuits generated by white collar crimes usually are aimed at one of two targets—the violators or the regulatory agencies. The specific legal mandates given the newer regulatory agencies have led to the numerous suits claiming that they have not lived up to or have exceeded the requirements of the law. Business interests, for instance, have mounted legal challenges to every OSHA health regulation except its 1972 asbestos standards,[77] and the EPA has repeatedly been sued by environmentalists seeking tougher action and by polluters seeking the opposite end. The net effect of this litigation is difficult to gauge, for both the public and the corporations have won important legal victories. However, to the extent that all the legal maneuvering tends to slow the enforcement process, it works to the benefit of the offenders.

Businesses also bring suits against each other, of course, but most involve disputes over contracts and other everyday business relations, not white collar crimes. However, allegations of fraud, false representation, or antitrust violations are not uncommon. The impact of this type of litigation is difficult to measure, but the fear of suits from individual victims certainly imposes a significant restraint on illegal business practices.

The legislators of the 1890s apparently had such confidence that the treble-damage act of the Sherman Act would stimulate effective civil actions that no funds were voted to enforce the act until well into the twentieth century. But the task of challenging the anticompetitive practices of the major corporations has proven far too formidable for individual citizens, and the same has held true for most other corporate crimes. In the 1960s, however, the courts began to allow the victims of antitrust violations to band together in a class action suit against a corporate offender. Although decisions by the more conservative Supreme Court of the 1980s have placed new procedural obstacles in the way of class action suits, they still greatly increase the victims' chances of legal success. Indeed, several law firms now specialize in this difficult kind of litigation in the hopes of sharing in the multimillion dollar judgments sometimes handed down.[78]

Another important legal development of recent years is the product liability suit. Current laws differ substantially from state to state, but individuals who have been injured by a defective product, or their survivors, now clearly have the right to sue the manufacturer for damages. A manufacturer's liability can run into hundreds of millions of dollars when a widely used product, such as the Ford Pinto, the Firestone 500, or the Dalkon Shield is involved. There has also been an increasing number of suits over the injuries caused by unsafe working conditions. Although occupational injuries and some occupational diseases are covered by workman's compensation statutes that restrict private suits, the courts have held that a worker can still bring legal action if he or she can show that the company deliberately concealed information about occupational health hazards. These rulings have, for example, opened the door for suits from the tens of thousands of asbestos workers who are dying from exposure to this deadly substance.

Despite the huge size of the judgments, civil court actions seldom result in the compensation for all the victims of a dangerous product. For one thing, individual plaintiffs are usually outgunned by highly paid corporate lawyers, whose legal maneuvers have often succeeded in obstructing whole groups of suits. For example, the makers of DES, the cancer-causing pregnancy drug, were able to win rulings that required the victims to prove which one of the 267 manufacturers of DES made the particular drug they took—a ruling that blocked most of the victims' suits. Years of legal battles were required before the courts finally formulated a new, and still not universally accepted, legal doctrine apportioning the liability among all the manufacturers based on their share of the market.[79] But while the battle dragged on, needy victims were denied compensation or were forced to accept out-of-court settlements for only a fraction of the money they deserved. A different sort of legal tactic was recently tried by the Manville Corporation, the world's largest manufacturer of asbestos. Despite healthy profits and billions of dollars in assets, the company declared bankruptcy in August 1982, claiming that it could not pay all the potential judgments that might be made against it in the asbestos cases. After five years of litigation, the issue still has not been resolved. But it now appears that Manville's maneuver will not succeed in denying compensation to its victims, and they may actually end up owning a controlling interest in the company.[80] Long-established restrictions on the right to sue the government have enabled it to be far more successful in avoiding responsibility for the victims of its mistakes. In 1987, for example, a federal appeals court ruled that the 250,000 workers exposed to nuclear radiation in atmospheric tests in the 1950s could not sue the government, even though the safety precautions were grossly inadequate, and the government failed to issue a warning on the potential dangers of radiation until 1977.[81]

But even without such legal maneuvers, civil action still takes years, and many victims are forced to agree to quick settlements to meet their medical expenses. Moreover, victims are often unaware of their right to sue or cannot for one reason or another prove their case. Thus, it is quite common for a few victims to receive huge settlements and for many others to get nothing. Nevertheless, the threat of civil litigation is one of the strongest controls on corporate crime. The staggering potential liability involved in the decision to market an unsafe product is a powerful deterrent to the kind of corporate irresponsibility exhibited by Firestone, Richardson-Merrell, and Manville, and some corporations have apparently begun to realize that a better program of product-testing and quicker recalls of faulty merchandise are much cheaper in the long run than public denials and legal maneuvering.

THE EFFECTIVENESS OF ENFORCEMENT

Enforcement is just as critical to the outcome of the struggle for reform as the legislative battles discussed in chapter 4. Because policies and priorities change from year to year and decade to decade, it is difficult to make a flat statement about whether the elitist or the pluralist account of the enforcement process is more accurate. On the whole, however, the data we have examined come far closer to confirming the elitists' contention, that the criminal activities of the elite receive only token punishment, than the pluralists' notion that pressure from other organized interests forces the justice system to treat the crimes of the privileged and the crimes of the powerless equally. But the overall picture is a complex one and a more detailed analysis is necessary.

The principal goal of professional self-regulation is clearly to protect the interests of the professionals, not the public, and it need not concern us further. The operations of the various regulatory agencies are of much more importance. Some agencies appear to do a reasonably good job of meeting their statutory obligations, whereas others seem to fail completely. Much of this difference can be explained by the different configurations of pressure groups with which the agencies must contend. The success of the SEC can be attributed to the fact that, unlike most of the other agencies examined here, it enjoys strong business support. Of course, particular rulings and procedures are subject to attacks from business interests, but on the whole the business elite recognizes the need for the kind of control and regulation that the SEC provides.

The EPA has certainly not had such support, but in addition to the business lobby, the EPA must also confront a well-organized environmental lobby, a fact that goes a long way toward explaining why the EPA has been more successful than most other regulatory agencies. But although the EPA has made an undeniable contribution to the public health and environmental protection, it has still fallen far short of the urgent task it was created to accomplish. Every year more wilderness is destroyed, more animals are driven to extinction, more pollutants are dumped into the environment, and the cancer rate continues to go up. (The National Cancer Institute estimates that up to 90 percent of all cancers are environmentally induced. [82])

Many of the Reagan administration's appointees to the EPA have been openly hostile to the environmentalists, and some have even expressed philosophical objections to the very kind of government regulation they are called upon to carry out. In addition, there have been sharp cuts in the agency's already meager resources. Between 1980 and 1983, more than one-quarter of the EPA's staff positions were eliminated. Even under these highly adverse conditions, however, the environmentalists have been able to mount a counteroffensive. Leaks of embarrassing information about the manipulation of EPA programs for political purposes and "sweetheart deals" with polluting industries led to a public scandal and the resignation of more than a dozen top EPA officials, including the chief administrator. Moreover, strong pressure from a public concerned about the dangers of pollution won a change in budgeting priorities and made the EPA the only regulatory agency to grow from 1983 to 1986. [83]

Although its mission is much the same as that of the EPA, OSHA has been markedly less successful. OSHA has not promulgated an adequate number of regulations to control exposure to dangerous substances, and its enforcement efforts have been grossly inadequate. To make matters worse, the current antiregulatory assault on OSHA has gone almost unchallenged. Soon after their appointment, Secretary of Labor Raymond Donovan and OSHA Director Thorne Auchter revoked or withdrew numerous rules instituted by the previous administration, including requirements for the labeling of hazardous chemicals, "walk around" pay for workers accompanying OSHA inspectors, and exposure standards for cotton dust (the cause of "brown lung" disease). In the first year of the Reagan administration, the number of OSHA inspectors declined by 18 percent, the number of serious citations dropped by 37 percent, and the total amount of the fines levied dropped by 65 percent. [84] Although OSHA appears to be improving its performance under Auchter's successor, John A. Pendergrass, its staff and its budget are still being whittled away. A 1987 study by the Safe Workplace Institute found that, while 128,000 workers had been killed on the job since the creation of OSHA in 1970, not a single person was sent to prison as a result of federal action in any of those cases. [85]

A major factor in the failure of OSHA has been the lack of a grass-roots movement for occupational safety comparable to the environmental movement. Although rank-and-file union members have often expressed concern about this issue, organized labor has never accorded top priority to health and safety issues. Conversely, business interests have mounted strong opposition to any effort to improve working conditions that involves significant financial costs.

The FDA presents a mixed picture, because it carries out two different tasks in regulating food and drugs. The FDA's reliance on the safety tests conducted by the drug manufacturers clearly weakens its regulatory effectiveness, but on the whole, the FDA exercises tighter supervision of the U.S. drug market than similar agencies do in other nations. The international community has grown so dependent on the

FDA's supervision of the multinational pharmaceutical companies that the Australian expert on corporate crime, John Braithwaite, concluded that: "The FDA is no longer only the guardian of the health of Americans; it is the guardian of the health of the world."[86] In contrast, the FDA's supervision of the quality and healthfulness of the food sold in our supermarkets has not met the statutory mandates. The agency has failed to issue timely bans on carcinogenic substances, it does not adequately inspect the food supply, and it has promulgated lax labeling standards for potentially hazardous substances.

The reasons for this difference once again lie outside the regulatory bureaucracy in the wider political arena. The consumer movement, which has been concerned with the quality of both food and drugs, is much weaker than the environmental movement and, generally speaking, no match for powerful agribusiness and pharmaceutical interests. But there are crucial differences between the kinds of harmful effects produced by food and by drugs. The effects of dangerous pharmaceuticals are much more immediate and dramatic, and they win far greater media attention. Even without a strong popular movement, the publicity surrounding DES mothers and Thalidomide babies brought massive outpourings of public indignation that no regulatory agency could ignore. Unsafe food additives or poorly labeled products, on the other hand, produce few banner headlines.

Of all the regulatory agencies, those dealing with antitrust enforcement have one of the most unbroken records of failure. Time after time, these agencies have won insignificant cases and ignored or lost the important ones. The crux of the problem lies in the lack of public involvement. Although many people recognize the problems created by the concentrated power of big business, there is little understanding of the complex legal technicalities involved in antitrust action. The antimonopoly movement of the late nineteenth and early twentieth centuries, which helped create the antitrust laws, has long since died away. Moreover, antitrust violations do not have the drama that attracts media attention, as the more violent white collar crimes sometimes do.

A review of the enforcement efforts of the criminal justice system presents another complex picture. The available evidence on prosecution and sentencing shows that occupational criminals receive more lenient treatment than common street criminals. Enforcement agencies devote few resources to occupational crimes, and even after cases are filed and defendants convicted, white collar offenders still receive lighter punishment. Convicted occupational offenders, however, do run a risk of imprisonment: one chance in four for a securities thief and one in five for a postal or bank embezzler.[87] Organizational criminals, in contrast, run little risk of significant punishment of any kind. The data examined in this chapter have shown that only a tiny fraction of the actions brought against deviant corporations end up in criminal court, and that even when convictions ensue, the "punishment" is often so insignificant as to be meaningless. For example, the criminal action against the Richardson-Merrell employees who had falsified the MER/29 test data (see chapter 2) was one of the toughest actions ever taken against crime in the pharmaceutical industry, yet the offenders received only six-month suspended sentences. But the failure to prosecute is a far greater problem than judicial lenience. There are no statistics on how many serious organizational crimes are never prosecuted, but we do know that criminal prosecution is so rare that even the most notorious and most deadly cases, such as those involving the Firestone 500, the Dalkon Shield, or the asbestos manufacturers, seldom result in criminal charges (see chapter 2).

The tort system was never intended to serve as a tool of criminal justice, but it has proven to be a much more effective restraint on organizational crime than has the criminal justice system. To confirm this conclusion, one need only compare the miniscule criminal fines given corporate offenders with the huge civil judgments passed against them. Although many factors contribute to this difference, the most important appears to be the nature of the plaintiffs involved. Even though private litigants lack the financial resources of the government enforcement agencies, they usually are firmly convinced of the justice of their claims and resolutely pursue the maximum possible recompense. In contrast, the government's enforcement efforts have repeatedly been compromised by political pressure. In the absence of unusually strong counterpressure to offset the political influence of the offenders, the government simply fails to do the job. It would, nonetheless, be a mistake to ignore the serious limitations the civil actions by victims have as a restraint on white collar crime. As we have already noted, such tactics represent a viable alternative for only a small percentage of those harmed by white collar offenses.

ANTITRUST AND THE PETROLEUM INDUSTRY

The broad strokes of our institutional analysis and the cumulative statistics generated by the enforcement process have painted a clear picture of the failure of enforcement. But to understand the reasons underlying this failure, we must also explore the way the justice system has dealt with specific individual cases and the political and economic pressures they generate. Many examples were discussed in chapters 2 and 3, and we will not reexamine them here, but a more explicit treatment of the enforcement process is necessary for the purposes at hand. Accordingly, this section will explore a case that holds extraordinary importance for the U.S. economy—antitrust enforcement in the petroleum industry.

Among the numerous antitrust cases brought against big oil, four stand out as serious efforts to break up the concentration of economic and political power in the petroleum industry: the early cases brought by the individual states under their own antitrust laws; the first federal case, instituted by President Theodore Roosevelt; the oil cartel case that began shortly after the end of World War II; and finally, the "Exxon case" instituted by the FTC in the early 1970s.

The first legal challenge to the Standard Oil monopoly came in 1889, when Ohio Attorney General David Watson happened across the text of the Standard Oil Trust Agreement in the appendix of a legal treatise. He was surprised to find that it violated the law in at least two important ways: first, it created a monopoly and was thus void and unenforceable at common law; and second, it forced Standard of Ohio to violate its state charter by operating under the direction of an out-of-state company. Watson took Standard to court, and after an extended legal battle, Standard of Ohio was ordered to withdraw from the trust. Although it appeared to commentators at the time that a death blow ad been dealt to the oil trust's operations in Ohio, the use of delaying tactics combined with the court's failure to set a time limit for withdrawal from the trust allowed Standard to continue its operations without substantive change. In response to the original court order, Standard merely consolidated some of its companies and reshuffled its trust certificates. When Watson's trust-busting successor, Frank Monnett, discovered the deception, he launched a new case against Standard. The company's response was to reorganize itself as a holding company instead of a trust and to continue its delaying tactics. Finally, Monnett was replaced by an orthodox Republican who refused to continue the case, and the oil trust carried on with business as usual. [88]

Texas's assault on the Standard monopoly was carried out in a very different environment from the one in conservative, industrial Ohio. Not only was Texas a predominantly agricultural state, but its farmers were undergoing a long period of hard times that they blamed on the machinations of the Eastern industrialists. Moreover, Texas had an exceptionally strong antitrust tradition bolstered by a constitution that contained explicit antitrust provisions.

The Texas representative of the Standard Trust, the Waters-Pierce Company, was renowned for the ruthless tactics it used against its competitors. The first moves against Waters-Pierce were made in 1894 by Governor Jim Hogg, who had already received wide acclaim for his contribution to the framing of a new state antitrust act. Although the early stages of the enforcement effort were marked by considerable ineptness on the part of the state prosecutors, they eventually won confirmation of the constitutionality of the Texas antitrust statutes in February 1897, a court ruling ordering the revocation of Waters-Pierce's Texas business license in the same year, and a final victory before the U.S. Supreme Court in March 1900.

After six years of legal battles, it appeared that the trust busters had finally won. Henry Clay Pierce, however, continued to fight to retain control of the lucrative Texas market, and he began cultivating friends in high places. His most notable recruit was a rising young congressman, Joseph Bailey, who received over $12,000 in interest-free loans from Pierce and his associates. Bailey was influential in persuading new Texas Governor Tom Smith to grant Waters-Pierce a series of extensions. And when the court order could no longer be evaded, Pierce reorganized his company, signed an affidavit certifying that Waters-Pierce (the company hadn't even changed its name) was no longer part of the Standard Trust, and won a new business license. The company continued to do business as usual in Texas until 1906, when Henry Pierce exploded a bombshell at a Missouri antitrust hearing by admitting that Standard Oil still controlled his company. The Texas attorney general filed suit ten days later and won a conviction in June 1907 that resulted in a $1,623,000 fine and another revocation of Waters-Pierce's business permit. Although the attorney general later ran for governor on the strength of the successful antitrust case, his success was more appearance than reality. Standard continued to operate in Texas through its other subsidiaries until 1909, when a court ordered its holdings in the state be placed in receivership and sold. However, it later was discovered that the purchaser, John Sealy, was himself a trustee of Standard Oil. The Waters-Pierce Company, meanwhile, was sold to a St. Louis businessman, Sam Fordyce, who turned out to be an old friend of Henry Pierce's; together they promptly formed the Pierce-Fordyce Oil Association. Thus, although the Texas trust busters had certainly made things difficult for the Standard Trust they ultimately failed to expel the monopoly from their state.

Altogether, ten states and the Oklahoma Territory filed antitrust suits against the Standard Oil combination between 1890 and 1911, but all the suits ultimately failed. In Tennessee, the combination dodged a 1909 court order banning Kentucky Standard from operating in that state simply by transferring its business to newly created Louisiana Standard; in 1910 Louisiana Standard sold 85.5 percent of the kerosene and 81.7 percent of the naptha and gasoline sold in Tennessee. In Kansas, a petition charging Standard of New Jersey with antitrust violations led the state supreme court to appoint a commissioner to investigate the oil industry. The investigators took an incredible five years to come to the obvious conclusion that Standard did in fact monopolize the oil business in that state, and even after the report was completed, the attorney general still took no action except to negotiate a meaningless consent decree. In 1908 the Missouri Supreme Court found three Standard companies guilty of antitrust violations. Each company was fined $150,000, the charter of one company based in that state (the infamous Waters-Pierce) was canceled, and the business licenses of the other two were revoked. But intense economic and political pressure from Standard, including the suspension of the construction of a large Missouri oil refinery, forced the court to back down and reverse its decision.

On the federal level, the passage of the Sherman Act was met with administrative apathy. No federal charges were brought against Standard, the nation's most notorious monopoly, for seventeen years. Although the act directed federal district attorneys "under the direction of the Attorney General" to institute antitrust proceedings against violators, in practice the decision to move against such politically powerful criminals was made by the President, not by the Attorney General. Despite widespread public hostility toward the Standard combination and its obvious antitrust violations, Presidents Cleveland and McKinley still took no action against the company. This was hardly surprising, for not only were they both conservatives strongly allied with big business, but both received substantial campaign contributions from Standard.[90]

The Justice Department finally brought suit against Standard for Sherman Act violations in May 1907. Although the case was marked by the same kind of legal maneuvering used in the state cases, the government won its final victory in May 1911, when the Supreme Court unanimously upheld a lower-court decision against Standard and ordered the combination dissolved into its constituent companies.

This decision was widely hailed by the press as a devastating blow to the oil trust. Passing largely unnoticed was the fact that the technique of dissolution ordered by the court, on the recommendation of the prosecutor, virtually assured Standard's continued domination of the petroleum market. One problem with the dissolution order was structural. The different companies in the Standard combination had always specialized in the production, distribution, or marketing aspects of the business, and because the court broke up Standard along the lines of existing companies, the newly created independent firms were virtually required to maintain close business relationships. A more serious problem resulted from the technique of stock distribution adopted by the court. Instead of assigning stockholders blocks of stock in one of the new companies, the court gave each stockholder a prorated share in each of the new companies. Because just eight stockholders held over 50 percent of the shares in Standard, this plan ensured that the same small group would own a controlling interest in each of the newly independent companies. Thus, even the dissolution of Standard Oil failed to break its hold on the domestic petroleum market. The question of why the prosecutors proposed such an obviously inadequate remedy cannot be answered with the available evidence, but one expert concluded that "they were more interested in winning a politically important case than restoring competition to the industry."[91]

Ironically, some measure of competition was soon to return to the petroleum industry—not as a result of the federal court's actions, but because of the discovery of large new oil fields in Texas and Oklahoma, which helped spawn the Texaco and Gulf petroleum companies. Moreover, Standard's foreign competitors, principally Shell and British Petroleum were also growing stronger. In fact, the outbreak of competition eventually became so worrisome to the heads of the largest companies that they met in Achnacarry Castle in Scotland to hammer out the illegal cartel agreement discussed in chapter 3.[92]

Details of the operation of the oil cartel were first uncovered by the Federal Trade Commission in the early 1950s. Although efforts were made to suppress the ensuing report on the grounds of national security, the news leaked out, and parts of the report were soon published. These disclosures came on the heels of evidence that some of the big oil companies had cooperated with the Germans during World War II. Together, these revelations generated a wave of public hostility that led President Harry Truman to order the Justice Department to begin a grand jury investigation of the oil cartel.[93]   Shortly before leaving office, Truman decided to drop the criminal charges pending against the petroleum companies but ordered that the civil action be "vigorously prosecuted." When President Eisenhower came to office, the oil cartel case, once seen as one of the most important cases ever brought by the Antitrust Division of the Justice Department, was slowly whittled away into insignificance. In the words of the director of the investigation, "The pressures were continuous from month to month, sometimes week to week, to downgrade the importance of the prosecution of the cartel case."[94] The final outcome of fifteen years of litigation was what Blair termed a "virtually meaningless consent decree."[95]

The last major challenge to the oligopolistic power of big oil was a suit launched by the FTC shortly after the first "oil crisis" in 1973—another time of strong public resentment against the petroleum industry. The suit charged Exxon and seven other major petroleum firms with collusive actions and sought to cut them up into separate production, pipe-line, refining, and marketing companies in order to break their control of oil from wellhead to gasoline pump. Like all matters of this nature, the so-called Exxon case was massive and complex, consuming 12 to 14 percent of the FTC's entire antitrust budget for much of the 1970s.[96] Despite this effort, the FTC was hopelessly outmatched, and little progress was made. The oil industry's legal team bogged down the government in endless maneuvers and finally swamped FTC investigators with massive requests for information and documents. With the coming of the Reagan administration, the political winds shifted against their effort and in September 1981 the FTC finally gave up. The FTC's staff report recommended dropping the Exxon case because of the obstructionist tactics of the oil companies and the glacial slowness of the suit. One staff attorney was quoted as saying that the case "could continue without a final judgment on the merits or implementation of remedial provisions until 15 or 20 years years after the filing of the complaint."[97]

The effort to prosecute antitrust violations in the petroleum industry has been a long and at times intense struggle with key victories on both sides, but it is clear that the interests of the petroleum companies ultimately prevailed. Despite all the government's efforts, the petroleum companies succeeded in minimizing competition and maintaining the control of a small cartel. It was not a one-sided battle. The antitrust movement did succeed in limiting some of the worst abuses of the oil companies both through direct court action and through the companies' fear of inciting more public demands for government action. But the fact remains that corporate interests ultimately defeated the antitrust laws.

WHY ENFORCEMENT FAILS

The evidence leaves little doubt about the failure of the criminal justice system to bring white collar criminals to justice. It now remains only to explain why enforcement fails. At a general level, we can say unequivocally that the enforcement effort against white collar crime has failed because the wealth and influence of the criminals have enabled them to avoid the full weight of the law. A growing body of evidence, however, allows us to go beyond such generalities and to specify some of the particular techniques that have been used to stymie the enforcement process.

Two Red Herrings

Our first order of business is to dispose of two widely held misconceptions that simply do not fit the facts. One is based on the belief that white collar crimes are nonviolent offenses that cause little real harm to the public. If one accepts that assumption, it follows that fewer enforcement resources should be spent on white collar crime than street crime. But the data reviewed in the first chapter of this book clearly show the fallacy of this argument. Not only do white collar crimes cost the public considerably more money than do all other types of crime combined, but many white collar crimes are very violent crimes indeed. The evidence indicates that white collar offenses kill and cripple more people than all the street crime put together.

A more widely accepted derivative of the first argument holds that whatever the actual harm caused by white collar crime, the public is less concerned about it than street crime and consequently puts less pressure on the enforcement agencies to do a thorough job.[98] But once again the evidence fails to support this contention. Although the public is unlikely to show interest in any individual crime unless the media publicizes it, three decades of opinion polls have shown a great deal of resentment about the crimes of those in positions of trust and responsibility. In a 1969 Harris poll, 68 percent of the people questioned felt that a businessman who illegally fixes prices was worse than a burglar, as opposed to only 28 percent who thought the burglar was worse.[99] A 1968 survey found that the public considers an embezzler to be a more serious offender than a burglar, prostitute, or looter, but not an armed robber or murderer.[100] In a 1972 sample, 120 Baltimore residents were asked to rate the seriousness of several different criminal acts. "Manufacturing and selling drugs known to be harmful to users" and "knowingly selling contaminated food which results in a death" were held to be more serious than such crimes as armed robbery or assault with a gun. A later replication of that study in a rural area of Illinois found even stronger resentment against white collar criminals. To the Illinois residents, the intentional sale of a contaminated drug that results in the death of a user was more serious than forcible rape or selling secrets to a foreign nation. A study published by the U.S. Department of Justice in 1984 with over sixty thousand respondents showed the same intense concern about white collar crime among the general public. A factory that polluted a city's water supply and kills twenty people was ranked seventh out of the 204 offenses studied. This research also made it clear that the more physical harm an offense causes, the more serious it is considered to be. A factory that killed one person with its waste was ranked thirteenth of the 204 offenses, a factory that made 20 people sick was ranked thirty-first, while a factory that was said only to pollute a city's water without mention of any injuries was ranked sixty-fourth.[102]

The evidence also shows the public favors tougher penalties for white collar offenders than are given out by the justice system. A study by Donald Newman asked 178 people to recommend the penalties for a number of actual violations of the Food, Drug and Cosmetic Act. Four out of the five respondents recommended harsher penalties than were given in the real case.[103]   Gibbons's sample of residents of the San Francisco area showed that 70 percent favored prison sentences for antitrust violators, and 43 percent agreed that incarceration was the appropriate penalty for advertisers who misrepresent their products.[104] In the Gibbons survey, 85 percent of the respondents favored prison sentences for embezzlers, as did 88 percent of the subjects in a national sample taken by other researchers at about the same time.[105] In a 1982 survey taken in Illinois, almost 90 percent of the respondents agreed with the statement, "White-collar criminals have gotten off too easily for too many years; they deserve to be sent to jail for their crimes just like everyone else." Less than 15 percent agreed with the statement, "Since white-collar criminals usually don't harm anyone, they shoudn't be punished as much as regular criminals."[106]

Hollow Laws

A cursory examination of the laws designed to control white collar crime reveals an imposing structure of rules and regulations. But a closer look uncovers numerous flaws, loopholes, and omissions that benefit elite interests, while the penalties provided by many laws are grossly inadequate to the tasks they are supposed to achieve. The courts have, on occasion, also helped to thwart the enforcement process. The Supreme Court's original ruling that the Sherman Act applied only to "unreasonable" restraints of trade, even though the legislation contained no such language, certainly made the federal regulators' job more difficult, as did the more recent decision requiring OSHA investigators to obtain a warrant before inspecting a workplace that an employer wished to conceal. Court rulings favorable to advertisers have allowed them to make false statements without legal penalty, so long as those statements remain sufficiently general. But by no means have all the rulings been one-sided, and court-imposed restrictions do not seem to have been as critical to the failure of justice as the inherent shortcomings in the laws themselves.

Complaints have often been voiced about the vague, general language in the enabling legislation for many regulatory agencies, but a case can be made both for and against this practice. On the one hand, the battle over the interpretation of ambiguously worded legislation inevitably ends up in court, where elite interests enjoy the advantages of vast financial resources and the best legal talent. On the other hand, it can also be argued that more specifically worded legislation cannot deal effectively with the subterfuges white collar criminals so often use to get around the letter of the law. As a congressional report on the original proposals to create the FTC put it, there is "no limit to human inventiveness in this field. If Congress were to adopt the method of definition, it would undertake an endless task."[107]

The penalties available to enforcement agencies vary enormously from crime to crime and agency to agency. In many cases even the maximum penalties are hopelessly inadequate. The largest fine OSHA can levy is only $10,000, and FDA fines are limited to $1,000 for the first offense and $10,000 for the later ones. The fines levied by other agencies can be much greater, however. The EPA can levy fines up to $50,000 a day for repeat offenders. Consumer Product Safety Commission fines can be as much as $500,000, and the maximum fine for antitrust violations is now $1 million.[108] To the average citizen, those figures may seem staggering, but to a giant multinational corporation such fines are still of little financial significance. For example, the offenders in the electrical equipment price-fixing case outlined in chapter 2 were fined a total of $1.8 million, yet they are estimated to have made almost $2 billion in profits from their crimes. Of course, various criminal penalties can also be imposed on corporate executives, but as we have seen, they are seldom used.

The Paucity of Resources

One of the most fundamental reasons for the failure of the enforcement effort is a chronic shortage of personnel and resources. Major agencies, such as the Securities and Exchange Commission, the National Highway Traffic Safety Commission, and the Consumer Product Safety Commission, have *total* enforcement budgets of less than $20 million.[109] Of the over one-half million police officers and tens of thousands of government prosecutors and enforcement officials in the United States, only a handful are assigned to deal with the nation's most serious crime problem. The combined manpower of the fraud sections of all the federal prosecutors' offices around the country is less than two hundred, yet they must handle the bulk of all federal prosecutions of occupational crimes. In the words of August Bequai, "They are asked to do a Herculean task, which is far beyond the resources and the power at their disposal."[110] At the Internal Revenue Service, only about sixty lawyers are assigned to criminal tax cases, and they have virtually ignored major corporate offenders.[111] The Consumer Product Safety Commission has the staggering responsibility of not only creating regulatory standards to ensure the safety of the millions of products sold in the American marketplace, but they must also enforce those standards. Yet its total staff in 1986, including administrators, rule makers, and

enforcement agents was 475 persons.[112] Moreover, these acute shortages of resources have been getting worse, not better. Between 1980
and 1983 the total staff of the federal agencies with responsibility for
antitrust enforcement and the protection of the health and safety of the
public declined by 19 percent;[113] and with the exception of the EPA,
which increased by 19 percent, the staff of these agencies, declined by
another 7 percent between 1983 and 1986.[114]

In addition to the severe shortage of personnel, the fact that government employees receive much lower pay than they would in the
corporate sector poses another serious problem. The lure of a higher-
paying job in private industry has led many government staffers to cultivate the favor of private interests at the expense of their legal duty.
Federal regulatory agencies also have a difficult time hiring top quality
professionals, especially lawyers and scientists. Quirk reported that the
FDA has had "trouble recruiting high-caliber scientific and medical personnel" and had to hire many practicing physicians with no expertise
in drug research because the agency cannot match the salaries specialists are paid in private industry."[115] Similar problems at the FTC and
the Antitrust Division of the Justice Department have led to extremely
rapid turnover in their legal staffs and the loss of much of their best
legal talent.[116] Thus, these agencies are forced to fight long legal battles
against some of the nation's best attorneys with a constantly changing
team of young, inexperienced lawyers.

The Personal Advantages of Privilege

The wealth and influence of white collar criminals give them a
significant advantage over the lower-class offenders typically involved
in street crime. It has often been claimed that the common cultural
background shared by judges and the white-collar defendants leads
to greater leniency than for street criminals.[117] In its most simplis-
tic form, this argument holds that judges give white collar criminals
lighter sentences because they have greater personal sympathy for
and understanding of a high-status defendant than for a low-status
defendant. The evidence suggesting that higher-status defendants
may receive slightly more severe punishments appears to contra-
dict this argument, however. But whether or not a high socioeconomic background leads to more lenient sentences in and of itself,
the cultural biases of the courts unquestionably manifest themselves
in the treatment of different types of offenses. As we have seen,
the courts show greater leniency toward defendants who commit
crimes as part of white collar occupations than those who commit
similar nonviolent street crimes. It appears that judges understand

the pressures that lead white collar workers to abuse their positions but have much less sympathy for those living in the alien world of the street criminal.

The white collar defendant's ability to hire a first-rate defense—the best lawyers, numerous appeals, and if necessary, private investigators and expert witnesses—is probably of even greater importance. Many former defendants have openly admitted that their ability to "hire the best" was the decisive factor in their cases. Conklin cited the example of a Texas oil millionaire who admitted that he was acquitted on wire-tapping charges because he spent over $1 million on his defense. A different businessman put it this way: "Law is like a cobweb; it's made for flies and smaller kinds of insects, so to speak, but lets the big bumblebees break through. When technicalities of the law stood in my way, I have always been able to brush them aside as easy as anything."[118]

The Advantages of Corporate Organization

In addition to the benefits of wealth and status, those involved in organizational crimes enjoy another special advantage: the law is written with a strong individualistic bias that makes it difficult to deal with such crimes. In order to convict someone of a criminal offense, the law normally requires not only that he or she be shown to have committed the criminal actions, but also that the person acted with criminal intent. For example, a corporate spokesman who falsely claims that a deadly product was safe has committed a criminal act only if he or she knows that statement to be false. But a press spokesman would be unlikely to be given such information, even if the dangers of the product were common knowledge in other parts of the organization. Somewhere in the corporate organization there would undoubtedly be an individual who both knew about the dangers of the product and ordered or permitted the release of the false statement—but that is an extremely difficult thing to prove. If corporations as a collectivity were put on trial, criminal intent (i.e., knowledge that the statement was fraudulent) would be much easier to prove. Although there are clear legal precedents for this kind of criminal case (see chapter 4), such charges are seldom filed.[119]

Another important advantage enjoyed by corporations is the legal confusion caused by their great size and complexity. Even when a low-er-level employee is caught red-handed in some illegal activity, it is extremely difficult to trace criminal responsibility back to the higher-ups who are ultimately responsible. Because of this diffusion of responsi-bility, it is often difficult to identify who actually ordered the illegal action. Many top corporate managers intentionally avoid any direct knowledge of their subordinates' illegal activities, even while indirectly encouraging them. Such was the case in the price-fixing conspiracy in the heavy electrical equipment industry. The conspirators testified that, although their bosses did not order them to fix prices, the company demanded a level of profitability than both parties knew could be achieved only by illegal means. A special committee of outside experts created by Merck & Company, America's largest pharmaceutical company, reached the same conclusion about middle level management's involvement in international bribery. The committee found that they did not report details of their bribery operations to top management "on the assumption that, despite the atmosphere of acceptance, top management did not want to be involved."[121]

The Techniques of Obstruction

Secrecy is the white collar criminal's first line of defense. Of course, street criminals also do their best to conceal their crimes, but white collar criminals enjoy some very significant advantages in this endeavor. Unlike the victims of most street crimes, the victims of white collar criminals are often unaware of the causes of their problems. Because the costs of such offenses as price fixing or environmental pollution are spread over a very large number of people, individual victims often suffer so small a loss that they have little to gain in pressing for legal action—if they even know they have been victimized. Organizational criminals enjoy the added protection of working behind the walls of secrecy the government and the corporations erect around themselves. Moreover the extreme complexity of corporate financial transactions makes it relatively easy to conceal illegal dealings from understaffed government agencies.

The corporations' influence on the media enables them to minimize public indignation about their crimes. Not only are most newspapers and radio and television stations owned by big corporations, but the media's almost complete dependence on advertising revenue for financial survival gives corporations with big advertising budgets added leverage. For example, the 1961 heavy electrical equipment price-fixing case was probably the most highly publicized antitrust case of its time, yet a study of major American newspapers found that only 16 percent featured the story on page one, and about a third made no reference to it at all. Even after the precedent-setting jail sentences were handed down, 45 percent of the newspapers still relegated the story to the back pages.[122] In an effort to see if this pattern of underreporting still prevailed in the 1970s, Evans and Lundman selected a very similar antitrust case—the folding carton price-fixing scandal of 1976—and replicated the earlier study. Even though the 1976 case involved about the same amount of damages over a similar period of time, it received even less coverage than its predecessor. They concluded that "newspapers protect corporate reputations by failing to provide frequent, prominent, and criminally oriented coverage of common corporate crimes such as price-fixing."[123]

One of the most effective techniques of obstruction is the delaying game. A corporation will often refuse to turn over data and documents requested by government regulatory agencies, thus forcing a time-consuming legal battle to obtain the information. And if a court orders that the information actually be divulged, the alternative tactic of "overcompliance" is commonly used. In one case, IBM responded to a private suit seeking information for an antitrust case with over 75 million pages of material.[124] Many government enforcement agencies also have been swamped in a similar sea of paper.

Our review of the antitrust actions against the petroleum industry showed how that industry used an almost endless chain of legal appeals and maneuvers to bog down understaffed government agencies. The efectiveness of this tactic can be seen in the FTC's capitulation in the Exxon case, when the government openly admitted that it gave up because the case would take too long to pursue. The delaying game has often been used against other regulatory actions as well. In an article on the Ford Pinto case, Mark Dowie gave the following description of the common techniques used to combat safety standards: "a) Make arguments in succession, so the feds can be working on disproving only one at a time; b) claim that the real problem is not X but Y; c) no matter how ridiculous each argument is, accompany it with thousands of pages of highly technical assertions that will take the government months or, preferably years to test."[125]

Some techniques of obstruction are far less subtle than the ones just discussed. Outright threats and coercion have also been used to prevent the law from being enforced. This is a particularly effective tactic against prosecutions carried on at the state or local level. Just as Standard Oil threatened economic reprisals against the state of Missouri if it continued its antitrust action, so numerous other businesses have threatened to leave states that pursue tough enforcement actions. Even the federal government is subject to this kind of blackmail, when multinationals threaten to move their operations to Third World countries that have virtually no environmental or safety legislation. Another kind of intimidation is brought to bear when corporations make dire predictions about the economic damage regulation would cause. But as Green and Waitzman pointed out, when new regulations have actually been put into effect, they seldom have produced the economic horrors predicted by the corporations.[126]

The Corruption of Enforcement

On top of chronic shortages of resources and all the difficulties inherent in proving charges against powerful white collar defendants, the enforcement process is further weakened by its own corruption. A host of political and economic rewards may await employees who are willing to neglect their legal responsibilities, whereas those who show too much zeal may risk arousing the displeasure of their superiors. To complicate matters further, bonds of friendship, sympathy, and common background may give the agents of enforcement reason to pause before demanding that the full weight of the law be brought to bear against white collar defendants.

Political pressure is the elite's most powerful weapon in its effort to corrupt the enforcement process. The history of enforcement in the petroleum industry, for example, shows that major antitrust cases are seldom initiated without prior political approval. The impetus for the major cases against big oil came from periodic waves of public indignation, not from routine administration actions on the part of the enforcement agencies. When public concern died down, the same cases that were launched with so much fanfare were either settled quietly through meaningless consent decrees or simply dropped. [127]

Even the regulatory agencies charged with the protection of the health and safety of the public operate in the same highly politicized environment. When Assistant Secretary of Labor George Guenter wrote a memo to his Nixon administration superiors promising to promulgate "no highly controversial standards (cotton dust, etc.)" so as to use "the great potential of OSHA as a sales point for fund raising and general support by employers," [128] he was unusual only in his willingness to put in writing the kinds of political considerations that often guide regulatory agencies. Moreover, Guenter's tactics were apparently highly effective, for after his nonenforcement pledge, textile interests contributed $1 million to Nixon's reelection effort. [129] Of course, other political forces may push for tougher enforcement—particularly after a highly publicized disaster or scandal—but the constant, day-to-day pressure usually runs in the other direction.

By no means is this pressure always transmitted via outside politicians. Business interests also operate effective lobbies aimed directly at the enforcement agencies. These lobbyists attempt to curry favor with regulators and enforcement officials, often offering free seminars, dinners, and travel. Corporations also can hold out the alluring possibility of high-paying jobs in private industry for those who "understand" business interests. The so-called revolving door between regulatory agencies and the industries they regulate fosters a probusiness attitude that makes it difficult to pursue tough enforcement actions. Paul Quirk defended the FDA's "revolving door" by arguing that "the incentives to adopt industry views are negligible as long as they [the staff] avoid identification as extremists."[130] This defense, however, seems more like an indictment, for what other law enforcement agents would fear being labeled as extremists by the criminals they are charged to prosecute? Moreover, corporations often go far beyond the use of ingratiating lobbyists and the lure of future employment. As the cases described in earlier chapters have shown, outright bribery is commonly directed at enforcement agents—especially field inspectors. Legal and illegal campaign contributions and direct payoffs also are used to gain allies among influential politicians who are in a position to obstruct the process of justice.

NOTES

1. Robert Derbyshire, as quoted in Boyce Rensberger, "Few Doctors Ever Report Colleagues' Incompetence," *The New York Times*, 29 January 1976, 1.

2. Martin Garbus and Joel Seligman, "Sanctions and Disbarment: They Sit in Judgment," in Ralph Nader and Mark Green, eds., *Verdicts on Lawyers* (New York: Thomas Crowell, 1976), 50.

3. Eliot Freidson, *The Profession of Medicine* (New York: Dodd & Mead, 1970), 71–72.

4. These figures were computed from data for the years 1971 to 1974 from the Federation of State Medical Boards. See Rensberger, "Few Report Incompetence," 24.

5. See, Robert C. Derbyshire, *Medical Licensure and Discipline in the United States* (Baltimore: Johns Hopkins Press, 1969); Sylvia Law and Stephen Polan, *Pain and Profit: The Politics of Malpractice* (New York: Harper & Row, 1978).

6. Garbus and Seligman, "Sanctions and Disbarment."

7. Jethro K. Lieberman, *Crisis at the Bar: Lawyers' Unethical Ethics and What to Do About It* (New York: W. W. Norton, 1978), 207.

8. Quoted in Garbus and Seligman, "Sanctions and Disbarment."

9. Quoted in Lieberman, *Crisis at the Bar*, 206.

10. Marshall B. Clinard and Peter C. Yeager, *Corporate Crime* (New York: The Free Press, 1980), 76; James Q. Wilson, *The Politics of Regulation* (New York: Basic Books, 1980), 357-394; Bruce Ackerman and William T. Hassler, *Clean Coal-Dirty Air* (New Haven: Yale University Press, 1981), 1-12.

11. See Clinard and Yeager, *Corporate Crime*, 76, n. 3.

12. Clean Air Amendments of 1970, 304, 42 USC (Supp II 1978).

13. John Lynxwiller, Neal Shover, and Donald Clelland, "The Organization of Inspector Discretion in a Regulatory Bureaucracy" *Social Problems* 30 (April 1983), 425-436.

14. See Arthur Belonzi, Arthur D'Antonio, and Gary Helfand, *The Weary Watchdogs: Governmental Regulations in the Political Process* (Garden City, N.Y.: Avery Publishing Group, 1977), 31-32.

15. See Mark J. Green, Beverly C. Moore, and Bruce Wasserstein, *The Closed Enterprise System: Ralph Nader's Study Group Report on Antitrust Enforcement* (New York: Grossman, 1972); Suzanne Weaver, " Antitrust Division of the Justice Department," in Wilson, *Politics of Regulation*, 123-151; Robert A. Katzman, "Federal Trade Commission," in Wilson, *Politics of Regulation*, 152-187.

16. Clinard and Yeager, *Corporate Crime*, 77.

17. See James S. Turner, *The Chemical Feast* (New York: Grossman, 1970), for a thorough, although now somewhat dated, examination of the FDA.

18. On this point see Paul J. Quirk, "Food and Drug Administration," in Wilson, *Politics of Regulation*, 191-235.

19. Ackerman and Hassler, *Clean Coal-Dirty Air* provides an insightful examination of the effects of the specific legislative mandates on the effort to minimize the air pollution from coal-generated electric power.

20. For example, see Alfred Marcus, "Environmental Protection Agency," in Wilson, *Politics of Regulation*, 267-305.

21. Marshall B. Clinard, Peter C. Yeager, Jeanne Brissetts, David Petrashek, and Elizabeth Harries, *Illegal Corporate Behavior* (Washington, D.C.: U.S. Government Printing Office, 1979), 41.

22. Clinard et al., *Illegal Corporate Behavior*, 45.

23. For a more detailed description of this case and its outcome, see Clinard et al., *Illegal Corporate Behavior*, 45.

24. For a good discussion of the role of the states in the enforcement efforts against corporate crime, see Clinard et al., *Illegal Corporate Behavior*, 41-53.

25. Calculated from the data in Katzmann, "Federal Trade Commission," 246.

26. Turner, *Chemical Feast*, 5-29.

27. See Turner, *Chemical Feast*, 138-168.

28. Katzmann, "Federal Trade Commission," 157.

29. Robert L. Jackson, "FTC Drops Huge Antitrust Suit Against Eight Oil Firms," *Los Angeles Times*, 17 September 1981, 1, 13.

30. Steven Kelman, "Occupational Safety and Health Administration," in Wilson, *Politics of Regulation*, 247; Jeanne Stellman and Susan Daum, *Work Is Dangerous to Your Health* (New York: Pantheon, 1973), 8.

31. Robert S. Smith, *The Occupational Safety and Health Act* (Washington, D.C.: American Enterprise Institute, 1976), 62.

32. Henry Weinstein, "OSHA Showing New Teeth In Its Watchdog Role" *Los Angeles Times*, 10 August 1987; Gordon Bock, "Blood, Sweat and Fears: Is Federal Crackdown Making Jobs Safer?" *Time* 28 September, 1987, 50–51.

33. Turner, *Chemical Feast*, 35.

34. Ibid., 145.

35. Ibid., 84–106.

36. Edward F. Cox, Robert C. Fellmeth, and John E. Schultz, *The Nader Report on the Federal Trade Commission* (New York: Baron, 1969); Green et al., *Closed Enterprise System*.

37. American Bar Association, *Report of the Commission to Study the Federal Trade Commission* (Chicago: American Bar Association, 1969).

38. See Clinard and Yeager, *Corporate Crime*, 77.

39. See, for example, Mark Green and Norman Waitzman, *Business War on the Law: An Analysis of the Benefits of Federal Health/Safety Enforcement*, rev. 2nd ed. (Washington, D.C.: Corporate Accountability Research Group, 1981.)

40. Michael A. Hiltzik, "Laws Against Monopolies Under Attack," *Los Angeles Times*, 19 March 1984, I: 1 *passim*.

41. Clinard and Yeager, *Corporate Crime*, 122.

42. Clinard et al., *Corporate Crime*, 291.

43. Clinard and Yeager, *Corporate Crime*, 125.

44. Ibid., 291.

45. Albert E. McCormick, "Rule Enforcement and Moral Indignation: Some Observations of the Effects of Criminal Antitrust Convictions upon Societal Reaction Processes," *Social Problems* 25 (October 1977): 30-39.

46. Philip Taubman, "U.S. Attack on Corporate Crime Yields Handful of Cases in 2 Years," *The New York Times*, 15 July 1979, 1.

47. S. Anthony McCann, *County-Wide Law Enforcement: A Report on Survey of Central Services in 97 Urban Countries* (Washington, D.C.: National Association of Counties, 1975), 1.

48. See August Bequai, *White-Collar Crime: A 20th Century Crisis* (Lexington, Mass: Lexington Books, 1978), 139.

49. William H. Webster, "An Examination of FBI Theory and Methodology Regarding White-Collar Crime Investigation and Prevention," *American Criminal Law Review* 17 (Winter 1980): 275-286.

50. Bequai, *White Collar Crime*, 148.

51. Bureau of National Affairs, "White-Collar Justice: A BNA Special Report on White-Collar Crime," *The United States Law Week* 44 (April 13, 1976): 3.

52. Economic Crime Project of the National District Attorneys Association, *Annual Report: Fighting the $40 Billion Rip-Off* (Chicago: National District Attorneys Association, 1976), 6, 7, 61.

53. National Association of Attorneys General, *Selected Statistics on the Office of Attorney General* (Raleigh, N.C.: National Association of Attorneys General, 1975), 1.

54. Bureau of National Affairs, "White-Collar Justice," 4.

55. Bequai, *White Collar Crime*, 149.

56. Michael L. Benson, William K. Maakestad, Francis T. Cullen, and Gilbert Geis, "District Attorneys and Corporate Crime: Surveying the Prosecutorial Gatekeepers," presented at the meetings of the American Society of Criminology, Montreal, Canada (November, 1987).

57. Ibid., 12.

58. See John Hagan, Ilene Nagel, and Celesta Albonetti, "The Social Organization of White-Collar Sanctions: A Study of Prosecution and Punishment in the Federal Courts" in Peter Wickman and Timothy Daily, eds., *White-Collar and Economic Crime* (Lexington, Mass.: Lexington Books, 1982), 259-275.

59. Kenneth Mann, *Defending White-Collar Crime: A Portrait of Attorneys at Work* (New Haven: Yale University Press, 1985).

60. See Clinard and Yeager, *Corporate Crime*, 285-286; Bureau of National Affairs, "White-Collar Justice," 12.

61. Green et al., *Closed Enterprise System*, 163.

62. Bureau of National Affairs, "White-Collar Justice," 12.

63. See, for example, William Chambliss and Robert Seidman, *Law, Order and Power*, 2nd ed. (Reading, Mass: Addison-Wesley, 1982).

64. Stanton Wheeler, David Weisburd, and Nancy Bode, "Sentencing the White-Collar Offender," *American Sociological Review* 47 (October 1982): 641-659.

65. John Hagen and Alberto Palloni, "'Club Fed' and the Sentencing of White-Collar Offenders," *Criminology* 24 (1986): 603-622.

66. John Hagen and Patrice Parker, "White-Collar Crime and Punishment: The Class Structure and the Legal Sanctioning of Securities Violations," *American Sociological Review* 50 (June 1985): 302-316.

67. Susan P. Shapiro, "The Road Not Taken: The Criminal Prosecution for White-Collar Offenders" *Law and Society Review* 19 (1985): 179-217.

68. Whitney North Seymour, Jr., *Why Justice Fails* (New York: William Morrow & Company, 1973), 45-46.

69. See Clinard and Yeager, *Corporate Crime* 296; Bureau of National Affairs, "White-Collar Justice," 11.

70. Donald A. Manson, *Tracking Offenders: White-Collar Crime*, Bureau of Justice Statistics: Special Report, (Washington, D.C.: Government Printing Office, November, 1986).

71. Clinard and Yeager, *Corporate Crime*, 291.

72. McCormick, "Rule Enforcement."

73. See Hans B. Thorelli, *The Federal Antitrust Policy: Origination of an American Tradition* (Baltimore: Johns Hopkins University Press, 1955).

74. Wheeler et al., "Sentencing the White-Collar Offender," 648, 651-652.

75. The Public Integrity Section, Criminal Division, U.S. Department of Justice, "Federal Prosecution of Corrupt Public Officials, 1970-1976," Department of Justice, February 8, 1977.

76. Barbara J. Hayler "Criminal Prosecution of Corporate Crime: The Illinois Corporate Murder Case," presented at the meetings of the Western Political Science Association, March 20-22, 1986, Eugene, Oregon; Larry Green, "3 Officials Guilty of Murder in Cyanide Death at Plant," *Los Angeles Times*, 15 June 1985, 1 & 5; Gibson and Mount, "3 Former Executives."

77. Kelman, "Occupational Safety and Health Administration," 259.

78. For a description of the origins of these legal developments see Barry Siegal, "Class-Action Suits Spur Misgivings," *Los Angeles Times*, 11 March 1982, 1 *passim*.

79. See Cynthia Laitman Orenberg, *DES: The Complete Story* (New York: St. Martin's Press, 1982), 137-157; Edwin Chen, "Liability Suits: Few Guidelines," *Los Angeles Times*, 6 October 1982, 1 *passim*.

80. See Henry Weinstein, "Manville Move Brings Asbestos Battle to Head in Courts and Congress," *Los Angeles Times*, 27 August 1982, IV: 1 *passim*; Martin Baron, "Asbestos Maker Files for Bankruptcy, Cites Lawsuits," *Los Angeles Times*, 27 August 1982, 1, 13.

81. Kim Murphy, "A-Test Victims Can't Sue U.S. Court Decides," *Los Angeles Times*, 23 June 1987, I: 1 & 19.

82. Richard T. Cooper and Paul E. Steiger, "Occupational Health Hazards—A National Crisis," *Los Angeles Times*, 17 June 1976, I: 1 *passim*.

83. *Budget of the United States Government Fiscal Year 1984* (Washington, D.C.: U.S. Government Printing Office, 1983); *Budget of the United States Government, Fiscal Year 1988* Washington D.C.: U.S. Government Printing Office, 1987.

84. *Budget of the United States Government, Fiscal Year 1983* (Washington, D.C.: U.S. Government Printing Office, 1979), Kitty Calavita, "The Demise of the Occupational Safety and Health Administration: A Case Study in Symbolic Action," *Social Problems*, April 1983: 437–448.

85. Weinstein, "OSHA Showing New Teeth."

86. John Braithwaite, *Corporate Crime in the Pharmaceutical Industry* (London: Routledge and Kegan Paul, 1984), 277.

87. Bureau of National Affairs, "White-Collar Justice," 11.

88. Bruce Bringhurst, *Antitrust and the Oil Monopoly: The Standard Oil Cases, 1890-1911* (Westport, Conn.: Greenwood Press, 1979), 10-39.

89. Ibid., 40-68; Carl Solberg, *Oil Power* (New York: Mason/Charter, 1976), 52-54.

90. Solberg, *Oil Power*, 49.

91. Brighurst, *Antitrust and the Oil Monopoly*, 147.

92. For details see John M. Blair, *The Control of Oil* (New York: Vintage Books, 1976), 54-71.

93. Burton I. Kaufman, *The Oil Cartel Case: A Documentary Study of Antitrust Activity in the Cold War Era* (Westport, Conn.: Greenwood Press, 1978), 19-37.

94. Quoted in Blair, *Control of Oil*, 75.

95. Blair, *Control of Oil* 75.

96. Katzmann, "Federal Trade Commission," 157.

97. Robert L. Jackson, "FTC Drops Huge Antitrust Suit Against Eight Oil Firms," *Los Angeles Times*, 17 September 1981, 1, 13.

98. Various versions of this argument can be found in George B. Vold, *Theoretical Criminology* (New York: Oxford University Press, 1958), 259; Ernest W. Burgess, "Comment," *American Journal of Sociology* 46 (July 1940): 38; Vilhelm Aubert, "White Collar Crime and Social Structure," *American Journal of Sociology* 58 (November 1952): 265; and Marshall B. Clinard and Richard Quinney, *Criminal Behavior System: A Typology* (New York: Holt Rinehart and Winston, 1967), 137.

99. "Changing Morality: The Two Americas: A Louis Harris Poll," *Time* 93 (June 6, 1969):26.

100. Joint Commission on Correctional Manpower and Training, *The Public Looks at Crime and Corrections* (Washington, D.C.: Joint Commission on Correctional Manpower and Training, 1968).

101. Peter H. Rossi, Emily Waite, Christine E. Bose, and Richard E. Berk, "The Seriousness of Crimes, Normative Structure and Individual Differences," *American Sociological Review* 39 (April 1974): 224-237; Francis T. Cullen, Bruce G. Link, and Craig W. Polanzi, "The Seriousness of Crime Revisited: Have Attitudes Toward White-Collar Crime Changed?" *Criminology* 20 (May 1982): 83-103.

102. Bureau of Justice Statistics, *Bulletin: The Severity of Crime* (Washington, D.C.: U.S. Government Printing Office, January 1984).

103. *Time*, "Changing Morality."

104. Don C. Gibbons, "Crime and Punishment: A Study of Social Attitudes," *Social Forces* 47 (June 1969): 395.

105. Joint Commission on Correctional Manpower Training, "The Public Looks."

106. Francis I. Cullen, Richard A. Mathers, Gregory A. Clark, and John B. Cullen, "Public Support For White-Collar Offenders: Blaming the Victim Revisited?" *Journal of Criminal Justice* 11 (1983): 481-493.

107. U.S. House of Representatives, Report 1142, 63rd Congress, 2nd session 19, 1914, as quoted in Clinard and Yeager, *Corporate Crime*, 76.

108. See Clinard and Yeager, *Corporate Crime* 30-333, for a list of the penalties that can be used against corporate criminals.

109. Clinard and Yeager, *Corporate Crime*, 96.

110. Bequai, *White Collar Crime*, 150.

111. Clinard and Yeager, *Corporate Crime*, 96.

112. *Federal Budget, 1983*, 1017.

113. Calculated from data given in the federal budgets for 1980 and 1983. The totals for the FDA, OSHA, CPSC, EPA, NHTSC, FTC, and the Antitrust Division of the Justice Department are 25,818 allocated positions for 1980 and 20,864 for 1983.

114. The exact allocations of positions for the Antitrust Division of the Justice Department for 1986 were not given in the budget; however, their budget declined from $44,245,000 in 1983 to $42,531,000 in 1986. The figures for the FDA, OSHA, CPSC, NHTSC, and FTC are: 1983-11,695 full-time positions; 1986—10,838 full-time positions.

115. Quirk, "Food and Drug Adminstration," 207.

116. See Katzmann, "Federal Trade Commission," 175.

117. For example, John E. Conklin, *Illegal But Not Criminal: Business Crime in America* (New York: Spectrum Books, 1977), 112-113.

118. Quoted in Frank Pearce, "Crime, Corporations, and the American Social Order," in Ian Taylor and Laurie Taylor, eds., *Politics and Deviance: Papers from the National Deviancy Conference*, Baltimore: Penguin Books, 1973), 22.

119. For an interesting treatment of this subject, see Christopher Stone, *Where the Law Ends: The Social Control of Corporate Behavior* (New York: Harper & Row, 1975).

120. Gilbert Geis, "The Heavy Electrical Equipment Antitrust Cases of 1961," in Gilbert Geis and Robert F. Meier, eds., *White Collar Crime: Offenses in Business, Politics and the Professions*, rev. ed. (New York: The Free Press, 1977), pp. 117-32.

121. Quoted in John Braithwaite, *Corporate Crime in the Pharmaceutical Industry* (London: Routledge and Kegan Paul, 1984), 19; Clinard & Yeager, *Corporate Crime*, 279–280.

122. "Notes and Comment: Corporate Crime," *Yale Law Journal* 71 (December 1961): 288-289.

123. Sandra S. Evans and Richard J. Lundman, "Newspaper Coverage of Corporate Price-Fixing: A Replication," *Criminology* 21 (November 1983): 529-541.

124. Lewis Beman, "IBM's Travails in Lilliput," *Fortune* (November 1973): 158.

125. Mark Dowie, "Pinto Madness," in Jerome Skolnick and Elliot Currie, eds., *Crisis in American Institutions*, 4th ed. (Boston: Little Brown, 1979), 33-34.

126. Green and Waitzman, *Business War on the Law*.

127. On this point see Bringhurst, *Antitrust and the Oil Monopoly*.

128. Green and Waitzman, *Business War on the Law*, 99.

129. Ibid., 108.

130. Quirk, "Food and Drug Administration," 213.

6

The Causes

In all the social sciences, no notion is more elusive than the concept of causality. Although its meaning seems clear enough in everyday conversation, the task of constructing a precise, scientific explanation of the cause of even the simplest human behavior is maddeningly complex. As the researcher painstakingly isolates and quantifies the factors that are presumed to have caused the behavior, new theories continually pop up to offer rival explanations. The interaction between the numerous variables and the procedures of measurement and investigation render the interpretation of even the most straightforward data ambiguous and uncertain. Thus, more than a little hubris is involved in any attempt to lay out a unified theory of the causes of as diverse a group of phenomena as those housed under the rubric of white collar crime. It is not a hopeless endeavor, however, as long as one is willing to accept the inherently probabilistic and tentative nature of any conclusions. Although the white collar crimes are diverse, there are, as we have seen, many underlying commonalities. There is also a growing body of research and analysis on the etiology of these crimes that can guide our efforts.

The aim of this chapter is to bring this research together into a unified theoretical structure that can make sense out of the complex phenomenon of white collar crime. Our final product will, however, bear little resemblance to the neat, monocausal explanations for which many scientists long. The theory of white collar crime more closely resembles a tapestry in which numerous causal strands are woven together into an integrated, if as yet incomplete, whole.

No effort will be made to review the entire body of research on the etiology of white collar crime. It contains too many divergent perspectives and approaches, and its quality is too uneven. Individual studies are included only if they make a material contribution to the analysis or have special historical significance.

Most theories of the origins of white collar crime focus on either the social-psychological forces that motivate individuals to violate the law or on the structural forces that account for the prevalence and distribution of those offenses. The objective of our analysis is not only to explore these two dimensions of white collar crime but to bring them together in a single theoretical structure.

The theory presented here is based on the notion that all criminal behavior requires two basic elements—motivation and opportunity— that must coincide before a crime can occur. At first it may appear that this analysis reflects a strict division between the social-psychological causes (motivation) and the structural causes (opportunity) of white collar crime, but that is not the case. An opportunity must ultimately reach down and become psychologically available to individual actors, or it will remain merely a theoretical possibility. And conversely, the roots of individual motivation can be found in the structure of industrial society.

Because of the complexity of the problem of motivation, we will break down our analysis of this topic into two parts. The first explores the formulation of the original motivation for white collar crime. But a mere attraction to the rewards of criminal behavior is not enough, for society erects strong ethical barriers to restrain it. The second part, therefore, deals with the ways in which white collar criminals, or the organizations in which they work, neutralize those controls. Finally, we will conclude this chapter with an analysis of the creation and distribution of the opportunities for white collar crime.

FORMULATING THE MOTIVATION

Understanding human motivation is no easy task, and we will begin, paradoxically enough, with a theoretical dead end. From there we will move on to a discussion of the ways in which individuals construct the personal realities that guide their behavior and explore the structural roots of those systems of meaning.

The Personality Factor

The public tends to see criminals as a breed apart from "normal" men and women. The deviants among us are commonly branded as insane, inadequate, immoral, impulsive, egocentric, or with any one of a hundred other epithets. In seeing the deviant as a wholly different kind of person from ourselves, we bolster our self-esteem and help repress the fear that under the right circumstances we, too, might violate the same taboos. But this system of facile psychological determinism collapses when applied to white collar criminals. The embezzling accountant or the corporate functionary serving in an employer's illegal schemes conforms too closely to the middle-class ideals of American culture to be so easily dismissed.

Sutherland repeatedly used the belief in the psychological normality of the white collar criminal as an argument against psychological explanations of any crimes: "The criminal behavior of businessmen cannot be explained by. . .feeblemindedness or emotional instability. We have no reason to think that General Motors has an inferiority complex or that Aluminum Company of America has a frustration-aggression complex or that U.S. Steel has an oedipus complex. . . .The assumption that an offender must have some such pathological distortion of the intellect or the emotions seems to be absurd, and if it is absurd regarding the crimes of businessmen, it is equally absurd regarding the crimes of persons in the lower classes."[1] Whether or not Sutherland's conclusions concerning the causes of street crimes are accurate, it is generally agreed that personal pathology plays no significant role in the genesis of white collar crime. In fact, this conclusion has been so widely accepted that only a few empirical studies of this issue have actually been done, but they all do support the notion that the white collar criminals are indeed psychologically normal.[2]

The fact that most white collar offenders are free from major psychiatric disorders does not prove, however, that their personality structures played no part in the genesis of their crimes. Recognizing this problem, Sutherland tried to show that the rates of corporate crime were unrelated to the personality of corporate employees, and he argued that individual personality was therefore not an important etiological factor in white collar crime. To support his case, Sutherland pointed out that a corporation may violate the law in some parts of its operations but not in others, whereas the entire operation is under the direction of the same individuals. He also emphasized the fact that many corporations continue long-term patterns of criminal activities despite complete changes in personnel.[3] The problem with this line of argument is that, even if it can be shown that variations in the personalities of corporate employees have little effect upon the rates of corporate crime, that does not prove that personality is not an important factor in an individual's decision whether or not to become involved in illegal corporate activities, or that personality has no influence upon the rates of other types of white collar crime, such as embezzlement. Sutherland did not even prove his claim that personality variations play no part in the genesis of corporate crime, for it is possible that corporate managers intentionally select individuals with a particular type of personality orientation for advancement. In other words, the mere fact that top management has changed does not prove that the personality characteristics of top management have also changed. But despite these objections, the empirical evidence still supports Sutherland's rejection of the notion that white collar crime is caused by the personal failings of individual executives.

The handful of studies that have attempted to analyze the personality or background experience of white collar offenders has reached rather divergent conclusions, but some traits do recur in sufficient numbers to be worthy of mention. All four studies examined here agreed on one point: white collar offenders are psychologically "normal," if by that term we mean that they are free from the symptoms of major psychiatric disorder (hallucinations, delusions, neurotic compulsions, etc.). In addition, two studies agreed that white collar criminals were "egocentric," and two characterized white collar offenders as "reckless." In his study of war crimes such as spying and sabotage, Selling concluded that such offenders were egocentric and antisocial. However, Selling's conclusions, formed from interviews with convicted offenders he encountered in the course of his psychiatric practice, are in many places so obviously prejudiced and ill-conceived as to cast grave doubt about the validity of his entire study. [4] Bromberg's methodology was similar to Selling's in that he examined criminals he happened to encounter in his work (at Bellevue Psychiatric Hospital), but despite the obvious flaws in his sampling technique, the moderate tone of his writings at least gives us hope of greater objectivity. Bromberg cited the case of a successful banker, convicted of various illegal financial manipulations, as typical of many white collar criminals. He, Bromberg wrote, "impressed the examiners as a realistic, though relatively uncompromising, individual, independent rather than stubborn, yet unaware of his rather strong tendency toward recklessness. On a deeper level, one could sense in him a certain rigidity of character expressed openly in stubbornness, independence, and lack of compromise. Egocentricity and an unconscious feeling of omnipotence shown through [his] character structure." [5]

In an interview with a sample of thirty white collar offenders from Leyhill Prison in Great Britain, John Spencer also found a high degree of recklessness among his subjects. He described the outstanding feature of these offenders' personalities as "their ambition, their drive, their desire to mix with people of higher social position than their own, and to give their children an expensive private education, and their willingness to take financial risks in the process." Spencer went on to characterize their behavior as "reckless and ambitious." [6] However, he was more careful to qualify his conclusions than was Bromberg, noting that "it would be a mistake to see the adventurous and ruthless gambler as typical of the white-collar criminal. Such men did not account for more than one-third of the sample."[7] Spencer found that just as many of his subjects were "muddlers and incompetent men" without firm principles who simply drifted into criminal behavior.

Blum's study of industrial spies was the only one to use a control group of nondeviant subjects, but the methodological advantages of this procedure were outweighed by the extremely small sample used—only three industrial spies and six controls. Like other psychologically oriented researchers, Blum found the white collar offenders he studied (and, for that matter, the control group as well) to be "remarkably free from instability or disabling psychopathology."[8] Blum focused his investigation on the life histories of his subjects. The main difference Blum discovered between the two groups was that the offenders reported a far greater number of troubling "life experiences," especially during childhood. The average was only three such experiences for the controls and eleven for the offenders.[9]

Taken as a group, these studies provide scant evidence for the proposition that white collar criminals have significant psychological differences from other white collar workers. The empirical evidence on this point is so weak, however, that it would be unwise to disregard the personality factor completely, pending the arrival of more conclusive data. One can easily imagine how personality differences could lead one executive to embrace criminal activities and another, similarly placed executive to reject them. It seems likely, however, that a particular personality orientation will facilitate criminal activities in one occupational situation and discourage them in another, so that no single set of characteristics is conducive to crime in all situations. For example, nonconformists might well be more likely to become involved in an occupational crime directed against an employer but less likely to go along with an organizational crime the employer demanded. A strict conformist could be expected to show the opposite tendencies. Nevertheless, it still seems likely that the reckless, egocentric personality described in some of this research will be associated with criminal activities in more situations than will most other personality types.

The overall impact of personality on the problem of white collar crime still seems slight for at least two important reasons. First, because the culture of industrial capitalism tends to encourage values, attitudes, and personality structures conducive to white collar crime, there are always a large number of people with the needed characteristics. Moreover, the operation of the corporate system and the competitive struggles of small business give such individuals a far greater chance of reaching key decision-making positions. As Willem Bonger put it back in 1905, "As always it is the environment that is the cause of the crimes taking place; it is the individual differences which explain in part *who* is the one to commit them."[10]   A second reason personality is of limited value in explaining white collar crime is because the structural demands in many occupational positions virtually force their occupants to violate the law, regardless of their psychological characteristics. For example, when Armstrong asked business students to play the role of board members of a pharmaceutical company and presented them with a problem faced by an actual company—a very profitable drug was found to be dangerous to the public—79 percent of the students made the same decision as the real company's management. They not only refused to withdraw the drug from the market, but they undertook legal and political maneuvers to prevent the government from banning it.[11]

The Culture of Competition

Whether or not the personality of the offender is considered important, conventional wisdom offers an even more popular explanation of the motivation for white collar crime. White collar criminals break the law, according to this view, because it is the easiest way for them to make a lot of money. Robert Lane, for example, found that the business and government officials he studied saw the desire for financial gain as the principal cause of white collar crime: "Most businessmen and most responsible government officers, at least from the sample interviewed, believe that businessmen run afoul of the law for economic reasons— they may want to 'make a fast buck.' "[12] Those familiar with criminological theory will recognize these views as an unknowing restatement of the principles of the classical criminology propounded in the late eighteenth and early nineteenth centuries by Beccaria and Bentham.[13] According to that school of criminology, people violate the law because they believe it will bring them more pleasure and less pain than the other courses of action available to them.

The longevity of this kind of explanation is not hard to understand. Although it may not provide a very convincing account of the reasons a woman would murder her husband in a fit of rage, it is persuasive when applied to rational, calculating crimes. But Lane's formulation is too narrow, for although the desire to get rich quick is certainly a motivating factor in many white collar crimes, other kinds of financial motivations are often equally important. Many white collar offenders are driven, for example, by the fear that they will lose what they already have. Several studies show, for example, that illegal activities are more common in firms that are doing poorly than in firms that are making big profits.[14] Of course, the desire to make more money and the desire to protect what one already has are two closely related aspects of the same phenomenon, which may be termed financial self-interest. But the numerous case studies we have examined make it clear that financial self-interest, even in its most general sense, is only part of a larger motivational complex that is deeply engrained in white collar workers. Along with the desire for great wealth goes the desire to prove oneself by "winning" the competitive struggles that play such a prominent role in our economic system. And this desire to be "a winner" provides another powerful motivation for white collar crime.

One illustration of the need to win without a concomitant financial motivation can be found in the Soap Box Derby. Although no great financial rewards are involved, the Derby creates fierce competition among the entrants. The rules of the Derby require that the young contestants build their own cars, but the desire to win is so strong that many use illegal outside help, and some racers have been built by professionals at a cost of as much as $20,000. The conventional wisdom among the contestants has been that forbidden modifications to the cars are necessary to win in the final heats. In addition to prohibited modifications to chassis and wheels, one winner was found to have installed a magnet in the nose of his racer, so that its attraction to the swinging starting gate would give him a quicker start.[15] Clearly, these contestants and their supporters were driven by a consuming desire to be winners in the competitive struggles of American life.

Interestingly, Bromberg found virtually identical motivations among the adult white collar criminals he and his associates examined. He concluded that those offenders had "become identified with the common business ideal of success at any price."[16] But such attitudes are apparently learned long before entering the business world. Only a few ever participate in the soap box derby, but 75 percent of the high school students in a 1985 survey in California admitted cheating on their tests.[17]

The definition of wealth and success as the central goals of individual economic activity is part of what may be termed the "culture of competition," found to one degree or another in all societies whose economies are organized upon the principles of industrial capitalism. In addition to giving great importance to wealth and success, the culture of competition defines the competitive struggle for personal gain as a positive, rather than a negative or selfish, activity. Competition is seen not only to build the character and endurance of the competitors (one of the theoretical benefits of the Soap Box Derby) but also to produce the maximum economic value for society as a whole. Not surprisingly, the competitive economic struggles typical of industrial capitalism are seen by and large as a fair battle in which the most capable and the hardest-working individuals emerge victorious. This belief in turn becomes an important legitimation for social inequality, as it implies that the poor deserve their inferior position because they are lazy or incompetent.[18]

The winners, on the other hand, are admired for the ability and drive that made them successful.

This adoration of the rich and successful and the stigmatization of the poor not only provides strong reinforcement for the drive for personal success but also contributes to the pervasive sense of insecurity and the fear of failure that make up a powerful undercurrent in the culture of competition. Malcolm X expressed these feelings well in his autobiography: "Full-time hustlers never can relax to appraise what they are doing and where they are bound. As is the case in any jungle, the hustler's every waking hour is lived with both the practical and subconscious knowledge that if he ever relaxes, if he ever slows down, the other hungry, restless foxes, ferrets, wolves, and vultures out there with him won't hesitate to make him their prey."[19] Although Malcolm X was describing a subculture of the lower classes of capitalist society, the same insecurities are equally common among respectable business people and politicians.

Neither the desire for wealth and success nor the fear of failure, however, can account for all the motivations behind white collar crime. Some of these crimes, for example, are clearly rooted in the desire of the offenders to live up to the expectations of the significant others in their occupational world. This is particularly true of the various functionaries who, out of an unreflective sense of obedience, carry out their superiors' orders to commit some illegal act, and of the members of occupational subcultures who go along with illegal activities in order to win the acceptance and support of their peers. In such cases, the offenders ignore the larger society's condemnation of their crimes and accept their occupational associates' definition of such actions as normal behavior.

Yet, when one extends this analysis beyond single individuals to encompass the entire group that sustains such criminogenic attitudes, the influence of the culture of competition usually reappears. While the lower-level functionaries involved in organizational crimes may act out of conformity and obedience, the executives giving the orders are usually pursuing those elusive goals of wealth and success. Similarly, while individual members of a deviant occupational subculture, such as that found among the police, may merely be conforming to the expectations of their peers, the collective desire for financial gain is the primary force that creates and sustains those expectations.

Of course, the culture of competition is only one of the many diverse strains of contemporary culture, and there are other constellations of values that reject or mitigate this kind of orientation. But how, then, do we explain why one individual comes to see the world in a way that is highly conducive to criminal behavior and another does not? Sutherland answered this question with his famous theory of differential association: "The hypothesis of differential association is that criminal behavior is learned in association with those who define such behavior favorably and in isolation from those who define it unfavorably, and that a person in an appropriate situation engages in such criminal behavior if, and only if, the weight of the favorable definitions exceeds the weight of the unfavorable definitions."[20] Sutherland argued that criminal behavior is learned like any other behavior, and that the criminal must learn both the techniques of crime and motivations favorable to criminal behavior. He further held that the "specific direction of motives and drives is learned from definitions of the legal codes as favorable or unfavorable."[21]

Sutherland's contention that criminal behavior is learned can hardly be challenged, and his forceful insistence on this point has been of lasting benefit to modern criminology. In other respects, however, his theory is clearly too narrow. Positive or negative definitions of the law comprise only one small component of the attitudes that influence criminal behavior. Many people with positive attitudes toward the law still break it, and many with negative attitudes do not. In other cases, criminals may be ignorant of the law, or the law itself may change.

Another problem with Sutherland's theory is his insistence that the construction of personal reality is entirely a product of one's associations with others. He felt that individuals automatically adopt the definitions of those with whom they have the greatest frequency, duration, and intensity of association. But if that were true, how could those definitions ever change? For that matter, how could they have originated in the first place?

In fact, individuals constantly create new ideas and definitions. Most are quickly discarded because they do not conform to the accepted structure of social reality, but a few have what Weber called an "elective affinity" for the social conditions of a particular group, and so are integrated into its cultural system.[22] Some individuals also persist in maintaining idiosyncratic conceptions of reality with little social support, despite the stigma that it may involve. Sutherland's view was that all criminals are ultimately conformists, but true deviance does in fact exist. Contemporary society would hardly have been possible without it.

Despite these objections, it still seems fair to say that most of our attitudes, values, and definitions are learned from others. But that still doesn't explain the origins of those ideas. To do that, we must look for their structural causes.

Anthropological studies of the few remaining hunting and gathering societies indicate that, in general, their people are not acquisitive or competitive. Most of those societies are, moreover, strongly egalitarian, with no social classes or even much in the way of permanent political leadership. The enormous differences between hunting and gathering societies and the industrial societies with which we are familiar can be traced to their relationship to the environment and the economic system it creates. The cooperative, egalitarian ethos of most hunting and gathering societies can be attributed, at least in part, to the fact that such societies produce little surplus wealth. Thus, the economic base cannot support the system of status competition based upon the accumulation of wealth that is found in the industrial societies. Significantly, the Indians living along what is now the Northwest coast of the United States and Canada, whose fishing activities generated a more substantial surplus, were in some important respects less egalitarian and more competitive than other hunting and gathering peoples. [23]

Willem Bonger, one of the first criminologists to systematically examine the relationship between crime and economic conditions, realized the important role that surplus wealth plays in the displacement of egalitarian social relations. He argued that the growth of commercial exchange made possible by an increasing surplus had a profound sociological impact:

> As soon as productivity has increased to such an extent that the producer can regularly produce more than he needs, and the division of labor puts him in a position to exchange the surplus for things that he could not produce himself, at this moment there arises in man the notion of no longer giving to his comrades what they need, but of keeping for himself the surplus of what his labor produces, and exchanging it. Then it is that the mode of production begins to run counter to the social instincts of man instead of favoring it as heretofore. [24]

Whether or not social evolution proceeded in the order that Bonger postulates, his work clearly points out the important role of market exchange in the development of the culture of competition.

Ethnographic studies of hunting and gathering societies have shown that their system of exchange is generally based upon sharing and reciprocity. For example, Richard Lee found that the bands of !Kung Bushmen in the Kalahari desert share all the available food equally. [25] Each day a group of adults leaves camp and forages for food. When they return, all the food is divided among the members of the band. Everyone receives an equal share whether they have been foraging, hunting, or sleeping. Robert Dentan found similar patterns of distribution among the Semai of Central Malaya. [26] Even a hunter who succeeds in killing a large animal and dragging it back to camp through the dense jungle still has no more claim on its meat than any other member of the band. The meat is cut up into equal portions and distributed to all who are hungry. The hunter is not given a special status because of his accomplishments—indeed, he is not even thanked by the other members of the group, for, as Dentan put it, "Saying thank-you is very rude, for it suggests first that one has calculated the amount of a gift, and second that one did not expect the donor to be so generous."[27]

The culture of competition that plays such an important role in white collar crime is rooted in the structure of the industrial economy. Most obviously, the enormous surplus wealth generated through industrial production provides a vast store of material goods to be competed for—a condition largely absent from hunting and gathering societies. A second key factor is the displacement of the open sharing of reciprocal exchange with the calculated self-interest of market exchange. Of course, reciprocal exchange still persists in industrial capitalism, particularly among relatives and close friends, but market exchange is the dominant mode. And that mode of exchange fosters a very different kind of personal outlook from that found among hunters and gatherers.[28] Market exchange is inevitably tied to the notion of profit and loss: the gain of one trading partner often comes at the expense of the other. Thus, as production for market replaces production for immediate consumption, competition and the quest for personal gain replace the more cooperative sentiments fostered in reciprocal exchange. In addition, the use of money provides an objective, impersonal standard by which to measure profit and loss in industrial society, thus further reinforcing the spirit of competition and the goal of the personal acquisition of wealth.[29]

But is this strong culture of competition a product of industrialism in general or of industrial capitalism alone? The best way to answer this question naturally would be to undertake a comparative survey of communist and capitalist nations to gauge the strength of their beliefs in the values and attitudes associated with the culture of competition. Unfortunately, no such data are available at the present time. It is, nonetheless, clear that the same conditions that create a culture of competition in the capitalist nations can also be found in the industrialized nations of the communist bloc. For one thing, all advanced industrial economies produce a substantial amount of surplus wealth, even though the amount of those surpluses may be somewhat smaller in the communist nations than in the capitalist countries of the West. And although the markets in the communist nations do not operate as freely as do those in the West, goods and services are still allocated largely upon the basis of monetary exchange. As in the West, reciprocal exchange predominates only within the family unit. Ideological claims notwithstanding, the systems of stratification in the Soviet Union and other communist nations are surprisingly similar to those of the industrial nations of the West. Moreover, studies of postrevolutionary Soviet society show that there has been a great deal of social mobility—a phenomenon that must have stimulated much more competition and status-seeking than occurred under the Czarist regime with its predominance of ascribed status.

It therefore seems likely that a strong culture of competition exists in all industrialized nations. However, because education, the media, and other public institutions give more support to the values of the culture of competition in the West, it can be expected to be stronger there. Whereas socialist societies attempt to motivate individual workers through constant ideological appeals to help advance the collective good, capitalist societies rely much more heavily upon a direct appeal to personal self-interest. The bombardment of mass advertising and its message that possessions, and the wealth to buy them, are the road to happiness provide a particularly strong socializer into the values of competitive materialism.

But if communist ideology provides a counterweight to the narcissism of the culture of competition, there is a heavy price to be paid. The communist nations are equally subject to the cultural impact of industrialization, and their attempts to impose a rigid ideology from above, whether or not actual economic and material conditions support it, is a major contributor to the crushing totalitarianism found in most communist states. The inevitable contradiction between the ideological decisions of the economic planners and the demands of the industrial system is itself a major cause of white collar crime—albeit in a very different form from that found in capitalist nations. [30]

It is, moreover, a serious mistake to divide all the industrialized nations into two rigid categories and then assume that all the members of those categories are essentially similar. The culture of competition may vary significantly among the various nations classified as capitalist or communist, just as their economic systems show considerable variance. Edwin Schur, for example, has argued that the United States puts a greater emphasis upon competitive individualism than can be accounted for solely on the basis of its capitalist economic system: "It is difficult not to conclude that American society has what might be termed capitalism with a vengeance—a reverence for the values of individualism, competition, and profit of such intensity as to provide incentives to crime that go well beyond a level that must be considered inevitable in a modern complex society, even a basically capitalist one." [31] Although there is little hard empirical work on this point, Schur is certainly not alone in this belief. Many observers have argued that the nexus of values we have called the culture of competition is stronger in the United States than in any of the capitalist nations of Western Europe, Oceania, or Asia.

NEUTRALIZING SOCIAL CONTROLS

The culture of competition receives strong social support in the Western nations, but so do the ethical standards that attempt to restrain it. Schools teach general moral principles at all grade levels, and religious institutions place even greater emphasis upon such values. Newscasts, popular television programs, and the pronouncements of corporate and government leaders proclaim the importance of maintaining high ethical standards, and even the shadiest operators claim to share them. The network of laws based on those values provides them with another powerful support. In addition to the threat of punishment, the law also has enormous symbolic importance. It provides official reinforcement for the principles it embodies and creates a stigmatizing label for those who violate its standards—a label that is, moreover, especially repugnant to the respectable business people, politicians, and professionals who comprise the majority of white collar criminals.

Rationalization

The conflict between the culture of competition and other ethical standards is carefully papered over in public. An elaborate pretense is maintained that there is no contradiction, and that unethical behavior is ultimately rewarded with failure and disgrace. In private, of course, the fact that "bending" the rules of the game provides an important competitive advantage is much too obvious to ignore, and other ways must be found to resolve this contradiction. Some people openly reject the ethical standards of their culture, while others find nothing appealing in the values of materialism and competition, but most people are attracted by both ideals. One way to construct a personal reality that accommodates both is through the use of what Sykes and Matza have called techniques of neutralization.[32] A technique of neutralization is essentially a device that enables individuals to violate important normative standards but to neutralize any definition of themselves as deviant or criminal. Such techniques take many forms, but in essence, they are rationalizations deviants use to justify their actions. A physician may, for example, justify claiming Medicaid reimbursements for services that were never performed by telling himself that his actions didn't really harm anyone.[33]

Techniques of neutralization are not just *ex post facto* rationalizations—they are available to the potential deviant before the offense actually occurs and form part of the motivation for the original act. [34] A physician does not file fraudulent Medicaid claims and then suddenly make up a rationalization to justify his actions. Rather, he is aware from the beginning that his schemes will not cause any direct harm to his patients, and that rationalization makes it psychologically feasible for him to carry out his plans.

Of all types of white collar criminals, embezzlers have been the subject of the most scientific study, perhaps because so many people have difficulty understanding why trusted, well-paid employees would jeopardize their position by stealing from their employers. Most of the research on embezzlement has attributed the offenders' crimes to their need for money. More specifically, these studies found the major causes of embezzlement to be gambling, extravagant living, and costly personal problems. [35] But the fact that embezzlers feel they need more money than they can legitimately earn is hardly a sufficient explanation in itself, for the culture of competition and the advertising that supports it have planted the desire for more money and more possessions in the minds of most people. The question still remains: Why do some individuals embezzle to get that extra money, while others do not?

Donald Cressey's detailed study of the motivations for embezzlement was the first to provide an answer to this question. [36] From intensive interviews with incarcerated embezzlers, Cressey concluded that three distinct elements are necessary for embezzlement to occur: the perpetrators must have a nonshareable financial problem, they must have the opportunity and the knowledge necessary to commit an embezzlement, and they must apply a suitable rationalization to "adjust" the contradiction between their actions and society's normative standards. Of these three propositions, the first is the most questionable, for there appears to be no necessary reason why an embezzlement must result from a nonshareable problem instead of from a simple desire for more money. Indeed, Gwynn Nettler interviewed several embezzlers who did not have such nonshareable problems, at least until after they committed their crimes, and Zietz's study of female embezzlers reached a similar conclusion. [37] Cressey's second proposition, in contrast, is almost self-evident: in order to be an embezzler, an individual must obviously have the opportunity and knowledge necessary to commit the crime. Of greatest relevance to our discussion is Cressey's third proposition and his investigation of the specific types of rationalizations embezzlers use to justify their actions.

Most embezzlers, according to Cressey, rationalize their crimes by telling themselves they are just borrowing the money and will soon return it. As one subject put it, "I figured that if you could use something and help yourself and replace it and not hurt anybody, it was all right."[38] Cressey found that his respondents continued to use this rationalization to justify embezzlement while they became more and more deeply involved in crime. Eventually they were either caught or realized they could never pay back all the money they had taken and were finally forced to accept the criminal nature of their behavior. Cressey's respondents reported using several other rationalizations as well, but the borrowing rationalization was by far the most common, probably because it is so well suited to neutralize the ethical standards condemning embezzlement.

The borrowing rationalization doesn't work as well for other white collar crimes. But fortunately, there are numerous studies that examine the rationalizations criminals use to justify other kinds of white collar crimes. One of the most common is the claim that the crimes do not harm anyone. If one's actions do not hurt other people, the argument goes, then there is nothing unethical about them. When a Westinghouse executive on trial for price fixing was asked if he thought his behavior had been illegal, he responded, "Illegal? Yes, but not criminal. . .I assumed that a criminal action meant damaging someone, and we did not do that."[39] Similar justifications were expressed in Zeitlin's study of workers discharged for stealing from their employers. As one of the subjects put it, "It's not really hurting anybody—the store can afford it."[40] Survey data have shown that the public is more tolerant of theft from large businesses and the government than it is of theft from smaller, more vulnerable organizations—probably because theft from a larger organization is perceived as less harmful to the victim.[41]

Those involved in business crimes frequently justify their behavior by claiming that the law itself is unnecessary or unjust. Business people complain loudly about "government interference" in their affairs, often using the ideology of laissez-faire capitalism to point out what they consider to be inappropriate statutes and regulations. According to such beliefs, it is the law that causes harm to the public and not the illegal activities of business. Given this system of beliefs, a host of business crimes can easily be justified. Clinard, for example, concluded that gasoline dealers' belief that the wartime rationing of gasoline was unnecessary was a "rationalization for the violations which were occurring."[42] Among small businesses, ideological considerations are probably less important than the owners' perception of whether or not the regulations are fair to them. In a study of rent control in Honolulu, Ball found no significant difference in violation rates among landlords who felt that rent control was necessary and those who did not. But he found significantly higher rates among landlords who felt that the rent ceilings applied to their property were less than the "fair" rental value. [43]

Another common technique of neutralization is the claim that one's criminal behavior was necessary in order to survive or to achieve vital economic goals. Many employees use this appeal to necessity to explain why they went along with illegal activities expected by their employer. Sutherland cited the case of an idealistic young college graduate who had lost two previous jobs because he refused to become involved in unethical activities. After taking his third job, this time at a used car dealership, he found out that they, too, expected him to become involved in shady business practices. "When I learned these things I did not quit as I had previously. I sometimes felt disgusted and wanted to quit, but I argued that I did not have much chance to find a legitimate firm. I knew the game was rotten, but it has to be played—the law of the jungle and that sort of thing." [44] Ian Smith, a former city councilman in Britain, used a similar argument to justify his part in a corruption scandal: "I am by nature a wheeler-dealer. How else can you be a successful politician. . .?" [45]

Even representatives of giant corporations use this justification, although such firms are unlikely candidates for economic extinction. The Westinghouse executive quoted earlier went on to justify his involvement in the price-fixing conspiracy by saying, "I thought we were more or less working on a survival basis in order to try to make enough to keep our plant and our employees." The former sales manager of a "competing" company made the same point: "The spirit of the [price fixing] meetings only appeared to be correcting a horrible price level situation,. . .[there was no] attempt to actually damage customers, [or] charge excessive prices. There was not personal gain in it for me [sic]. The company did not seem actually to be defrauding [anyone]. Corporate statements [show] that there have been poor profits during all these years." [46] It is also worthy of note that this executive, like most other white collar criminals, freely combined different justifications of his behavior. In addition to claiming that his activities were necessary to his employer, he also denied that his illegal activities harmed others.

Another version of this argument of necessity often used to justify occupational offenses is that the crime was necessary to help one's family. There is, however, evidence of significant gender differences in the use of this rationalization. Kathleen Daly's study of the presentence reports of convicted white collar offenders found that female embezzlers were about twice as likely to cite the needs of their family members as a justification than male embezzlers, while the males were much more likely to cite business needs. [47]

A justification that is often combined with the argument of necessity is the claim that "everybody else is doing it." As one of Cressey's subjects put it, "In the real estate business you have to paint a pretty picture in order to sell the property. We did a little juggling and moving around, but everyone in the real estate business has to do that. We didn't do anything that they all don't do."[48] This kind of rationalization is frequently used to justify "fudging" on income tax returns, and Benson found it to be just as popular among those convicted of criminal tax fraud. According to one respondent: "Everybody cheats on their income taxes, 95% of the people. Even if it's ten dollars, it's the same principle."[49]

Another version of the "everybody's doing it" justification holds that it is unfair to condemn one violator unless all the other violators are condemned. A defendant in a British corruption case said, "I will never believe I have done anything criminally wrong. I did what is business. If I bent any rules, who doesn't? If you are going to punish me, sweep away the system. If I am guilty, there are many others who should be by my side in the dock."[50] Another version of this justification is that criminal behavior must be some sort of individual choice, and that people are not responsible for their actions when they are merely conforming to the expectations of others. Corrupt employees often claim that they haven't done anything wrong, because they were merely going along with a pattern of behavior accepted among their peers.[51]

Finally, many occupational crimes are justified on the grounds that the offender deserves the money. This rationalization is particularly common in cases of employee theft. In his study of dock workers, Gerald Mars found that pilferage was defined as a "morally justified addition to wages" or an "entitlement due from exploiting employers."[52] Lawrence Zeitlin found similar attitudes among employees who stole from retail stores. One of his subjects felt that the "store owed it to me," while another said, "I felt I deserved to get something additional for my work since I wasn't getting paid enough."[53] The same rationalizations have also been used to justify corruption among government employees, who often see themselves as underpaid in comparison to their counterparts in private industry. One former city councilman gave the following account of his reasons for becoming involved in corruption:

> People like me are expected to work full time without salaries, without staff, or even postage stamps. I for one couldn't afford such a situation. And that is where Poulson [a businessman seeking special favors] filled the gap. . . .I came to the conclusion that I was missing out, that I could combine my real desire to give public service with what they call a piece of the action.[54]

Of course, many other justifications are used to neutralize normative controls, but the six rationalizations just discussed seem to be the most common. Before moving on, however, we must explore an important question concerning their origins. Cressey argued that individual offenders do not invent their own rationalizations but simply apply to their own behavior definitions that are already present: "Each trusted person does not invent a new rationalization for his violation of trust, but instead applies to his own situation a verbalization which has been made available to him by virtue of his having come into contact with a culture in which such verbalizations are present."[55]   While this is probably true much more often than not, individuals do construct their own particularistic justifications based upon individual circumstances and rework previously learned rationalizations to better fit their own experience. For example, employees who justify their thefts by holding that the company will not be harmed generally pick up this rationalization directly from other employees or from widely held cultural beliefs. But employees who find themselves confronted with a special problem not shared by their co-workers may develop more unique rationalizations. A woman singled out as a target for her boss's sexual advances and the jealousy of her male co-workers might, for example, use those facts to construct a particularistic justification for her criminal behavior.

With all this said, it is still clear that most of the techniques of neutralization are culturally learned. Of particular importance in this regard are the various occupational subcultures that not only supply their members with a set of appropriate rationalizations, but also help to isolate them from contact with those who would pass harsher judgment on their criminal activities. Many of the ways occupational subcultures encourage criminal behavior were examined in chapter 2. Police subcultures, for example, often distinguish between "clean" payoff money and "dirty" payoff money and hold that there is nothing unethical about accepting the former. Then, too, the workers in many factories make clear distinctions between which property it is permissible to steal and which property it is not, while many politicians learn to see the swapping of political favors for campaign contributions or personal rewards as a normal part of their job.

Such deviant subcultures need not be confined to a single employer or even to a single profession. The business culture that is shared to one degree or another by most business people not only provides incentives for illicit activities but also contains justifications that can be used to neutralize ethical restraints. The common expression that "business is business" reflects the subculture's belief that harsh necessity justifies both the unethical and the illegal activities of the business world. Polls indicate that the "everybody else is doing it" rationalization also has a strong affinity to the attitudes and opinions of the business subculture. Most business people apparently believe, not only that their peers and competitors are willing to commit unethical acts, but that they are actually doing it. Four out of five executives surveyed by the *Harvard Business Review* felt that some of the generally accepted practices in their industry were unethical, and four out of seven believed that other executives would violate a code of ethics if they felt they would not be caught.[56]   A 1975 study of top officials in the fifty-seven largest U.S. corporations found that the officials believed unethical behavior to be so widespread that it had to be accepted as part of everyday business activities.[57]   A study of business attitudes undertaken by the Uniroyal Corporation found that "most managers believed that their peers would not refuse an order to market off-standard and possibly dangerous products (although a majority insisted they would personally reject such orders), and a majority thought young managers automatically go along with superiors to show loyalty."[58]

The perceptive reader will have noticed that we have dealt only with the neutralization of the symbolic controls on white collar crime. There is, of course, another set of controls on criminal behavior imposed by the criminal justice system, and the logic of our analysis would normally require a section devoted to that topic. But because the operation of the criminal justice system was discussed in detail in chapter 5, another treatment of this subject would be redundant. It is sufficient to note here that the criminal justice system has thus far proved itself incapable of mounting a sufficient enforcement effort to deter most types of white collar crime.

Organizational Conformity

Up to this point we have been discussing the causes of white collar crime in general, but now some special attention must be devoted to organizational crime. Although the same process of motivation and rationalization occurs in both occupational and organizational crime, the structural demands of formal organizations create unique pressures that require careful analysis. Modern organizations are, in a sense, machines for controlling human behavior. In order to survive, a large corporation must directly control the behavior of thousands of employees and indirectly influence the activities of much larger groups on the outside. And although organizations may well encounter special problems in persuading employees to engage in illegal activities, the mechanisms for achieving conformity to organizational expectations are much the same whatever the legal standing of the organization's demands.

One of the most powerful techniques to win conformity with organizational demands is the threat of dismissal. John Z. DeLorean, a for-

mer top executive of General Motors and founder of his own unsuccessful automobile firm, gave the following description of the pressure
applied to an engineer who objected to dangerous design elements in
the notorious Chevrolet Corvair: "Charlie Chayne, vice-president of
engineering, along with his staff, took a very strong stand against the
Corvair as an unsafe car long before it went on sale in 1959. He was
not listened to but told in effect, 'You're not a member of the team.
Shut up or go looking for another job.' "[59] Of course, such threats are
seldom made so blatantly, but even so, employees understand what is
involved in going against the company's demands.

The fear of losing an important assignment or being passed up
for the next promotion is just as much a threat for the achievement-
oriented executive as the possibility of dismissal. In the social world of
the modern corporation, dedication to the company and conformity to
the wishes of one's superiors are seen as essential to success. Regular
promotions are an expected part of the climb up the corporate ladder,
and overly scrupulous managers are likely to find the promotions they
expected going to those who have been more cooperative. For example,
court testimony from General Electric executives involved in the heavy
electrical equipment cases indicates that they were under intense pressure from their superiors to participate in the price-fixing conspiracy.
Their primary fear was not so much the loss of their jobs (although,
ironically, many of them were fired after the scandal broke) as the loss
of the particular assignments they had been given, and the negative
effects that event might have had on their career.[60] As one executive put it, "If I didn't do it, I felt someone else would. I would be
removed, and somebody else would do it."[61] The consuming desire
for success and the notion that conformity and obedience to superiors
are essential to achieve that goal make executives fearful of question-
ing their orders, even if those commands involve illegal activities. As
a report to the Securities and Exchange Commission concerning Lockheed's involvement in the overseas bribery scandals noted, "Employees
learned not to question deviations from standard operational procedure
and practices. Moreover, the Committee was told by several witnesses
that employees who questioned foreign marketing practices damaged
their claims for career advancement."[62] Thus, top corporate leaders are
able to persuade their subordinates to engage in illegal activities, often
without specifically ordering them to do so, because their position in
the organization gives them control of rewards and punishments that
are enormously important to those below them.

Organizational control nonetheless involves much more than
simply handing out sufficient rewards and punishments to ensure
employee obedience. A large organization harbors a unique social world
all its own, and the subculture embodied in the organization influences

its members' behavior in ways of which they are not even aware. Most fundamentally, the way an organization defines the employee and his or her work discourages some actions and encourages others. The ethos of a corporation also helps shape the moral sensibilities and perspectives of its employees—especially those in managerial positions. Moreover, the initial decision to engage in illegal activity is profoundly affected by the social world sheltered within the organization.

One important element of this social world is its "moral tone"— that is, its ethical system and its attitudes toward illegal behavior. As one student of the Equity Funding case wrote,

> Corporations can and do create a moral tone that powerfully influences the thinking, conduct, values, and even the personalities of the people who work for them. The tone is set by the men who run the company, and their corruption can quickly corrupt all else. A startling thing about Equity Funding is how rarely one finds, in a cast of characters big enough to make a war movie, a man who said, "No, I won't do that. It's wrong." [63]

In describing his research sponsored by the accounting firm of Peat, Marwick, and Mitchell, Donald Cressey writes that: "I interviewed about two dozen internal and external auditors. Every one of these financial executives said that the ethical behavior of a company's personnel is determined by the example set by top management." [64] Clinard and Yeager found the same attitudes in a series of interviews they conducted among top corporate managers. [65]

But while such beliefs are accurate, they are also misleading, because they hinge on a single fact taken out of the social and economic context in which it is embedded. Of course top management influences the ethical tone of the organization—but top managers' ethical standards are not simply their own personal beliefs. The ethics and outlook of those who come to hold the most powerful positions are molded and shaped by the same process of socialization that influences other, less successful managers. Indeed, promotion to the highest ranks generally requires a much higher degree of ethical conformity than is expected of lower-level employees. [66] Those who refuse to change personal standards that are incompatible with the demands of their corporate employer never reach the top.

Much has been written about the numbing effects modern bureaucracies have upon the moral sensibilities of their employees. Numerous writers have chronicled the growth of what Whyte called the "organization man," [67] who is under such overwhelming pressure to conform that individuality and personal ethical standards must be sacrificed for the sake of a career. According to Margolis, the "new men" who took over American business as it became more routine and more bureaucratic "had to be less autonomous and more passive, less ambitious and more malleable; team players, not loners—in short, other-directed, not inner-directed."[68] Howton used similar terms in describing the modern-day corporate functionary as a "new kind of man who in his role of servicing the organization is morally unbound. . . .His ethic is the ethic of the good soldier: take the order, do the job."[69]

Howton argued convincingly that these amoral functionaries have become so common because they are necessary to bureaucratic organization. A bureaucracy, as Weber pointed out, is an impersonal system of interrelated roles whose rights and duties are spelled out in formal rules.[70] One of the principal strengths of bureaucratic organization is that individual employees are dispensable—one employee can be replaced by another with a minimum of disruption. But this interchangeability requires that individual employees think and act in a similar fashion, and the existence of widely divergent ethical standards and attitudes among the work force might interfere with the smooth operation of the organization. Thus, the efficient bureaucracy breeds moral conformity—or, perhaps more often, a kind of amoral pragmatism.

The process of socialization into the corporate ethic occurs at all levels of the organization, but a particular effort is made to shape aspiring managers according to the corporate image. The transfer is one of the devices commonly used to achieve this goal. By continually moving young executives from one area to another, the firm weakens outside ties that might interfere with their socialization. These transfers make managers more dependent upon the corporation to satisfy their social needs and bring them ever more deeply into its social world. The long hours of work required of up-and-coming executives have a similar effect. The burden of overwork disrupts commitments to family, friends, community, and other interests that might place conflicting pressures upon the manager. As Margolis put it,

> What is to be accomplished is not a total change in the young man's values or attitudes but merely their reorder. The priority of the corporation must be established. For that to happen, exhausting workloads are less strategic than work situations that put the corporation into competition with other institutions or persons who might lay claim on the man. These competitions, which always have the appearance of accidents, are in fact intentional enforcers or tests of the man's loyalty to the corporation.[71]

This rigorous process of socialization can produce a kind of "moral numbness" in corporate managers.[72] The well-socialized executive tends to display a narrow, pragmatic approach to his or her work, acting in the best interests of the corporation with little thought of its moral implications. C. Wright Mills held such attitudes to be part of the "structural immorality" of American society.[73] But perhaps the phenomenon can more appropriately be termed "structural amorality," for the well-trained bureaucrat does not oppose or reject popular morality—he or she is simply indifferent to it.

Socialization into a bureaucratic organization does much more than just dull the initiate's ethical sensibilities, however. As March and Simon, Perrow, and other sociologically oriented organizational theorists have pointed out,[74] an organization also controls its members through its influence on the definition of the situations they face on the job. The organization provides definitions about what needs to be done, the importance of various tasks, and the effects of those tasks upon the company and the community. The organization defines the goals it is pursuing and the ways those goals are to be achieved. It provides repertoires of actions to be used in response to given situations, and it teaches employees to direct their attention to certain aspects of their environment and to ignore others.

This network of definitions often makes unethical or illegal activities appear to be a normal part of the daily routine. Time after time, individuals unlucky enough to have been caught committing corporate crimes have expressed surprise and even shock that their actions were really considered criminal by the world outside their organizations. One General Electric executive involved in the heavy electrical equipment scandals said that price fixing "had become so common and gone on for so many years that we lost sight of the fact that it was illegal."[75] Carey's description of the attitudes of those involved in the marketing of MER/29 applies equally well to many other organizational criminals: "No one involved expressed any strong repugnance or even opposition to selling the unsafe drug. Rather, they all seemed to drift into the activity without thinking a great deal about it."[76]

The organizational structure of modern bureaucracy greatly facilitates its ability to manipulate employees' definition of their occupational world. The mammoth size of many of these organizations, their labyrinth of organizational units, and the ever-increasing trend toward specialization fragment the responsibility of individual employees. Most employees work on only a small part of a much larger overall operation, and many never see—or choose to ignore—the potential impact of the project as a whole. Employees who question the ethical or legal implications of their work are told to carry out their duties and not to worry about things that are the responsibility of top management.

At the same time, top managers often make an intentional effort to avoid legal responsibility for the programs they encourage. In the heavy electrical equipment price-fixing cases, for example, top management first set quotas and goals that virtually required price fixing to achieve, and then they made it clear that they did not want to hear anything about the criminal activities of their subordinates.[77] Surveys indicate that many middle-level managers are afraid to be honest with their bosses. Moreover, the number of managers reporting this problem almost doubled from the late 1950s to the middle 1970s.[78] This same process goes on in government as well. The scandal that developed around the sale of arms to America's enemies in Iran, and the use of some of the profits to illegally support the rebels seeking to overthrow the government of Nicaragua, provides a classic example. It is clear that President Reagan ordered his subordinates to find some way to aid the Nicaraguan rebels, even though a specific prohibition on the use of government funds for such a purpose had already been enacted into law. Former National Security Adviser John M. Poindexter, who directed the "Iran-Contra" scheme, testified before Congress in July 1987, that although he was confident that the President would have approved of the plan, he did not ask his permission in order to protect him from the political damage that would occur if the plan became public.[79]

Another factor that facilitates corporate control of its managers is their relative isolation from the outside world. In one of his most well-known works on business administration, Peter Drucker compared the isolation of the executive with that in a monastery. He went on to note that the executive's "contacts outside of business tend to be limited to people of the same set, if not to people working for the same organization. The demand that there be no competing outside interests and loyalty applies to the corporate executive as it does to the army officer. Hence executive life not only breeds a parochialism of the imagination comparable to the 'military mind,' but places a considerable premium on it."[80] This isolation is important, because it insulates the white collar criminals from the condemnation they would otherwise receive from those outside the social world of their organization, and also because it discourages normal skepticism about attitudes and goals executives learn on the job.

THE DISTRIBUTION OF OPPORTUNITY

No matter how strong an individual's motivation, by itself it can never provide a complete explanation of criminal behavior. If there is no opportunity, there is no crime. In this short discussion, we cannot hope to list all the opportunities associated with different occupational positions. We can only provide a general description of the overall distribution of the opportunities for white collar crime and examine some of the causes of that distribution. But before we proceed, one more point must be made. In everyday speech, "opportunity" has a positive connotation—an opportunity is a favorable set of circumstances that allows us to do something we desire. Thus, we speak of an opportunity to double an investment, not an opportunity to have cancer surgery. Here, however, the term will be used in a more neutral way. For our purposes, an opportunity is merely a possible course of action, and different opportunities can be evaluated on the basis of their attractiveness to different individuals or groups. Generally speaking, the more attractive opportunity is one that appears to hold greater possibilities for gain, less chance of punishment, and to be more compatible with an individual's values and beliefs.

There has, unfortunately, been little effort to measure criminal opportunities directly. But because the culture of competition has diffused the motivation for white collar crime so widely, it seems reasonable to assume that high crime rates reflect the presence of attractive criminal opportunities. The only other important factor would appear to be the distribution of rationalizations, for some types of crime are more easily justified than others. But in light of the ingenuity people have shown at creating flattering definitions of their own behavior, there is little doubt that crime rates and the distribution of criminal opportunity are strongly correlated. A more serious problem arises from the fact that virtually all the quantitative measures of white collar crime used in criminological research are based on reports by regulatory and criminal justice agencies. Although those statistics are certainly influenced by the underlying crime rate, they also reflect a number of extraneous variables such as the likelihood of detecting a particular crime, and the priorities and procedures of the agencies themselves. Yet in spite of these difficulties, some preliminary conclusions are still necessary, both as a summary of the current state of our knowledge and as a basis for further research. [81]

The Legal System

Since it defines what is and is not a crime, the legal system is the ultimate cause of the distribution of criminal opportunities. Whenever the law is changed to create new types of crime or to eliminate old ones, the structure of opportunity changes as well. As noted in chapter 4, the laws that create white collar crimes reflect a struggle for power among many different groups. Although the corporate elite has far greater influence than its usual opponents, periodic crises and the social unrest they create have led to a host of legal restrictions on the elite's power. One of the reasons contemporary capitalism is so uniquely conducive to organizational crime is that popular mass movements have had much more success in influencing elected officials who make the laws than in influencing the bureaucrats who enforce them. Consequently, a network of legal restrictions on the abuses of the elite has been created, but those "crimes at the top" often carry little or no real penalty. Under such circumstances, white collar workers naturally find many illegal activities to offer very attractive possibilities.

In Third World nations ruled by small oligarchies and in the industrialized nations of the communist bloc, there is a very different legal structure. Centralization of power and the lack of legitimate political opposition allow the ruling elite greater control of the legal system, which therefore becomes more a tool of social policy than a product of social conflict. In communist societies, the government's direct control of industry provides many more ways to influence organizational behavior without the use of the criminal law. However, the ideological nature of many of the decisions made by the economic planners creates pressure on managers to use extralegal means to meet their production goals, and the communist economy thereby creates its own forces promoting organizational crime.[82] All things considered, it seems likely that organizational crimes are less common in communist nations than among the profit-seeking private firms of the capitalist nations, but there is little reliable data upon which to base any conclusion.

But if the organizational crimes are less common in communist countries, the same is not true of occupational offenses. One of the principal objectives of the communist legal system is to prevent individual deviants from interfering with the goals of the central administrative hierarchy, and this priority is reflected in the activities of the criminal justice system. In one of the few available breakdowns of criminal statistics from the Soviet Union, S. S. Ostroumov indicated that 5 percent of all reported offenses were economic crimes (violations of laws restricting speculation and other private economic enterprise), 4 percent were "official crimes" (the abuse of office by state functionaries), 5.5 percent were offenses against the system of justice or administration (often involving bribery and corruption), and 17 percent involved the theft of state property (principally, it seems, by employees).[83] The broad categories and the uncertain accuracy of these figures do not permit an estimation of exact percentages, but the data do suggest that as many as 25 to 30 percent of all officially recognized offenses in the Soviet Union are occupational crimes.[84]

Industries

Both the distribution of opportunities and their relative attractiveness vary significantly from one industry to another. One question that has created a great deal of interest among scholars is the relationship between market structure and corporate crime. However, many contradictory claims have been made about which type of market structure has the greatest criminogenic effects. On the one hand, it can be argued that competitive markets in which many different firms struggle to keep afloat are the most likely to have high crime rates, because the combatants will use every possible means to survive and prosper. On the other hand, it appears that price fixing and other antitrust conspiracies are far easier in highly concentrated industries. Thus, it would seem that industries with many small, highly competitive firms would be characterized by a high rate of crimes that are intended to improve competitive performance, such as fraud, false advertising, and espionage, and that collusion and antitrust activities are most common in more concentrated industries.

Most of the empirical research on this issue has focused on the antitrust laws. Although it would seem to be impossible for hundreds of small firms to join together in an illegal conspiracy without being detected, many researchers have compared the rate of antitrust violations in moderately concentrated and highly concentrated industries. Pfeffer and Salancik, Burton, and Riedel[85] all found the greatest number of antitrust violations in industries with intermediate levels of concentration, whereas Hay and Kelley[86] found more violations among highly concentrated firms. Asch and Seneca[87] concluded that high concentration is associated with higher rates of crime in consumer goods industries and with lower rates of crime in producer goods industries. Finally, Posner[88] and Clinard[89] found little relationship of any kind between these two variables. As Clinard and Yeager suggested, quantitative research on this topic is extremely difficult, and more-sophisticated methodology is needed before these contradictory findings can be resolved.[90]

The much slimmer body of research on bribery also concentrates on the issue of market structure. Pointing out the numerous bribery scandals involving the sale of such products as phonograph records and beer, Clinard and Yeager argued that bribery is most likely to occur in highly competitive industries.[91] This position has obvious appeal, because it pictures bribery as simply one more type of competition between firms seeking to sell their products—the more competition, the greater the need to resort to bribery. Kugel and Gruenberg, however, argued that oligopolistic markets are most conducive to bribery: "Since oligopoly markets are characterized by lack of price competition, international payoffs become a kind of nonprice competition."[92] The data from the international payoff scandals in the 1970s appear to support Kugel and Gruenberg's thesis. Of the thirty-two companies that were found to have spent more than $1 million in "questionable payments" abroad, half were in just four industries. The heaviest concentration of offenders was in the drug industry, where seven different firms admitted making over $1 million in foreign payments. The second greatest concentration of offenders was in the aircraft industry, where four firms surpassed the $1 million mark, followed by the oil industry with three million-dollar offenders and the food industry with two.[93] In all these industries, a few firms control the bulk of production and sales in the United States.

The matter is, however, more complicated than it may appear, for a high concentration ratio in the United States does not necessarily mean that there is no international competition. Despite a high degree of domestic concentration in the aircraft industry, the international aircraft market is often fiercely competitive, and most of the reported bribery in this industry was indeed intended to promote aircraft sales. In contrast, the petroleum industry has long been characterized by cartels and collusion, and there generally is little competition in either domestic or international markets. Significantly, most of the bribery reported in the petroleum industry was intended not to directly promote the sales of a particular company's products, but to preserve and enhance a political climate favorable to the operations of all international oil companies. Thus, intense competition appears more likely to be associated with commercial bribery intended to promote the sale of a firm's products, whereas firms in noncompetitive industries may have a tendency to be involved in political bribery aimed at influencing government policies and programs.

Because all of the quantitative studies just discussed rely on official records and reports as their only measure of white collar crime, it is difficult to know how much confidence we should place in their conclusions. The case study method, which analyzes the conditions that contribute to the rates of particular white collar offenses in particular industries, has so far produced better results. Farberman[94] and Leonard and Weber,[95] for example, both concluded that the economic organization of the automobile industry virtually forces individual dealers to engage in shady business practices. They argue that the oligopolistic firms that control the supply of new automobiles pressure their franchises to sell their cars at an extremely low price in order to increase their sales volume, and dealers are therefore forced to make up their losses through repair and service rackets and other fraudulent activities. Denzin found similar conditions in the liquor industry.[96] Distillers impose rigid sales quotas on their distributors that force them to give untaxed, under-the-table incentives to retailers in order to keep their volume up. Needleman and Needleman have, however, criticized the assumption in such studies that the participants are coerced into criminal activity.[97] They argue that in most cases, it is more accurate to talk about "crime facilitative" rather than "crime coercive" systems. Their study of the securities industry, for example, found many conditions that made criminal activities easier but did not actually force individuals to participate. More specifically, the Needlemans found that the legal doctrines limiting the financial risk in handling stolen securities, the strong financial incentives to keep up market flow, and the traditions of trust and professional solidarity in the industry all combine to facilitate securities theft. These conclusions are supported by Weisburd, Waring, and Wheeler's analysis of convicted white collar offenders, which found a higher crime rate in the securities industry than in any of the six other industries they analyzed.[98]

Another variable influencing the opportunity structure within an industry is what Edward Gross called "organizational sets"— groups of similar organizations whose actions are visible to each other.[99] The key point is that these sets tend to have an internal system of stratification with dominant organizations, middle level organizations, and marginal organizations. The relatively small number of firms at the top of these stratified organizational sets greatly increases the attractiveness of antitrust conspiracies, because it reduces the number of firms that must become involved and thus reduces their chances of being uncovered. Citing the Equity Funding case, Gross also argued that both the tendency for organizations to focus their attention almost exclusively on the activities of other members of their set and the great complexity of relations among participants in different sets make it easier for outsiders to conceal fraudulent schemes that cut across set boundaries.

Variations in the regulatory environment also play a major role in determining the opportunity structure in different industries. The more tightly an industry is regulated, the more attractive opportunities are likely to be illegal, and the more white collar crime we can expect. One of the most important influences shaping an industry's regulatory environment is the products it makes. Industries whose products cause serious and clearly identifiable harm to the public or the environment tend to be subject to more stringent regulation than those that do not.

Examples include the manufacturers of pharmaceuticals, whose products may mean life or death for their users, the automobile industry, which has been subject to an increasing number of safety and environmental regulations, and the chemical and petroleum industries, which produce a wide variety of hazardous substances, often using industrial processes that pose great environmental risks. It is not surprising, then, that the Wisconsin study found all these industries to have unusually high crime rates.[100]

There is also considerable evidence that illegal practices spread from one organization in an industry to another.[101] Some of this tendency can be attributed to the diffusion of motivations and rationalizations discussed earlier in this chapter, but other processes appear to be involved as well. Knowledge about the availability of criminal opportunities and the specific techniques necessary to carry them out also diffuse within an industry.[102] The illegal activities of a firm also have a direct impact on its competitors. For one thing, seeing a competitor increase its profits by illegal means is likely to enhance the attractiveness of such behavior, while the failure of a competitor's illegal enterprise is likely to have the opposite effect. Profits generated by illegal means may also allow a firm to lower its prices or take other advantages over its competition, thus reducing the attractiveness of the competition's legitimate opportunities and encouraging all the firms in the industry to become involved in similar illegal practices.

Organizations

According to the theory of capitalism advanced by Adam Smith and his followers, the principal goal of all private enterprise is profit. Corporations are money-making machines, and if they fail to make money, the logic of capitalism says they should go bankrupt. However, some defenders of contemporary business downplay the importance of profit as a business goal, pointing out that business firms pursue many other objectives as well. J. K. Galbraith has held that the giant multinational firms typical of the corporate sector have become increasingly conservative, in that their sights have turned from achieving the maximum possible profits to the quest for security and self-protection.[103] In this view, managers aim for a "satisfactory" level of profitability that offers stability and security, rather than taking greater risks to achieve higher profits. The size and influence of the firm, Galbraith has argued, are often more important to today's professional managers than are exorbitant profits. Because managers are no longer the major stockholders in their firms, high profits and dividends are supposedly less attractive than the status derived from being at the helm of a huge firm with vast power and influence. Even among the owner-operated firms of the small business sector, the argument goes, there are still constraints on the pursuit of profit, such as limitations on how much time and effort the owner is willing to devote to the business.

Although there is some truth in these arguments, the central importance of profit to contemporary business must not be underestimated. Modern-day managers may not struggle for every last dime in profits, but they know that a decline in profitability poses a direct threat to their careers. Once "satisfactory" levels of profitability have been achieved, firms may pursue other goals, but the primacy of the profit motive quickly reemerges if profits decline. After a careful statistical analysis of the reasons for the dismissal of top corporate executives, James and Soref concluded that "profit criteria appear to be the most important standard by which corporate chiefs are judged, and dismissal is the ultimate sanction that conditions their behavior."[104] Thus, the corporate executive who lets the profitability of his or her firm decline runs a very real risk of being fired.[105]

Modern corporations are, however, far too complex to operate with only a single goal. A corporation can hardly tell its manufacturing division or sales division that its goal is simply to make profits. Each organizational unit must be given specific subgoals that ultimately contribute to the overall organizational goals. The sales division, for example, might be given a particular quota to reach, while the manufacturing division is told to produce a certain number of items at a particular cost.

Corporate managers have little discretion in selecting the primary corporate objective (profitability), but they are responsible for the subgoals. Moreover, the specific targets selected by top management may have an important influence on the decisions of middle-level employees whether or not to stay within the confines of the law. For example, Ronald Kramer argues that the goals set for the Ford Pinto—that it weigh less than two thousand pounds and cost less than $2,000—ultimately caused the safety problems for which it became famous, because such goals led to the rejection of safety modifications that would have increased the weight and cost of the car.[106]

The retired middle managers studied by Marshall Clinard expressed the belief that top management is responsible for setting the overall ethical standards of the corporation. Many of them drew a distinction between "financially oriented" managers and "technical and professional types." The interviewees believed that financially oriented managers were primarily interested in quick profits and personal prestige and were therefore more inclined to criminal activities. Professionally oriented managers were held to be less willing to risk criminal activities and more concerned with the long-term well-being of the corporation. [107]

It would be a mistake, however, to attribute too much independence to those at the top. Even the highest ranking managers are often as constrained by the structural realities of the organization and its external environment as are lower-level employees. For one thing, top management is confronted by a complex balance of political forces within the organization that places clear limits on its discretion. Individuals and groups who occupy strategic lower positions within the organization may have great power over certain types of corporate operations. One study of the Australian Trade Practices Act, for example, concluded that most violations did not originate at the top, but with other factions within the corporations involved. [108] Those at the top often find that they have great power only so long as they utilize it in the ways that are expected of them. The culture and traditions of an organization have a resilient strength that is difficult for even the most capable leader to overcome. Most upper-level executives have also been socialized into the same organizational culture as other employees, and it plays an important part in determining their decisions. [109]

In addition to those powerful internal forces, top management is also restrained by the external environment of the organization. Many critical definitions, ideas, and beliefs come from the industry in which a firm operates and the general ethos of corporate culture. Government controls and the climate of public opinion place another set of restraints on contemporary corporations, as do the economic realities of the marketplace. Under many circumstances, top management may have little choice but to engage in illicit activities, if it is to meet the overriding demand for profits. If, for instance, a competitor is cutting costs by violating pollution and safety standards, it may be impossible to maintain competitive prices without engaging in similar activities.

Given the primacy of the profit motive, it is not surprising that the research shows firms with declining profitability are more likely than others to break the law. In a study of wartime price control legislation, George Katona found that compliance in the meat and laundry industries "seemed to be more satisfactory among firms with rising profits than among those with declining profits." [110] Lane's study of New England shoe manufacturers also found fair trade violations to be more common when profits were declining, [111] and Geis concluded that there was more price fixing in the heavy electrical equipment industry when market conditions were poor. [112] In a study of five hundred major corporations, Staw and Szwajkowski found that firms cited for antitrust violations had been making lower profits than had other firms in their industry. [113] The Wisconsin study of corporate crime reached similar conclusions. In the words of Clinard and Yeager, "Firms in depressed industries as well as relatively poorly performing firms in all industries tend to violate the law to a greater degree." [114] One exception is Clinard's 1952 study of wartime price control violations, which did not find a relationship between profits and business offenses. [115] Finally, Simpson's study of antitrust violations found that firms in a difficult economic environment committed more serious violations, while in good economic times, firms committed more minor violations. [116]

Many observers have claimed that there is a relationship between the size of a firm and its involvement in illegal activities, but they do not agree on whether large or small firms are most likely to break the law. John Conklin, for example, suggested that the anonymity and impersonality of the large corporations and the way responsibility for important tasks is fragmented among many different employees promote crime in such firms. [117] Others, especially those working for large corporations, have claimed that small firms are more likely to violate the law, because they lack the professional expertise to decipher the maze of government regulations that controls business activities. [118]

The research on this point is as contradictory as the claims. Neither Katona nor Clinard was able to arrive at definitive conclusions about the relationship between the violation of wartime price regulations and firm size. Lane found that larger firms were much more likely to violate labor regulations and trade-practices legislation than were smaller firms. [119] But he found the opposite to be the case for violations of the Fair Labor Standards and the Public Contracts Acts in the metal and metal products industry. In two other industries, Lane found no relationship at all between size and legal offenses. His overall conclusion was that there is "no clear relationship between size and violation; each industry and each regulatory measure has a pattern of its own." [120] The Wisconsin study reached similar conclusions. Although larger firms were found to have more total violations, the relationship disappeared when controls were introduced to compensate for the greater volume of business carried on by the big firms. [121] Riis and Patric found some evidence that dishonest practices were more common among large than among small car and radio repair shops, [122] and a more recent study of income tax compliance found that erroneous returns were more commonly filed by large firms than by small ones. [123] Despite the efforts of these researchers, however, no clear relationship between firm size and criminal conduct has been established.

Occupations

All occupations offer some illicit opportunities, even if it is only to evade the taxes on the money we earn. These opportunities are, however, unevenly distributed, and some occupations clearly hold far greater possibilities for illicit gain than others. The great diversity of occupational categories and the paucity of sociological research on this subject unfortunately make it possible to present only a few basic generalizations and hypotheses. The attractiveness of the opportunities for bribery, for instance, appears to depend on the economic value of the services the holder of a particular job can offer in exchange for corrupt payments. One of the reasons police corruption is most common among officers involved in the enforcement of narcotics and vice laws is that organized criminals are willing to pay those officers large sums of money to look the other way. [124] Other occupations with rich opportunities for corruption include purchasing agents, government inspectors, and politicians.

The government's increasing role in regulating private business has created burgeoning opportunities for corruption as the number of rule makers and inspectors has increased. [125] Another structural condition that encourages government corruption is the increasing cost of running for public office. Because of the widely held belief that an expensive advertising campaign is necessary to win high office, even the most scrupulous politicians are tempted to trade political favors for the campaign contributions necessary for such efforts. The simultaneous expansion of the politicians' need for money and private industry's desire to purchase special favors from them has produced a situation uniquely suited to foster corruption.

The opportunities for embezzlement seem to vary with the degree of financial trust placed in the holders of different occupational positions. Accountants, bookkeepers, and clerks have many opportunities for embezzlement, while other employees in the same organizations may have none. Opportunities for fraud and other illegal financial manipulations appear to be greatest in occupations with direct involvement in financial dealings such as salespeople and upper level executives. A recent study of presentence reports in federal court by Weisburd, Waring, and Wheeler found that managers were convicted of the most serious crimes, the crimes of owners were second, and lower-level employees committed the least serious offenses. [126]

In general, it appears that the opportunities for employee pilfer-age are more widely dispersed than the opportunities for fraud or embezzlement. Most employees have the opportunity to steal from their employer at one time or another, and a great many actually do. Such opportunities are not, however, evenly distributed throughout the occu-pational structure. Hollinger and Clark's comprehensive survey found that employees with access to and knowledge about vulnerable targets for theft (e.g., sales clerks in stores, engineers in factories, and nurses and technicians in hospitals) were the most likely to report having actu-ally committed a theft.[127] Occupations also differ in the size of the reward they offer to the potential thief. Whereas the television assem-blers in Horning's study usually took small objects of little value,[128] stockbrokers and securities dealers have the opportunity to steal far more valuable items.

One of the most important determinants of the illicit opportuni-ties available to professionals is the financial arrangements determining their remuneration. Professionals working on a fee-for-service basis have numerous opportunities to persuade their clients to consent to profitable but unnecessary procedures, while those working on salary have nothing to gain from such activities. Another important factor is the ignorance of clients about what kind of services they really need, and the strong emphasis on mutual trust in the professional-client rela-tionship which leads many clients to an unquestioning acceptance of the professional's judgment. The fact that a substantial portion of med-ical and dental bills are paid by insurance further decreases the clients' concern about unnecessary services and overcharging, thus decreasing the chances of punishment for such actions.

Occupational subcultures facilitate white collar crime by promot-ing the spread of knowledge and techniques necessary to transform a potential course of criminal action into a psychologically available opportunity. Because these subcultures typically have members from many different industries, they provide a source of communication independent of the industry or organization in which an individual works. Accountants, physicians, and lawyers, for example, learn about opportunities for white collar crime as they learn their profession and are socialized into its subculture. Similarly, the striking similarities in the patterns of corruption found in the New York and Philadelphia police departments in the early 1970s strongly suggest the transmis-sion of criminal techniques through an occupational subculture shared by officers in those two departments. Although subcultures in law, medicine, and the other professions, do not directly condone criminal behavior, their sense of mutual solidarity and self-protection do make criminal opportunities more attractive by reducing the chances of receiving severe punishment. Occupational subcultures thus serve as part of a network of communication that transmits information about opportunities, techniques, and motivations, as well as a protective shield that reduces the visibility of professional misconduct.

Gender

Gender is one of the strongest predictors of criminality. In general, men commit far more crimes than women. A quick examination of the statistics on criminal arrests, however, appears to cast some doubt about the validity of this generalization for white collar crimes. Although only 17.4 percent of the persons arrested in the United States in 1985 were female, women made up 35.6 percent of those arrested for embezzlement and 42.6 percent of those arrested for fraud (a higher percentage than for any other crime except prostitution and vice). [129] However, Kathleen Daly's analysis of a sample of presentence reports from seven federal court districts indicates that there are indeed very great differences between male and female white collar offenders. [130] The women in Daly's sample were younger, less educated, and had lower-status positions and lower incomes than the men. She also found that the women made less money from their crimes and were less likely to commit their offenses as part of a group. Although this study included many offenses that do not fall within the definition of white collar crime used in this book (welfare fraud, for example), a comparison of the gender differences among specific white collar offenses produces some interesting results. Women were extremely underrepresented among those charged with the two offenses that are most likely to be corporate crimes. An overwhelming 98 percent of those charged with antitrust and SEC violations were male. In contrast, 45 percent of those charged with bank embezzlement were female. The women charged with bank embezzlement were more likely to be tellers, while the men were more likely to be bank officers or financial managers. The crimes of these women were also "generally less sophisticated than men's, of shorter duration, and less likely to be carried out with others." [131]

One possible explanation of these findings is that differences in social expectations and socialization create different motivational patterns for women and men. For example, some studies of moral reasoning indicate that women are more likely to see moral issues in terms of a network of interconnecting responsibilities, while men are more prone to see such issues in terms of individual rights based on formal rules. [132] Such differences might contribute to the lower overall crime rate among women and their relatively greater involvement in white collar than street crimes. Other social-psychological research indicates that men are more task oriented in their group behavior,[133] which might help explain why men's white collar crimes involved a larger group of conspirators. At this point, however, such contentions are mere speculation. Little empirical research has yet been done on gender differences in the motivation of white collar criminals, and none of it specifically addresses these points.

What the available research does show is that men and women tend to use different rationalizations to justify their white collar crimes. The most comprehensive study of this issue was conducted by Dorothy Zietz, who found that many of the generalizations Cressey had made about male embezzlers did not apply to the embezzlers she interviewed in the California Institution for Women.[134] Cressey's subjects needed money because of "non-shareable" problems they had brought upon themselves, and they rationalized their crimes by telling themselves that they were only borrowing the money. Zietz's subjects, on the other hand, cited problems for which they were not responsible and seldom used the borrowing rationalization. Zietz's embezzlers were far more likely to justify their offenses in terms of the needs of their spouse or children.

Zietz's findings have received mixed support from other researchers. In a small case study of convicted embezzlers, Sue Mahan concluded that Cressey's theory was very applicable to some female embezzlers.[135] Zietz's conclusion about the use of family based rationalizations by female offenders finds support in Daly's research. Although Zietz found that all of her subjects used the family rationalization, and only 29 percent of Daly's sample of embezzlers used that rationalization, Daly still found that the family rationalization was used about twice as often by women than men. The impact of the differences in the distribution of rationalizations among females and males is still unclear, however. For one thing, both genders appear to share many rationalizations. Moreover, the different rationalizations preferred by males and females all appear to provide effective justifications for white collar crime, and it is difficult to determine if this difference has any impact on the actual incidence of embezzlement or other crimes.

While the issue of motivational differences remains unresolved, differences in the opportunity structure for women and men clearly have a powerful effect on white collar criminality. Daly's finding that very few women are involved in corporate crimes obviously reflects the gross underrepresentation of women in the higher circles of corporate decision making. Of course, this same pattern of discrimination continues down through the middle and lower levels of the corporate hierarchy and has a similar effect in patterning the distribution of white collar offenses. The fact that female bank embezzlers are more likely to be tellers, while males have a greater likelihood of holding managerial positions, seems to be an obvious reason why women's crimes were less sophisticated, netted lower returns, and were less likely to be committed by a group of offenders. We cannot, however, assume that men and women in the same occupational position are necessarily presented with the same opportunities for white collar crime. Steven Box, for example, argues that female workers are more closely supervised than their male counterparts in the same job and, therefore, have fewer criminal opportunities.[136] Research on managerial women also indicates that they are often excluded from the social networks of their male colleagues[137] — another condition that might tend to reduce the availability of criminal opportunity.

REVIEW

As we have seen, the pattern of etiological factors that generate white collar crime is indeed a complex one. Although social scientists have tended to focus on either the social-psychological or the structural level, a complete understanding of the causes of white collar crime requires us to recognize the interdependence of those two approaches. On one hand, social-psychological analysis alone leaves us ignorant of the social and historical forces that shape all human behavior. An analysis focused exclusively on structural variables, on the other hand, neglects the personal dimension of human behavior and ultimately cannot account for any individual offenses.

Our analysis has shown that white collar crime is caused by the coincidence of three necessary conditions, the first of which is motivation. There must be some reason why an individual turns to white collar crime. In most cases, the motivation is the desire for financial gain or the wish to be seen as a success in the eyes of others. Although many people believe such motivations to be a part of human nature, that is clearly not the case. Rather, the political economy of industrial capitalism, with its enormous economic surplus and reliance on a system of market exchange, has given rise to a culture of competition that fosters these motivations.

The second requirement is the neutralization of the ethical restraints that inhibit criminal behavior. On the individual level, this is achieved through the use of various rationalizations that justify the offender's behavior. Oftentimes these rationalizations are learned on the job, but there are many other sources as well. In the case of organizational crime, this process of neutralization is greatly facilitated by the power of large organizations to shape the definitions that guide the behavior of their employees. Thus, criminal activities may be defined in such a way as to make them appear to be routine, unproblematic behavior, or at least a necessary part of the job.

Finally, along with the desire, there must also be an opportunity. The fact that popular mass movements have been able to force the adoption of legal restrictions on many abuses of the elite, but have been unable to win effective enforcement of those standards, creates a rich profusion of opportunities for white collar criminality. The distribution of those opportunities was found to be influenced by many different variables among the various occupations, organizations, and industries in which people are employed.

NOTES

1. Albert Cohen, Alfred Lindesmith, and Karl Schuessler, eds. *The Sutherland Papers* (Bloomington, Ind.: Indiana University Press, 1956), 96.

2. Richard H. Blum, *Deceivers and Deceived* (Springfield, Ill.: Charles Thomas, 1972), 145–157; Walter Bromberg, *Crime and the Mind: A Psychiatric Analysis of Crime and Punishment* (New York: Macmillan, 1965), 377–400; Lonell S. Selling, "Specific War Crimes," *Journal of Criminal Law, Criminology, and Police Science* 34 (January-February 1944): 303–310; John C. Spencer, "White Collar Crime," in Edward Glover, Hermann Mannheim, and Emanuel Miller, *Criminology in Transition* (London: Tavistock, 1965), 233–266.

3. Edwin H. Sutherland, *White Collar Crime* (New York: Dryden Press, 1949), 257–266.

4. Selling, "Specific War Crimes."

5. Bromberg, *Crime and the Mind*, 388.

6. Spencer, "White Collar Crime," 259.

7. Ibid., 261.

8. Blum, *Deceivers and Deceived*, 154.

9. Ibid., 145–157.

10. Willem Bonger, *Criminality and Economic Conditions*, abridged by Austin T. Turk (Bloomington, Ind.: Indiana University Press, 1969; originally published in 1905 as *Criminalité et conditions économiques*), 137, italics in the original.

11. J. Scott Armstrong, "Social Irresponsibility in Management," *Journal of Business Research* 5 (1977): 185–213.

12. Robert E. Lane, *The Regulation of Businessmen: Social Conditions of Government Economic Control* (New Haven: Yale University Press, 1954), 90.

13. Cesare Beccaria, *An Essay on Crimes and Punishments* (London: Almon, 1767); Jeremy Bentham, *An Introduction to the Principles of Morals and Legislation* (London: Pickering, 1823).

14. See notes 95 through 101.

15. Richard Woodley, "The Importance of Being Number One," in Leonard D. Savitz and Norman Johnston, eds., *Contemporary Criminology* (New York: Wiley, 1982), 117–125.

16. Bromberg, *Crime and the Mind*, 389.

17. David G. Savage, "High School Cheating: 75% Admit It, Cite Pressure" *Los Angeles Times*, 17 April 1986, I: 3 & 29.

18. Joe R. Feagin, *Subordinating the Poor: Welfare and American Beliefs* (Englewood Cliffs, N.J.: Prentice-Hall, 1975), does an excellent job of showing how the "ideology of individualism" serves to legitimate the American system of stratification and to subordinate the poor.

19. Malcolm X, *The Autobiography of Malcolm X* (New York: Grover, 1965), 109.

20. Sutherland, *White Collar Crime*, 234.

21. Edwin Sutherland, *Principles of Criminology* (Chicago: J. B. Lippincott, 1947), 6.

22. See Max Weber, *Ancient Judaism*, trans. by Hans Gerth and Don Martindale (New York: Free Press, 1932), esp. 80; Hans Gerth and C. Wright Mills, trans., *From Max Weber: Essays in Sociology* (New York: Oxford, 1946), esp. 280.

23. See Ruth Benedict, *Patterns of Culture* (Boston: Houghton-Mifflin, 1934). Also see Marvin Harris, *Culture, People, Nature*, 3rd ed. (New York: Harper & Row, 1980), 233–237.

24. Bonger, *Criminality and Economic Conditions*, 37. On this point, also see Eleanor Leacock, "Women's Status in Egalitarian Society: Implications for Social Evolution," *Current Anthropology* 19 (June 1978): 247–255.

25. Richard Borshay Lee, *The !Kung San: Men, Women, and Work in a Foraging Society* (Cambridge: Cambridge University Press, 1979).

26. Robert Knox Dentan, *The Semai: A Nonviolent People of Malaya* (New York: Holt, Rinehart and Winston, 1968).

27. Dentan, *The Semai*, 49.

28. Numerous scholars in the Marxist tradition have commented upon this point, including Freidrich Engels, *The Origin of the Family, Private Property, and the State* (New York: International, 1972); Leacock, "Women's Status in Egalitarian Societies"; Bonger, *Criminality and Economic Conditions*, esp. 37–38.

29. See Hans Georg Amsel, "Money and Criminality: A Reorientation of Criminological Research," *International Journal of Criminology and Penology* 1 (1973): 179–187.

30. See Maria Łoś, "Crime and Economy in the Communist Countries," in Peter Wickman and Timothy Dailey, eds., *White-Collar and Economic Crime* (Lexington, Mass.: Lexington Books, 1982), 121–138.

31. Edwin M. Schur, *Our Criminal Society: The Social and Legal Sources of Crime in America* (Englewood Cliffs, N.J.: Prentice-Hall, 1969), 187.

32. Gresham M. Sykes and David Matza, "Techniques of Neutralization: A Theory of Delinquency," *American Sociological Review* 22 (December 1957): 667–670.

33. Gilbert Geis and Robert F. Meier, eds., *White Collar Crime*, rev. ed. (New York: The Free Press, 1977), 149: "A major characteristic these behaviors [white-collar crime] share is that their perpetrators rarely regard themselves as criminals or, indeed, as deserving of censure or punitive treatment."

34. See Donald R. Cressey, *Other People's Money: A Study in the Social Psychology of Embezzlement* (Belmont, Cal.: Wadsworth, 1971). (Originally published 1953.)

35. G. E. Levens, "101 British White-Collar Criminals," *New Society*, 26 March 1964: 6–8; Virgil W. Peterson, "Why Honest People Steal," *Journal of Criminal Law and Criminology* 38 (July-August 1947): 94–103; "Postwar Embezzler Is Younger, Lives Faster, Is Less Inclined to Suicide," *Journal of Accountancy* 90 (October 1950): 344; Svend H. Riemer, "Embezzlement: Pathological Basis," *Journal of Criminal Law and Criminology* 32 (November-December 1941): 411–423; Cressey, *Other People's Money*.

36. Cressey, *Other People's Money*.

37. Gwynn Nettler, "Embezzlement Without Problems," *British Journal of Criminology* 14 (January 1974): 70–77; Dorothy Zietz, *Women Who Embezzle or Defraud: A Study of Convicted Felons* (New York: Praeger, 1981).

38. Cressey, *Other People's Money*, 101.

39. Quoted in Gilbert Geis, "The Heavy Electrical Equipment Cases of 1961," in Geis and Meier, *White-Collar Crime*, 122.

40. Lawrence R. Zeitlin, "A Little Larceny Can Do a Lot for Company Morale," *Psychology Today* 14 (June 1971): 22 *passim*.

41. Erwin O. Smigel, "Public Attitudes Toward Stealing as Related to the Size of the Victim Organization," *American Sociological Review* 21 (June 1956): 320–326.

42. Marshall B. Clinard, *The Black Market: A Study of White-Collar Crime* (New York: Rinehart and Co., 1952), 169.

43. Harry V. Ball, "Social Structure and Rent-Control Violations," *American Journal of Sociology* 65 (May 1960): 598–604.

44. Sutherland, *White-Collar Crime*, 236.

45. Steven Chibnall and Peter Saunders, "Worlds Apart: Notes on the Social Relativity of Corruption," *British Journal of Sociology* 28 (June 1977): 138–154.

46. Geis, "Heavy Electrical Equipment Cases," 122, 123.

47. Kathleen Daly, "Gender and White Collar Crime," presented at the Meetings of the American Society of Criminology, Atlanta, Georgia (October/November 1986).

48. Cressey, *Other People's Money*, 35.

49. Michael L. Benson, "Denying the Guilty Mind: Accounting for Involvement in White Collar Crime," *Criminology*, 23 (1985): 585–607.

50. Chibnall and Saunders, "Worlds Apart," 142.

51. See Geis, "Heavy Electrical Equipment Cases," 123.

52. Gerald Mars, "Dock Pilferage: A Case Study in Occupational Theft," in Paul Rock and Mary McIntosh, eds., *Deviance and Social Control* (London: Tavistock, 1974), 224.

53. Zeitlin, "A Little Larceny," 22.

54. Chibnall and Saunders, "Worlds Apart," 143.

55. Cressey, *Other People's Money*, 137.

56. Raymond C. Baumhart, "How Ethical Are Businessmen?," *Harvard Business Review* 39 (July-August 1961): 5–179.

57. L. Howard Silk and David Vogel, *Ethics and Profits: The Crisis of Confidence in American Business* (New York: Simon & Schuster, 1976).

58. Carl Madden, "Forces Which Influence Ethical Behavior," in *The Ethics of Corporate Conduct* (Englewood Cliffs, N.J.: Prentice-Hall, 1977). Also see Marshall B. Clinard and Peter C. Yeager, *Corporate Crime* (New York: Macmillan, 1980), 67–68.

59. *Time*, 19 November 1979, 85.

60. See Geis, "Heavy Electrical Equipment Cases," 124.

61. Ibid.

62. Quoted in Clinard and Yeager, *Corporate Crime*, 65.

63. William E. Blundell, "Equity Funding: I Did It for the Jollies," in Donald Moffitt, ed., *Swindled!: Classic Business Frauds of the Seventies* (Princeton, N.J.: Dow Jones Books, 1976), 46.

64. Donald R. Cressey, "Employee Theft: The Reasons Why," *Security World* (October 1980): 31–36.

65. Clinard and Yeager, *Corporate Crime*, 60.

66. See Diane Rothbard Margolis, *The Managers: Corporate Life in America* (New York: William Morrow, 1979).

67. William H. Whyte, Jr., *The Organization Man* (Garden City, N.Y.: Anchor Books, 1957).

68. Margolis, *The Managers*, 118.

69. Frank W. Howton, *Functionaries* (Chicago: Quadrangle, 1969), 5–6.

70. Max Weber, *The Theory of Social and Economic Organization*, trans. by A. M. Henderson and Talcott Parsons (New York: The Free Press, 1964), 329–341.

71. Margolis, *The Managers*, 63.

72. See Margolis, *The Managers*, 41–66, for an excellent description of this process.

73. C. Wright Mills, *The Power Elite* (New York: Oxford University Press, 1959), 343.

74. James G. March and Herbert A. Simon, *Organizations* (New York: John Wiley and Sons, 1958); Charles Perrow, *Complex Organizations: A Critical Essay* (Glenview, Ill.: Scott Foresman, 1972), esp. 145–176.

75. Quoted in Geis, "Heavy Electrical Equipment Cases," 123.

76. James T. Carey, *Introduction to Criminology* (Englewood Cliffs, N.J.: Prentice-Hall, 1978), 384.

77. See Geis, "Heavy Electrical Equipment Cases."

78. Baumhart, "How Ethical Are Businessmen?"; S. N. Brenner and E. A. Molander, "Is the Ethics of Business Changing?," *Harvard Business Review* 55 (January-February 1977): 59-70.

79. Sara Fritz and Karen Tumulty, "Did Not Tell Reagan of Funds Diversion, Poindexter Testifies" *Los Angeles Times*, 16 July 1987, I: 1 *passim*.

80. Peter F. Drucker, *Concept of the Corporation*, rev. ed. (New York: John Day Company, 1972), 88. Sutherland also examined the issue of the isolation of corporate executives, see *White Collar Crime*, 247–253.

81. For a more detailed analysis, see James William Coleman, "Toward an Integrated Theory of White Collar Crime," *American Journal of Sociology* (September, 1987): 406–439.

82. Łoś, "Crime and Economy in Communist Countries."

240 THE CRIMINAL ELITE

83. These figures are apparently for 1967. See Walter D. Connor, *Deviance in Soviet Society: Crime, Delinquency, and Alcoholism* (New York: Columbia University Press, 1972), 148–150.

84. On this topic, also see Valery Chalidze, *Criminal Russia: Crime in the Soviet Union* (New York: Random House, 1977), 195–196; Louise Shelley, "The Geography of Soviet Criminality," *American Sociological Review* 45 (February 1980), 111–122; Christopher S. Wren, "Graft and Embezzlement, Most Persistent Crimes in Soviet, Continue to Plague Economy," *The New York Times*, 13 April 1976, 17.

85. J. F. Burton, Jr., "An Economic Analysis of Sherman Act Criminal Cases," in J. M. Clabault and J. F. Burton, Jr., eds., *Sherman Act Indictments, 1955–1965: A Legal and Economic Analysis* (New York: Federal Legal Publications, 1966); Jeffrey Pfeffer and Gerald R. Salancik, *The External Control of Organizations: A Resource Dependence Perspective* (New York: Harper and Row, 1978), esp. 124–125, 183; Marc Riedel, "Corporate Crime and Interfirm Organization: A Study of Penalized Sherman Act Violations," *Graduate Sociology Club Journal* 8 (1968): 74–97. Also see Clinard and Yeager, *Corporate Crime*, 50–51.

86. George Hay and Daniel Kelley, "An Empirical Survey of Price-Fixing Conspiracies," *Journal of Law and Economics* 17 (April 1974): 13–39.

87. Peter Asch and J. J. Seneca, "Is Collusion Profitable?," *The Review of Economics and Statistics* 58 (February 1969): 1–12.

88. Richard Posner, "A Statistical Study of Antitrust Enforcement," *Journal of Law and Economics* 13 (October 1970): 365–420.

89. Marshall Clinard, Peter Yeager, J. M. Brissette, D. Petrashek, and E. Harries, *Illegal Corporate Behavior* (Washington, D.C.: U.S. Government Printing Office, 1979).

90. Clinard and Yeager, *Corporate Crime*, 51.

91. Ibid., 165–166.

92. Yerachmiel Kugel and Gladys W. Gruenberg, *International Payoffs* (Lexington, Mass.: Lexington Books, 1977), 36.

93. Kugel and Gruenberg, *International Payoffs*, 47.

94. Harvey A. Farberman, "A Criminogenic Market Structure: The Automobile Industry," *The Sociological Quarterly* 16 (Autumn 1975): 438–457.

95. William N. Leonard, and Marvin Glenn Weber, "Automakers and Dealers: A Study of Criminogenic Market Forces," *Law and Society Review* 4 (February 1970): 407–424.

96. Norman Denzin, "Notes on the Criminogenic Hypothesis: A Case Study of the American Liquor Industry," *American Sociological Review* 42 (December 1977): 905–920.

97. Martin L. Needleman and Carolyn Needleman, "Organizational Crime: Two Models of Criminogenesis," *The Sociology Quarterly* 20 (Autumn 1979): 517–528.

98. David Weisburd, Elin Waring, and Stanton Wheeler, "Examining Opportunity Structures in White Collar Crime: The Roles of Social Status and Structural Position," presented at the meetings of the American Society of Criminology, Montreal, Canada (November 1987).

99. Edward Gross, "Organizational Structure and Organizational Crime," in Gilbert Geis and Ezra Stotland (eds.), *White-Collar Crime: Theory and Research* (Beverly Hills: Sage, 1980), 52–77.

100. Marshall B. Clinard, Peter C. Yeager, Jeanne Brissette, David Petrashek, and Elizabeth Harries, *Illegal Corporate Behavior* (Washington, D.C.: U.S. Department of Justice, October, 1979), 102–107.

101. Edwin H. Sutherland, *White Collar Crime: The Uncut Version* (New Haven, Conn.: Yale University Press, 1983, originally published in 1949), 246–250; Clinard and Yeager, *Corporate Crime*, 60–63; Donald R. Cressey, "Restraints of Trade, Recidivism and Delinquent Neighborhoods," in James Short, Jr. (ed.), *Delinquency, Crime and Society* (Chicago: University of Chicago Press, 1976).

102. Harold C. Barnett, "Branch Culture and Economic Structure: Correlates of Tax Noncompliance in Sweden." Revised version of a paper presented to the American Society of Criminology, Cincinnati, Ohio, November 9, 1984.

103. John Kenneth Galbraith, *The New Industrial State* (New York: Signet Books, 1967).

104. David R. James and Michael Soref, "Profit Constraints on Managerial Autonomy: Managerial Theory and the Unmaking of the Corporation President," *American Sociological Review* 46 (February 1981): 1–18.

105. In further contradiction of Galbraith's thesis, Larner found no significant differences in the profit orientation of manager- and owner-controlled firms. Robert Larner, *Management Control and the Large Corporation* (New York: Dunellen, 1970).

106. Ronald C. Kramer, "Corporate Crime: An Organizational Perspective," in Wickman and Dailey, *White-Collar and Economic Crime*, 75–94.

107. Marshall B. Clinard, "Corporate Ethics, Illegal Behavior, and Government Regulation: Views of Middle Management," report to the National Institute of Justice (Washington, D.C., 1982).

108. Andrew Hopkins, "The Anatomy of Corporate Crime," in Paul R. Wilson and John Braithwaite, eds., *Two Faces of Deviance: Crimes of the Powerless and the Powerful* (St. Lucia, Queensland: University of Queensland Press, 1978), 214–231.

109. On the limitations on the power of those at the top of the corporate hierarchy, see Rosabeth Moss Kanter and Barry Stein, eds., *Life in Organizations: Workplaces as People Experience Them* (New York: Basic Books, 1979), 3–21; Warren Bennis, *The Unconscious Conspiracy: Why Leaders Can't Lead* (American Management Associations, 1976).

110. George Katona, *Price Control and Business* (Bloomington, Ind.: Indiana University Press, 1946), 241.

111. Robert E. Lane, *The Regulation of Businessmen: Social Conditions of Government Control* (New Haven: Yale University Press, 1954), 94.

112. Geis, "Heavy Electrical Equipment Cases."

113. Barry M. Staw and Eugene Szwajkowski, "The Scarcity-Munificence Component of Organizational Environments and the Commission of Illegal Acts," *Administrative Science Quarterly* 20 (September 1975): 345–354.

114. Clinard and Yeager, *Corporate Crime*, 129. Emphasis in the original.

115. Clinard, *The Black Market*. The conclusions of this study are, however, cast into doubt by the fact that Clinard erroneously cites Katona's work as part of the support for his conclusions. On p. 324, Clinard cites a table in Katona's book showing a weak relationship between profitability and *attitudes* toward price controls and then claims that "Katona concluded that sales and profits were not related to price violations." However, in Appendix III of his work, Katona clearly arrived at different conclusions.

116. Sally S. Simpson, "The Decomposition of Antitrust: Testing a Multi-level Longitudinal Model of Profit-Squeeze," *American Sociological Review* 51 (December 1986): 859–875; also see Sally S. Simpson, "Cycles of Illegality: Antitrust Violations in Corporate America," *Social Forces* 65 (June 1987): 943–963.

117. John E. Conklin, *Illegal But Not Criminal: Business Crime in America* (Englewood Cliffs, N.J.: Prentice-Hall, 1977), 64–65.

118. See Lane, *Regulation of Businessmen*, 96–97; Clinard, *The Black Market*, 325; Katona, *Price Control and Business*, 128–129.

119. Lane, *Regulation of Businessmen*, 97–98.

120. Ibid., 98.

121. Clinard and Yeager, *Corporate Crime*, 130.

122. Roger William Riis and John Patric, *Repairmen Will Get You if You Don't Watch Out* (New York: Doubleday, Doran & Co., 1942).

123. Eileen Shanahan, "Tax Errors Seen Among Concerns," *The New York Times*, 21 July 1975, 31–32.

124. Knapp Commission, *The Knapp Commission Report on Police Corruption* (New York: George Braziller, 1972); Pennsylvania Crime Commission, *Report on Police Corruption and the Quality of Law Enforcement in Philadelphia*, 1974.

125. For an interesting analysis of some of the factors contributing to corruption in local land use regulation, see John A. Gardiner and Theodore R. Lyman, *Decisions for Sale: Corruption and Reform in Land-Use and Building Regulation* (New York: Praeger, 1978), 138–180.

126. Weisburd, Waring, and Wheeler, "Examining Opportunity Structures in White Collar Crime."

127. John P. Clark and Richard C. Hollinger, *Theft by Employees in Work Organizations* (Washington, D.C.: National Institute of Justice, September, 1983).

128. Donald N. M. Horning, "Blue Collar Theft: Conceptions of Property Attitudes Toward Pilfering and Work Group Norms in a Modern Industrial Plant," in Erwin O. Smigel and H. Lawrence Ross, eds., *Crime Against the Bureaucracy* (New York: Van Nostrand Reinhold, 1970).

129. U. S. Department of Justice, Bureau of Justice Statistics, *Sourcebook of Criminal Justice Statistic—1986* (Washington, D.C.: GPO, 1987), 298.

130. Kathleen Daly, "Gender and White-Collar Crime," presented at the Meeting of the American Society of Criminology, Atlanta, Georgia, October 1986.

131. Daly, "White-Collar Crime and Gender," 18.

132. Carol Gilligan, *In A Different Voice: Psychological Theory and Women's Development* (Cambridge: Harvard University Press, 1982); Josephine Donovan, *Feminist Theory* (New York: Fredrick Ungar, 1985).

133. See Alice H. Eagly, *Sex Differences in Social Behavior: A Social-Role Interpretation* (Hillsdale, N.J.: Lawrence Erlbaum, 1987), 108–110.

134. Dorothy Zietz, *Women who Embezzle or Defraud: A Study of Convicted Felons* (New York: Praeger, 1981).

135. Sue Mahan, "Opportunities for Women in White Collar Crime," presented at the Meeting of the American Society of Criminology, Montreal, Canada 1987.

136. Steven Box, *Power, Crime and Mystification* (New York: Tavistock, 1983).

137. See Rosabeth Kanter, *Men and Women of the Corporation* (New York: Basic Books, 1977).

7

The Criminal Elite

Through the pages of this book we have seen that white collar criminals are indeed members of a criminal elite. In comparison with other criminals, they make more money from their crimes, they run fewer physical risks, their chances of arrest or conviction are lower, and if convicted they receive lighter penalties. Although precise quantitative data are lacking, we have also seen that criminal activities are surprisingly common among elite groups that might be thought to have little to gain from such behavior. Thus, we have a criminal elite in another sense as well—an elite frequently involved in crime, but one that seems able to ignore the laws that constrain the other strata of society.

White collar crime is, as we have seen, an enormously complex phenomenon. In order to handle so cumbersome a topic, it was necessary to break it down into many smaller units. But all the issues we have examined—the legal definition of white collar crime, its causes, the enforcement effort, and the characteristics of the crimes—are facets of a single problem. This topical approach tends to isolate these issues from one another, and as a result we risk losing sight of their subtle interconnections. Our next task is therefore to present an integrated restatement of the main points of this study that makes these interconnections explicit.

THE PROBLEM OF WHITE COLLAR CRIME: A SUMMARY

The problem of white collar crime is rooted in the social conflicts of industrial society. One of the most important of these is class conflict, and especially the struggle for power and profits waged between the dominant elite and the less privileged strata of society. Most of the laws creating organizational crimes were the product of the interaction between the efforts of farmers, consumers, workers, or the general public to limit abuses of the elite and the response of the elite to those social movements. The origins of the laws prohibiting occupational crimes such as embezzlement and employee pilferage can, on the other hand, be traced to the efforts to protect the interests of much more privileged groups by regulating the behavior of the lower classes. The same class conflicts can also be seen in the enforcement process, for example, in the success the elite has had in weakening the enforcement of legislation that threatens its interests or its use of law enforcement as a tool to suppress the political activities of its critics.

But the battle lines do not always coincide so neatly with the divisions of the class system. Environmental protection is apt to be as beneficial to the upper class as the lower. A specific antitrust action may benefit some corporate interests while harming others. And in many occupational crimes, the victims and the offenders come from the same social strata.

The laws defining the white collar crimes have diverse historical origins, but all of them can ultimately be traced back to the dislocations and conflicts caused by the growth of industrial capitalism. Antitrust legislation was a response to the economic squeeze put on small farmers and business people by the growth of the giant corporations. Consumer protection laws can be seen as substitutes for the informal controls that regulated commerce in small-town America. Legislation regulating political campaigns formed part of an effort to maintain and improve democratic institutions in the face of the growing centralization of economic power. Worker and environmental protection legislation can be traced to the recognition of the dangerous side effects of industrial technology. But such problems do not automatically generate new legislation. Rather, legislative change comes about as a result of the conflict between organized interest groups.

Most white collar crime legislation has been the product of struggles between popular mass movements (with occasional support from some segments of the upper class) and entrenched elite interests. The efforts of the antimonopoly, populist, consumer, and environmental movements all fit a similar pattern. At first, the reformers encounter a stone wall of elite opposition that frustrates their efforts. But if the movement is able to take advantage of such factors as well-publicized disasters and scandals, widespread popular support, and effective organization and leadership, they may ultimately win passage of new legislation. Yet even when elite interests fail to defeat reform legislation, they still exert great influence in shaping its final form.

The prohibition of such activities as embezzlement and industrial espionage followed a different pattern, which might be called "reform from the top." Because the changes were initiated by elite interests, they did not require popular pressure for enactment. Indeed, many of these reforms arose from new judicial interpretations that involved no changes in statutory law. When new laws were created, the legislative process generally occurred with a minimum of public involvement and without great media attention.

The passage of new legislation is not, as it is so often pictured, the end of the struggle for reform—it is the beginning. The same interests continue their conflict, this time over control of the enforcement process. And in this second struggle, elite interests are in an even stronger position than they are in the legislative arena. Despite the elite's power to manipulate the media, the political process is far more open to public view than the enforcement bureaucracy, and the voting power of the masses may help counter the political influence that inevitably flows from vast concentrations of wealth and power. However, the popular appeal of reformist movements is of considerably less strategic significance in influencing the enforcement process.

A comparison of the treatment of white collar criminals and street criminals demonstrates the justice system's double standard. For one thing, white collar criminals are much less likely to be arrested. And even if they are arrested and convicted, white collar criminals typically receive much lighter punishment than those who have committed street crimes of equal severity. Despite this overall pattern of leniency, many occupational criminals do receive jail sentences or other meaningful punishment; but the same is seldom true of those involved in organizational crimes. Organizational criminals are usually given nothing more than a warning or an order to stop their illegal activities. Even when punishments are meted out, in most cases they involve only small fines that do not even equal the profit the offenders made from their crimes.

The reasons for this unequal justice can be traced to the great structural advantages enjoyed by white collar criminals. For one thing, the organization of the justice system favors the white collar criminal. The investigation of occupational crimes is usually left in the hands of small, understaffed "fraud units" in the offices of state or local prosecutors, whereas local police departments with much greater investigative resources largely ignore the problem. Influential professions such as law and medicine have won broad powers of self-regulation that often serve as a shield against outside "interference" from the criminal justice system. And finally, most white collar defendants in criminal or civil court enjoy the advantages of wealth, prestige, and the best legal representation.

The responsibility for most organizational crimes has been shifted away from the criminal justice system to specially created regulatory agencies that are more inclined to negotiate cooperative settlements than to pursue tough criminal sanctions. Moreover, elite interests have generally been successful in preventing the allocation of sufficient resources to those agencies to enable them to carry out their legislative mandates effectively. Regulatory agencies are almost always underfunded and understaffed, especially in comparison with the vast resources at the disposal of the corporate offenders they must police. In criminal cases, organizational offenders also benefit from the individualistic bias of our legal system, which often makes it necessary to sift through complex networks of organizational interactions in order to prove the criminal intent of each individual defendant.

Compared to other offenders, the social and political power of corporate criminals puts them in an entirely different position vis-à-vis the justice system. Corporate criminals often have the strength to fend off, wear down, or even overpower the enforcement effort. Delaying tactics have proven to be one of the corporate criminal's most effective strategies. Whereas the strength of the enforcement effort waxes and wanes with the changes in the political climate, the profit-seeking private corporation never wavers in the pursuit of its own interests. Thus, corporate criminals seek to delay legal proceedings as long as possible, while waiting for a change in the political climate that will let them off the hook. In some cases, powerful corporate criminals use direct intimidation, threatening to close a large plant or to move overseas if enforcement agencies don't adopt a more "reasonable" attitude. In others, they attempt to corrupt individual officials with the lure of high-paying jobs in private industry, big campaign contributions, or sometimes even outright bribes.

Secrecy is one tool used by white collar and street criminals alike. But white collar criminals, and especially organizational criminals, enjoy some important advantages in its use. For one thing, the victims of white collar crime are often unaware of the causes of their problems and thus cannot complain to enforcement agencies. Another major advantage enjoyed by organizational criminals is the wall of secrecy that corporations and government agencies build to protect themselves from outside scrutiny. In many cases, there is a legitimate need to protect sensitive information, but the same security measures can also serve to conceal illegal activities.

It would be easy to conclude that the principal cause of white collar crime is the offenders' knowledge that they run little risk of significant punishment, but the matter is a good deal more complex than that. It is as necessary to explain the motivations of the offenders and the structure of illicit opportunities as it is to account for the failure of the mechanisms of social control. No monocausal explanation can account for the complex interrelationships between the social-psychological and structural variables that lie at the root of the problem of white collar crime.

On the social-psychological level, individuals are pushed toward white collar crime by the same craving for money and success that motivates so many other crimes. Such motivations are often combined with pressures, exerted by occupational subcultures or superiors, that encourage or even demand illegal activities. The occupational subculture in many urban police departments, for example, requires officers to participate in some petty corruption if they want to be considered "one of the gang." Similar pressures are often brought to bear on government or corporate employees to carry on criminal activities for the sake of their organizations.

The combination of such motivations can create strong psychological pressure to become involved in white collar crime; however, a belief in moral or ethical principles often generates a powerful contravening force of its own. Thus, the way an individual resolves this conflict will obviously have a great influence on his or her potential for criminal behavior. White collar offenders use a variety of common rationalizations to neutralize those ethical standards and maintain a positive self-image despite their deviant behavior. Typically, they justify their behavior by telling themselves that no one is really being harmed by their activities, that the laws are unjust, that some criminal activities are necessary for economic survival, that everybody else is doing it, or that they deserve the extra money their crimes produce.

Although many criminologists are content with such personal explanations, the roots of these psychological forces lie in the structure of contemporary industrial society. The desire for wealth and success, more than merely an individual personality trait, is part of the culture of competition found to one degree or another in all industrial societies. These societies generate large economic surpluses and are characterized by high degrees of inequality, yet unlike agricultural societies, they also have considerable social mobility. This combination inevitably encourages the desire to outdo one's fellows in the accumulation of material goods and the symbols of success. Moreover, the competitive nature of economic organization in capitalist nations serves to further strengthen the culture of competition in its position as a dominant cultural force.

The political economy of industrial capitalism and the diverse interest groups it creates also structure the definitions of criminal behavior. And once the laws and the enforcement priorities have been set, structural variables also determine the distribution of the most attractive opportunities for white collar crime. Thus, crime rates in the pharmaceutical and automotive industries are high because the dangers associated with their products create strong public pressure for government regulation and, thereby, the temptation to violate those regulations. In a more general way, the demand for profitability the economic system places on all private businesses is a primary motivation for organizational crime. A business must make profits in order to survive and prosper, and criminal activities often provide an effective way of making those profits.

WHAT CAN BE DONE?

Crime, as Emile Durkheim pointed out long ago, is inevitable in modern societies. The function of criminal law is to create crime by branding certain people and certain behaviors as deviant. A law that no one broke would be an unnecessary law. Thus, a certain amount of white collar crime is inevitable in any society that bases its legal system on standards that apply to all social strata. But as we have seen, the incidence of white collar crime goes far beyond this inevitable minimum. No other kind of crime—and indeed, few problems of any sort—can even approach the hundreds of thousands of lives and billions of dollars lost every year through white collar crime.

The aim of this final section is to explore some of the ways of dealing with this pressing problem. Although its conclusions are based on the preceding analysis, a crystal ball is not part of the standard inventory of sociological tools. The sociology of deviance has shown the unexpected damage done by past efforts to deal with such problems as drug use and prostitution through criminal law,[1] and there are no guarantees that any of the following proposals would have the desired effects. Yet there is good reason to believe that the growing body of research into the problem of white collar crime can help us avoid the mistakes of the moral crusaders of the past.

Ethical Reforms

One of the most common reactions to the news of some heinous crime is to ask, "What kind of a person would do such a thing?" and to blame the crime on the moral failings of the criminal. Sociologists have long opposed such one-sidedly individualistic explanations, and they are especially suspect when applied to white collar crime. Organizations and occupational subcultures generate powerful pressures on employees to conform to their expectations, and any effort to deal with the problem of white collar crime on this level must be aimed at changing the "ethical climate" within the corporations and the government. DeFleur argued that "because it is impossible to police everyone . . . a reduction in illegal corporate behavior depends on the development of stronger codes of ethics in business."[2]   But how can that be done? He recommended three ways in which those goals might be met: (1) courses in ethics should be made mandatory in business schools, (2) trade associations should establish uniform ethical codes for each industry, and (3) individual corporations should make systematic efforts to develop ethical codes and instill them in their employees.[3]

To more structurally oriented sociologists, however, such proposals appear extremely naive. It is hard to imagine that a single college class, or even a series of them, would be likely to stimulate achievement-oriented young managers to defy the expectations of the organizations on whose approval their futures depend. It is equally difficult to imagine that an industry trade association would promulgate any standards of behavior that ran counter to the financial interests of its members, or that the members would follow the standards if they did. High sounding codes of ethics may make for good public relations, but by themselves they are unlikely to have any effect on the "ethical climate" of the government or the business world. After a careful statistical comparison of corporations with codes of ethics with explicit penalties, corporations with codes but without penalties, and corporations with no codes at all, Marilynn Mathews concluded that: "It just didn't make a difference."[4]

A structural analysis suggests that ethical standards will change only when the structural rewards for unethical behavior change. What is necessary, then, is some way to make ethical behavior more rewarding than criminal behavior. The most obvious course of action would be to increase the civil and criminal penalties for such offenses, and we will examine those alternatives in the following section. Christopher Stone, Donald Cressey, and others have proposed another approach—the creation of a public award given to corporations that maintain proper ethical standards.[5]   Such awards would be highly publicized, and corporations would be encouraged to use them in advertising campaigns. Corporations that fail to meet ethical standards would then face negative publicity, especially since their competitors would be free to advertise their ethical superiority. This proposal still leaves many unanswered questions concerning the nature of those ethical standards and the best ways to evaluate corporate performance, but it does merit further study. A similar proposal made by W. Brent Fisse would also use publicity as a sanction against corporate offenses, but instead of a public award, he calls for new legislation requiring convicted corporate offenders to pay for advertising that would inform the public of their offenses. [6]

Because occupational criminals are not supported by large impersonal organizations, individual ethical standards are probably more important in controlling their behavior. Tougher punishments would once again be helpful, but there are limits to the effectiveness of even a well-organized and well-financed criminal justice system. As long as the culture of competition remains a central part of our culture, the level of occupational crime is likely to remain high. There are, of course, alternative value systems, both religious and secular, that stress the ethics of cooperation. But a significant weakening of the culture of competition would have to be accompanied by changes in the structural relations that support it. Such a change is by no means impossible—and perhaps not even unlikely—but cultural evolution of this sort tends to be a painfully slow process.

Enforcement Reforms

Of all the reforms discussed here, the idea that white collar criminals must be more severely punished is probably the most widely accepted. But there are many different proposals, and none of them has won universal acceptance by experts and political activists. Foremost among these suggestions are the calls for greater resources and new priorities for enforcement agencies, a greater effort to isolate those agencies from outside political pressures, and legislation that is less ambiguous and easier to enforce.

The data given in chapter 5 clearly show the need for greater resources. Regulatory agencies and prosecutors are often hopelessly outmatched by their corporate opponents, who command larger and more skilled legal staffs and much greater financial support. There are too few government inspectors to detect more than a small fraction of the pollutants illegally released into the environment, and the same is true of occupational health and safety hazards and dangerous consumer products. The regulatory agencies even lack the resources to test most potentially dangerous substances so that appropriate regulations can be promulgated. To remedy this situation, regulatory and enforcement agencies must be given very substantial increases in their budgets. Certainly, funding at five or ten times the current levels would not be out of line with the importance of the problem. The most pressing needs are for larger research budgets to permit regulatory agencies to actively search out threats to public health and safety before disaster strikes; for substantial increases in the ranks of the investigators and prosecutors; and for higher pay for the legal, medical, and scientific personnel who now are often lured away to higher-paying jobs in private industry. Greater support is also needed for the local agencies that bear the primary responsibility for dealing with occupational crimes.

An increase in resources must be accompanied by a greater effort to insulate enforcement agencies from undue political pressure. Although there appears to be no certain way to achieve that end, several possibilities have been suggested. First of all, along with an increase in pay, the employees of regulatory agencies could be required to sign an agreement, backed up by explicit legal penalties, promising never to work for any of the firms that fall under their regulatory jurisdiction. Currently, there is a two-year moratorium on such employment changes, but many people believe that a longer time period is necessary and that the regulatory agencies would be better off without an employee who would refuse to sign such an agreement. Secondly, in order to defuse the threat of punitive budgetary cutbacks for agencies that offend powerful special interests, as well as to lighten the financial burden on the public, enforcement and regulatory agencies could be made more self-supporting. This could be accomplished by legislation requiring that convicted offenders pay the full cost of the government's investigation and prosecution. This money, along with any punitive fines, would then be turned over to the agencies involved in the case.

The current system of fines and penalties needs restructuring for another reason as well. Far too often, penalties do not even equal the profits made from an organizational crime, much less pose a credible deterrent. To resolve this problem, the laws could be rewritten to require that convicted corporate offenders automatically pay a penalty at least equal to the amount of profit they made from their illegal activities. The judge or hearing officer would also be given the authority to impose additional punitive fines as appropriate. Where violent offenses are involved, much stiffer financial penalties are called for—perhaps based on the severity of the injuries and the number of deaths the offenders caused.

Many criminologists believe that even large fines have little impact on organizational crime, because corporate offenders merely pass them on to their customers in the form of higher prices. This is indeed a problem in some cases, but it is not always so. In a competitive industry, a corporate offender may be unable to pass on the cost of the fines to its customers, thus resulting in lower profits and trouble for top management. Fines are likely to have less impact in more oligopolistic industries, but if the penalties were sufficiently large and were assessed on only a single member of the oligopoly, they might still have the desired effect.

Other critics have charged that the imposition of large financial penalties may force some offenders into bankruptcy, thus punishing the innocent along with the guilty. There is little doubt that financial penalties based on a realistic estimate of the damage done by organizational crime would indeed cause some firms to go bankrupt. But there are good grounds for believing that such an event would ultimately work to the public good. Although some workers might lose their jobs, the assets of bankrupt firms do not vanish, they are purchased by other businesses. Most of the workers probably would be quickly rehired—hopefully, by a more reputable employer. If necessary, new legislation could be enacted mandating the bankruptcy courts to take special action to protect the interests of the workers in such cases. Stockholders would suffer a more permanent loss, but that is part of the risk investors take when they buy stocks rather than invest in more secure investments such as insured bank accounts. The example of a major corporation being forced into bankruptcy because of the penalties for its criminal behavior would certainly pose a powerful deterrent to other offenders and might also spur stockholders to monitor the activities of management more closely.

Another promising approach focuses on prevention rather than punishment. The idea here is to penetrate the organizational shell of the corporate offender by placing enforcement agents in a position to make it impossible for a corporation to repeat its crimes. For example, a firm that has committed repeated environmental violations would be required to pay the cost of hiring enough government inspectors to continually monitor the firm's compliance with the law. In order for such a system to function effectively, it would probably be necessary to rotate the inspectors periodically to prevent them from becoming too closely identified with a single firm.

There are also a number of ways in which current laws could be changed to improve the effectiveness of the enforcement effort. A simple modification of the laws concerning mergers could greatly strengthen the government's antitrust efforts. Instead of the current requirement that the government prove that a proposed merger would tend to restrain trade or create a monopoly, new legislation could simply forbid all mergers by the nation's five hundred or so largest corporations. Specific exemptions might then be granted if the firms involved could show that the proposed merger would have beneficial economic and social effects.

Under a bill introduced by Senator Edward Kennedy in 1979, corporations with over $2.5 billion in sales or $2 billion in assets would have been prohibited from merging, no matter how different their lines of business. Corporations with $350 million to $2.5 billion in sales and $200 million to $2 billion in assets would have had to prove that the proposed merger would lead to greater efficiency and more competition. Not only would such legislation simplify the current enforcement procedures and encourage competition, but it could be expected to yield other economic benefits as well. By reducing the tendency of big corporations to simply buy up an existing firm when they want to enter a new line of business, laws of this kind would encourage U.S. firms to build new plants and buy new equipment.

Lawyers associated with Ralph Nader have drawn up a much broader piece of legislation that has been proposed for adoption in several states. Were this model legislation, entitled "The Corporate Deviance Act," enacted by a significant number of states, it would certainly strike a forceful blow at corporate criminality. Among other things, it would make it a felony for a corporation to conceal any product or process that might cause death or injury, and it would also make it a crime to retaliate against "whistle-blowers" seeking to inform the public about such activities. A business license would be made contingent on the "good character" of the corporation and could be denied if the state found a consistent pattern of unethical or illegal activities. The legislation would require corporations to provide workers, consumers, and public with all available information about any hazards their activities may create.[7]

Another approach would be to enact legislation mandating the licensing of executives of the major corporations, in the same way we license other professionals. Such a license need not be difficult to obtain. A simple test on the legal and ethical requirements of corporate management would be sufficient. The main value of this licensing system would be to create a mechanism for disbarring corporate officers who violate their ethical obligations. A special regulatory agency might be established to hear the cases against individual executives. If the evidence warranted, the hearing officer would be empowered to prohibit an offender from working for any major corporation for a fixed number of years. Although many disbarment cases would undoubtedly be appealed to the federal courts, such a procedure would provide a means of sanctioning executive misconduct without having to prove criminal intent.

One largely untapped resource in the battle against organizational crime can be found in the outside auditors whom publicly traded firms must hire to examine their financial reports. These auditors are obviously in an excellent position to uncover many types of corporate illegalities. However, the American Institute of Certified Public Accountants, along with most individual practitioners, has traditionally held that "the normal audit arrangement is not designed to detect fraud and cannot be relied upon to do so."[8] Outside auditors face a built-in conflict of interest, for although their employer is an independent firm, it is still paid by the corporation whose books they are examining. Hence, a firm that gains a reputation for "overzealousness" in checking for corporate illegalities might find itself losing many important clients. The attitude of most accounting firms is reflected in the following statement by one member of a major firm: "We are not required to audit below the normal levels of materiality in search for illegal payments. *Our responsibility in this connection is to our clients.* It does not extend to informing the SEC about immaterial payments if we find them. We are not police for the commission."[9]

Auditors may not be policemen, but they are in a unique position to assist law enforcement, and a few basic reforms could greatly enhance their role in protecting the public from corporate fraud. Auditors could be legally required to search out fraud and deception in corporate financial statements and to report any suspected illegalities to enforcement agencies. But in order to carry out this new role, the accounting firms would have to be insulated from their clients' financial pressures. To achieve this goal, major corporations could be required to pay an audit fee to a government clearinghouse, which would then select the firm to do the actual audit. Thus, the auditors would feel no undue pressure to compromise the integrity of their report.

Honest employees who refuse to accept the idea that illegal activities are necessary to get the job done can be another important ally in the fight against white collar crime. But to win their help, a strong new law protecting the whistle-blowers who report the crimes of their employers is needed. Such legislation would make it a crime to retaliate against whistle-blowers in any way and require that substantial punitive damages be paid to the victim of such an action.

According to the polls discussed in chapter 5, the public is most concerned about white collar crimes that cause direct physical harm to people. It therefore makes sense to give such crimes as environmental pollution, occupational safety violations, and the manufacture of unsafe products a high priority in the enforcement effort. Those same polls show that the public believes that such violent white collar crimes deserve punishments as severe as those given for violent street crimes. A much more vigorous effort is therefore needed to investigate, prosecute, and imprison violent white collar offenders. For example, a greater volume of cases is necessary to establish clear legal precedents for the prosecution of negligent corporate executives for criminal manslaughter and to make such legal actions a routine and expected response to violent organizational crime.

"Supply side" economists have taken a very different approach to enforcement reform, arguing that the government ought not to be involved in economic regulation at all. They would write most white collar crimes out of existence and allow the economic system to operate on its own. Advocates of this position have argued that consumers can regulate unsafe products by refusing to buy them, that workers can regulate occupational safety by refusing to work at unsafe jobs, and so on. In this view, environmental pollution could be controlled through some system of taxation on emissions, so that corporations can decide whether or not to install antipollution devices on economic grounds. Although such a program of deregulation would eliminate many white collar crime by legal fiat, it is hard to imagine how it could help resolve the underlying problems that led to the creation of those laws. If it were true that an unfettered market naturally takes care of such problems, those laws would never have been enacted in the first place.

Another attack on the regulatory system came from President Reagan in February 1981, when he issued an executive order requiring a special cost/benefit analysis before any new regulation is put into effect. The goal of this cost/benefit analysis is to reduce "regulatory unreasonableness" and the burden the latter allegedly places on American business."[10] Our previous analysis has shown, however, that the regulatory process has always been most sensitive to the interests of the businesses being regulated, and that regulatory inaction is a much greater problem than regulatory unreasonableness. The imposition of one more level of review to the already cumbersome rule-making procedure only aggravates the failures of the enforcement process.[11]

Structural Reforms

Criminologists have long held that the best way to deal with any kind of crime is to attack it at the source rather than to rely on the criminal justice system to punish the offenders after the fact, and that is exactly what proposals for structural reforms try to do. Yet these proposals are highly controversial, both because they have strong ideological implications and because they threaten powerful vested interests. Nevertheless, this approach offers some of the most promising avenues for achieving long-range solutions to the problem of white collar crime.

Many proposals for dealing with organizational crime involve basic changes in corporate structure to reduce the incentives for illegal activities, or at least to make them more difficult. Christopher Stone has proposed that public representatives be added to the boards of directors of all the major corporations.[12] These directors would have their own staffs and be charged not only with representing the public interest in the boardroom but also with supervising corporate behavior, hearing complaints, and uncovering corporate illegalities. In a variation on this idea, several European nations, including Sweden and West Germany, now require worker representation on corporate boards. Such workers' representatives might well be combined with Stone's public representatives to further broaden the spectrum of interests participating in corporate decision making.

How effective would these new board members be at making corporations more responsible? Studies of the European experience have shown that worker representation on corporate boards has not brought radical changes in corporate policies, for the new board members' main concerns have been in the areas of job security and working conditions.[13] Thus, there is reason to doubt that, in itself, worker representation in corporate decision making would do much to improve the integrity of the business, discourage environmental pollution, or encourage safer products. Impetus for such reforms must come from public representatives. But as long as stockholders continue to dominate corporate boards, the likelihood of major internal reforms is obviously limited. If, however, the worker representatives and the public representatives worked together, and their combined votes exceeded those of the stockholders, some fundamental changes might well occur.

Ralph Nader's Corporate Accountability Research Group has argued that much stricter standards of corporate accountability can be imposed by means of the chartering process.[14] But if an individual state tried to impose tough new standards under the current chartering system, major corporations would simply move their headquarters to other states that gave them a better deal. The Nader group therefore proposed a system of federal chartering that would prevent corporations from playing one state off against another. Under the Nader proposal, the federal chartering agency would require corporate boards to take a much more active role in guiding firms. The boards also would be expanded to include worker representatives, and the corporations would be required to give the public much greater access to their records on such things as product safety research, plant emissions, and plans for factory closings.

However it is achieved, a freer flow of information among top management, corporate directors, regulatory agencies, and the general public would help discourage corporate crime and make the enforcement agencies' job an easier one. Too often, top managers and directors are able to cultivate selective ignorance about the criminal activities of their subordinates, the dangerous emissions of their plants, or the hazards of their products. Today, corporate spokesmen who make false public statements that cause serious harm to others can avoid criminal liability for fraud simply by claiming that they honestly believed their statements to be true.

One way to deal with this problem would be to require corporate decision makers to review explicit reports on such things as product safety research, environmental pollution, and unethical practices. As those reports moved up the chain of command, officials at each level would be required to describe their effort to conform to legal regulations and to report any knowledge they have of possible illegalities. After the reports had been signed by the corporate board, they would be given to an appropriate federal agency for legal review. In addition to alerting enforcement agencies to possible problems, such a reporting system would make it impossible for top managers to claim that they were unaware that, for example, the statements made by the sales division were contrary to the findings of the research department.

John Braithwaite has proposed a similar program. Whether by new legislation, by court order, or by voluntary corporate reform, Braithwaite argued that those assigned the responsibility for keeping a corporation in compliance with the law must be given greater strength within the corporation. Among other things, he suggested that: compliance personnel be given a more professional status; a high-level ombudsman be established to hear complaints; reports be made directly to the chief executive officer in writing (thus "tainting" him or her with the knowledge of potential criminal activities); and corporate decisions about ethical and legal matters be written down to create a kind of "corporate case law" that would then provide a guide for employees who must make a difficult decision. [15]

A different approach to the control of corporate crime would be the selective nationalization of firms that have long records of criminal violations. Nationalization may sound like an extreme measure, but it is a common practice in many nations around the world. All the government would have to do is buy up enough stock to gain a controlling interest in the criminal firm. The old management would then be replaced by a new group of managers, who would be instructed to reform and restructure the corporation. After the reforms had been effected and the corporation was operating in a responsible manner, the government could either sell its stock and return the firm to private ownership, or continue to operate it as a public trust.

A program of nationalization might also focus on industries rather than on individual firms. The rationale behind this approach is that some industries (petroleum, for example) have such a long history of antitrust violations that they clearly are no longer regulated by the free market, and the government therefore needs to step in to protect the public interest. This could be done in several ways. All the firms in the industry could be nationalized—but that, of course, would produce even less competition, albeit with public instead of private control.

Another alternative would be to nationalize a single large firm and to use it to reintroduce competition into the oligopolistic industry. A third alternative would be to start an entirely new, government-owned firm to compete with the existing oligopoly.

On the whole, occupational crimes are not as amenable to structural solutions as are organizational crimes. But there are two important exceptions—occupational crimes among government employees (discussed in the next section) and occupational crimes in the health care professions. Our previous analysis showed that the fee-for-service technique of payment is a major cause of crime in the health care industry. The motivation for performing unnecessary tests and treatments, for example, comes from the fact that physicians and laboratories are paid for each service they perform; thus, they are rewarded for "overdoctoring." If the health care system paid professionals on the basis of a salary rather than on the volume of services performed, the motivation for many offenses would be eliminated. This approach has already proven successful in private health maintenance organizations, as well as in nationalized health care systems such as the one in Great Britain.

Political Reforms

White collar crime differs from most other types of crime, in that there are so many promising proposals for dealing with it. There is little doubt that, if some reasonable combination of the proposals discussed above were vigorously applied to the problem, the incidence of white collar crime would decline. The difficulty in dealing with white collar crime lies not so much in discovering viable responses but in winning their implementation. In other words, this is primarily a political problem that can be solved only by reforming the political process.

The most urgent need is for radical changes in the present system of campaign financing. The fact that most politicians have to rely on campaign contributions from well-endowed special interests clearly has had a paralyzing effect on the battle against white collar crime. An aide to former Senator Gary Hart, during his campaign to win the 1988 Presidential nomination, revealed exactly what the problem was when he was asked about his candidate's position on corporate crime: "No Democratic presidential candidate has ever made corporate crime an issue," he said, because "the money will dry up."[16]

The simplest way to resolve this problem would be to create a system of federal and state financing for election campaigns. The current provision for matching funds in presidential elections is certainly an improvement over the old system, but it is only a halfway measure for a single office. It would be far better to provide complete government funding for all major elections. Each candidate would naturally be given the same amount of money to spend, and large blocks of free television and radio time would be set aside for the candidates to discuss the issues.

The main difficulty in formulating such a system is to create a fair way to determine who is to receive government funds. On the one hand, a large number of frivolous candidates might run for office if no cost were involved. But on the other hand, the large, established parties currently in power might well write the campaign financing legislation in such a way as to exclude small-party candidates. Nonetheless, some fair system could certainly be worked out. One promising approach would be to require petitions with a minimum number of signatures to qualify for funding in the primary, and then use the primary returns as the basis for funding eligibility in the general election.

Another essential step toward reform is the provision of stronger protections for individual civil rights and the freedom of political expression. As we have seen, the government has not only established systematic programs for the surveillance of those who challenge the political interests of the elite, but it has actually taken direct covert action to repress such political activities. It would be helpful to have a new federal law explicitly criminalizing any activities on the part of government agents that interfere with the freedom of expression. Although most such activities are already illegal, such a law would still have an important symbolic value.

A more difficult problem is to get the government to enforce existing laws that regulate the behavior of its agents. Many observers have suggested the creation of a permanent special prosecutor's office, similar to the temporary one first created during the Watergate scandals. This office, equipped with its own investigative force, would have unrestricted access to all government records, files, and reports. The selection of the head of this office would best be left up to the Supreme Court or some prestigious, nonpartisan group. With such a strong institutional base, the effort to control the government's abuse of power would seem to stand a much better chance of success than it has in the past.

But because there is some question about how effectively the government can ever police itself, it is crucial that the public be given access to the broadest possible range of information about the government's activities. When a government agency begins an investigation of a political group, it should be required to notify the group of that fact. The activities of all government agents, operatives, and informants involved in such political cases should be periodically reviewed by a panel of federal judges to make sure that the government is staying within the bounds of the law and the standards of ethical conduct. Individuals should be given speedy access to all files kept on them by public or private organizations, without having to take costly legal action. All citizens should also be able to get inaccurate information removed from their files and have the right to sue for any damages caused by the dissemination of false information.

A CONCLUDING NOTE

This book must convey a rather dismal picture of the world to most of its readers. The repeated examples of respected men and women using the most unscrupulous means to enlarge already ample fortunes, of major corporations' indifference to the injuries and deaths they cause innocent people, of the government's violations of human rights, and of the weakness and corruption of the enforcement effort, certainly cast our society in a dark light.

It is the responsibility of the sociological enterprise to probe the depths of society's problems, and such an endeavor is unlikely to produce comforting results. Good sociology often contains a disquieting glimpse behind the social illusions we erect to conceal unpleasant realities. It is, nonetheless, true that there are countless honest corporate executives, diligent government servants, and dedicated professionals who have been ignored in these pages. But social problems are not created or resolved on the basis of personal moral characteristics or individual decisions, but by the objective social conditions that underlie them.

In the last analysis, the problem of white collar crime is one strand in a seamless web of social relations that transcend the neat categories sociologists create to contain them. The kinds of changes necessary to provide a permanent solution will require a major restructuring of our social and economic relationships. If such changes are made, they will not come about because of the problem of white collar crime alone, but because of a confluence of many social forces pushing in the same direction. The one thing that is certain is that our social relations will indeed change—but only time will tell if those changes will leave us with a more humane society.

NOTES

1. See, for example, James William Coleman, "The Myth of Addiction," *Journal of Drug Issues* 6 (Spring 1976): 135–141; Troy Duster, *The Legislation of Morality* (New York: The Free Press, 1970); Edwin M. Schur, *Crimes Without Victims* (Englewood Cliffs, N.J.: Prentice-Hall, 1965).

2. Melvin L. DeFleur, *Social Problems in American Society* (Boston: Houghton Mifflin, 1983), 352.

3. Ibid.

4. Quoted in Paul Richter, "Big Business Puts Ethics in Spotlight," *Los Angeles Times*, 19 June 1986, I: 28; also see Marilynn Cash Mathews, "Codes of Ethics: Organizational Behavior and Misbehavior" in William C. Frederick (ed.), *Research in Corporate Social Performance and Policy* (Greenwich, Conn.: JAI, 1987). For a discussion of corporate codes of ethics, see Donald R. Cressey and Charles A. Moore, *Corporation Codes of Ethical Conduct* (New York: Report to the Peat, Marwick, and Mitchell Foundation, 1980).

5. Christopher D. Stone, *Where the Law Ends: The Social Control of Corporate Behavior* (New York: Harper & Row, 1975), 243.

6. W. Brent Fisse, "The Use of Publicity as a Criminal Sanction Against Business Corporations," *Melbourne University Law Review* 8 (June 1971): 113–130.

7. *Corporate Crime Reporter* 1 (27 April 1987): 5–60.

8. C. David Baron, Douglas A. Johnson, D. Gerald Searfoss, and Charles H. Smith, "Uncovering Corporate Irregularities: Are We Closing the Expectation Gap?," *Journal of Accountancy* (October 1977): 56.

9. Walter Guzzardi, Jr., "An Unscandalized View of Those 'Bribes' Abroad," *Fortune* (July 1978): 178. Italics added.

10. See, for example, Eugene Bardach and Robert A. Kagan, *Going by the Book: The Problem of Regulatory Unreasonableness* (Philadelphia: Temple University Press, 1982).

11. See, for example, Mark Green and Norman Waitzman, *Business War on the Law: An Analysis of the Benefits of Federal Health/Safety Enforcement*, rev. 2nd ed. (Washington, D.C.: The Corporate Accountability Research Group, 1981).

12. Stone, *Where the Law Ends.*

13. See Martin Carnoy and Derek Shearer, *Economic Democracy: The Challenge of the 1980s* (White Plains, N.Y.: M.E. Sharpe Inc., 1980), 249–257.

14. Ralph Nader, Mark J. Green, and Joel Seligman, *Taming the Giant Corporation* (New York: Norton, 1976).

15. John Braithwaite, *Corporate Crime in the Pharmaceutical Industry* (London: Routledge and Kegan Paul), 290–388.

16. *Corporate Crime Reporter* 1 (13 April 1987): 50.

Index